SME Managers Turnover in Modern China

Modern China Series

SME Managers Turnover in Modern China

Ji Yun

North American Business Press

SME Managers Turnover in Modern China

ISBN: 9781948915007

NORTH
AMERICAN BUSINESS
PRESS

North American Business Press
Atlanta, Georgia
Miami, Florida
New York, New York,
Toronto, Canada

FIRST PRINTING, 2019

About Modern China Series

China, as one of the oldest civilized regions in the world, has emerged as something of a "new world" because it is working to embrace its own essence and heritage and link them to viable economic strategies. In the last 25 years, China has made tremendous strides by doing so. The country and her people have every right to take pride in these accomplishments. With these successes under their belt, many Chinese leaders and intellectuals anticipate continuing growth. China's plans and strategies, furthermore, are often based upon this premise.

There is tremendous interest in the US on the Chinese economy and business environment. China has emerged as a global super power, and scholars and businessmen in the US are keenly interested in learning how this is going to continue to affect them and how they can do business with China. In response to growing interest from international and Asian scholars, North American Business Press is pleased to announce our Modern China Series (MCS) books, which is first of such series in the US and has garnered tremendous interest both in the US and around the world. With our first book reaching stores in September 2011, this initiative is aimed at developing relationships between NABP and Chinese scholars who desire to promote their academic and applied business writings to the rest of the world.

We have had overwhelming demand for the Modern China Series from both authors who would like to publish in the series and people who would like to read the books. Currently, there are ten books published in the series and, additionally, we have a couple of dozen books that we are considering for the series. The books have been viewed by tens of thousands of people from the U.S. and the rest of the world.

We have published books relating to several areas revolving around the Chinese business environment. We have a few that focus on the best practices in marketing in China; a couple relating to "best practices" in doing business in China; and a few on the outlook of the

Chinese economy. The market for the Modern China Series is huge. There are tens of thousands of scholars that are keenly interested in the continued growth of the Chinese economy and the implications that will have on the business world. Even more significant are the millions of businessmen that are interested in the impact that China will continue to have on the global economy. It is difficult to pin down the exact demand for the series, but it is very large.

We have big plans for growing the Moderns China Series. This has the potential to one of the most significant economic/business series ever produced. We are very selective with the books that we will add to the collection, but we encourage any scholars who think they have unique and interesting perspectives on China to submit their books to us. From the readers' perspective, we are committed to producing high quality books on a regular basis so that readers should expect a steady stream of insightful books to be coming out for many years to come.

This initiative is headed by Dr. Robert Tian, a renowned researcher and academic, who spearheads our efforts in partnering with foreign authors and administering day-to-day operations of this series. Dr. Tian, a Vice-President with North American Business Press and Editor of this series, spends much of his time in Beijing, Shanghai, and other Chinese cities, focusing on developing and managing our interests with authors and universities. Below is the list for the books we have published:

Enterprise Strategy: New Horizon authored by Zhang Xiuyu
Governance of Private Enterprises in Modern China authored by Qin Zhong
The Art of War and Enterprise Strategy Management authored by Fu Shouzhi
Marketing Issues in Modern China edited by Tian Guang et al.
The Footprints of the Academician authored by Fu Zhouzhi
Marketing and Economics in Modern China (I) edited by Qi Xiaoguang et al.

Marketing and Economics in Modern China (II) edited by Wang Tianjin et al.
An Islamic Heritage in China authored by Ma Zhanming
China Environmental Anthropology authored by Wang Tianjin, Tian Guang, and Ma Jianfu
Can China Rule the New World? Authored by Tian Guang and Chen Gang
Critiques on Pan-marketization authored by Li Cunlin, Liu Hongfei, and Tian Guang
Economic and Business Anthropology in China edited by Qi Xiaoguang and Tian Guang
SME Managers Turnover in Modern China authored by Ji Yun

Table of Contents

Preface

Small and medium-sized private enterprises (SME) occupy great share of Chinese economy. The potential and performance of SME have considerable influence on prospect of China. In recent years, it is a frequently discussed concern that management resources loss directly threatens the development of SME in China. It has become an increasingly critical issue for business circles and academia to attract and retain professional managers in company. By combining theoretical and empirical methods, this book probes into the process and influence factors of manager turnover in companies. It aims to explain the mechanism of influence factors, with a preliminary intend to establish the "intention forming process model", considering small and medium-sized private enterprise professional managers, and to put forward relevant management measures and solutions.

Main factors that influence manager turnover are investigated in this research, including personal factors, organizational factors, job factors, employer factors etc. Personal factors refer to the degree of job participation degree, commitment tendency, entrepreneurial motivation, risk aversion degree and traditional concepts. Organizational factors are composed by organizational rewards, salary satisfaction degree, organizational conditions, interpersonal atmosphere, procedural fairness and career development opportunities. Job factors consist job autonomy, job pressure and job challenge. Employer factors consist of employer value, employer leadership, employer integrity, leadership fairness, employer achievement motivation, and employer trust. Other factors are mainly that of job embeddedness, matching degree, other job opportunities and organizational change. These factors influence manager turnover directly or indirectly, through attitude variables such as job satisfaction, organizational commitment, work initiative, work status and job searching motivation.

According to the structural equation model, the basic process of professional manager turnover is formed by four stages. First, managers perceive on individuals, organizations, employers, jobs and other job opportunities. Second, the decline of perceived level reduces work satisfaction degree, organizational commitment degree and work initiative. Third, worsened managers' working state makes them search for other job opportunities, and finally, the intention of leaving the job occurs. The verified process model has a strong explanatory power on the variance of manager turnover.

In stage I, managers' perception on employers' attention, job autonomy, job participation degree and interpersonal atmosphere significantly affects their job satisfaction degree and organizational commitment degree. Meanwhile, employer leadership, employer equity and trust, job autonomy, job participation degree and job involvement degree to considerable extent affect the work initiatives. These perception variables ultimately affect managers' turnover intention through the mediation of attitude variables such as satisfaction and initiative, and the lower the degree of manager's freedom in work, the lower satisfaction degree with the job, and the lower the manager's loyalty to the organization. The lack of trust in subordinates would directly affect the initiatives, which is an important signal of manager turnover.

In stage II, satisfaction and commitment degree, employer's attention, work pressure and job autonomy etc. directly affect the working status of the manager. Employers' attention, work autonomy, work involvement degree, commitment orientation, organizational changes and other factors have a significant impact on the motivation of job searching.

In stage III, work pressure, other job opportunities, job searching motivation, work status and so on directly affect manager turnover intention. In case of manager turnover, the work status and job searching motivation act as the transmission mechanism, among which, the organizational changes and fluctuation may induce managers' job searching motivation. Some managers with low promise tendency usually pay attention to talent market information more frequently than those bear high promise tendency. Managers who already have other job opportunities directly quit the current job without any intermediate links. And in stage IV, manager turnover intention occurs.

Results show that managers' participation and commitment tendency can moderate the relationship between work status, work searching motivation and turnover intention. The motivation of entrepreneurship has the moderating effect on work searching motivation. Risk aversion and traditional concept have moderating effects on the state of work. At the same time, employer's leadership, employer's equity and trust can mitigate the impact of organizational factors on the intention to leave, which can reduce managers' turnover intention caused by the lack of organizational attraction, till to less than 60%. This finding is brand new to western literature on mainstream managers' turnover.

Economical explanations on professional manager turnover are made in this book. In the dual two-dimensional space, the employer attaches great importance to the managers' ability and loyalty, managers pay more attention to their position, manager turnover and family management of private enterprises can balance the managers' ability and their loyalty. The adverse selection of private enterprises in the process of introducing professional managers makes it difficult to enter the core layer of the enterprise, so that the operation of the enterprise is degraded to the closed mode dominated by family members. Seeing from the dynamic information disclosure model of interactive process between enterprises and managers, the dynamic information disclosure process, compared to situation of complete information asymmetry, would help stop manager turnover.

Some policy suggestions for professional manager turnover are put forward, in accordance with the formation process of turnover intention. As a result, attention should mainly be paid to the related factors of perception, work attitude change, low working status and job searching motivation. To really stop managers from resignation, some corporate governance measures must be made, concerning the overall human resource management system, including the recruitment, training, job design, job arrangement, motivation and career management etc.

New influential factors that influence the professional manager turnover in small and medium-sized private enterprises are expounded. By this way, the research materials in area of manager turnover are enriched. Furthermore, this research explains the mechanism of the affecting factors on manager turnover intention, and highlights the inner relationship between the influencing factors and the turnover intention. It builds a process model of the formation of professional manager turnover intention of small and medium-sized private enterprises, and makes a theoretical supplement to professional manager turnover. The policy recommendations suggested in this book also bear practical significance to small and medium-sized private enterprises, in the field of absorbing and retaining professional management resources.

Acknowledgements

First, I sincerely thank my Doctoral Supervisor Professor Zhang Jianqi. His profound academic knowledge and professional research attitudes have deeply influenced on my early scholastic stage and later career. This work was completed under his direction and guidance. I thank especially Professor Tian Guang, without his encouragement and help, it is impossible to have this book ready for publishing. The high quality of translation done by Dr. Li Wei is indispensable to this English version, thanks for her professional research assistance.

Finally, I am grateful for the financial support from the Academy of Financial Research and Business School of Wenzhou University.

Foreword

Tian Guang

The Chinese economy is gradually shifting from the stage of "extensive expanding" to "endogenous driving". With the gradual disappearance of the reform dividend, demographic dividend, and late-developing advantage, the marginal rate of return of investment is gradually decreasing, and the driving force for economic growth is increasingly dependent on the internal management and innovation of economic entities. One fact that cannot be ignored is that the management capacity of SMEs, which occupy a large share of China's economy, is relatively low. This is represented in that on one side, many SMEs are in low production efficiency, lack of innovation ability, and in inferior quality of products and services. On the other side, its life cycle is shortened, and the continuous operation period is much lower than the average life expectancy of enterprises in mature market economies. It indicates that the future Chinese economy, which relies on "endogenous driving", will face serious challenges. Without sufficient management and innovation capabilities, the Chinese economy will gradually lose its momentum of rapid growth, and eventually fall into low level of equilibrium.

Therefore, it is of great theoretical significance and realistic urgency to explore the reasons for the low management ability of SMEs, and propose feasible countermeasures accordingly. This monograph by Dr. Ji Yun reflects an effort and attempt in this regard. This research cuts in from the perspective of the loss of management resources of SMEs, and analyzes the threat of the survival and development of SMEs by analyzing the turnover of professional managers, emphasizing the importance of retaining the core management resources of enterprises. Based on a large amount of literature, the author uses in-depth field research data to summarize the factors affecting the turnover intention of professional managers, such as individual level, organizational level, employer aspect, job nature and external environment. Based on this, a multi-stage turnover intention forming process model with multiple mediating variables and moderating variables is constructed and tested. According to the model, many strategies and mechanisms can be devised to help reduce the turnover rate of SMEs' professional managers. Furthermore, the author uses adverse selection model of the professional manager market in China context to give an economic explanation for the loss of core management resources of SMEs at this stage, and proposes a series of countermeasures based on the dynamic matching model under information asymmetry.

By reading the book, readers interested in contemporary China issues can certainly benefit a lot. It provides a clear analysis of the status and prospects of SME management resources, and it gives wonderful comments in the right place. Based on rich empirical facts and unique theoretical discussions, the book draws a series of convincing conclusions. For example, through qualitative research, the author points out that two key facts leading to the loss of management resources of SMEs are: entrepreneur's obsession with equity and control rights, and the career orientation of middle- and high-level professional managers that "better be the chicken head than the phoenix tail". In addition, the empirical tests found that SMEs, which are relatively inferior in terms of organizational attractiveness, can reshape the trust and fair perception of professional managers through the adjustment of entrepreneurial behavior, and greatly reduce their turnover intention. These research results in Chinese contexts not only make a marginal contribution to the management literature, but also have important reference value for foreign companies interested in developing business in China.

In recent years, the international community has not only been interested in the economic governance system dominated by the Chinese government, but also concerned about the energetic SMEs in a fiercely competitive environment. In this special dualistic economic system, two types of economic entities, large state-owned enterprises and small and medium-sized private enterprises, which are extremely different in terms of enterprise scale, governance mechanism, development strategy, and operational system, jointly support China's huge economic aggregate. For researches on the large state-owned enterprises, many literatures at home and abroad have conducted in-depth and extensive investigations and studies, and given quite convincing analysis and explanation. For researches on the small and medium-sized private enterprises, most existing analyses cannot jump out of the Western theoretical framework. Most of the researches only repeat the existing findings in the Chinese context. In this sense, Dr. Ji Yun's monograph is impressive. Although the book continues the academic traditions of the research field, it creatively introduces many analytical elements with Chinese characteristics, such as relationship, loyalty, clannism, rule of man etc. Especially, for the information economics explanation of the familial tendencies of SMEs, the author skillfully combines the mainstream economic analysis tools with the special factors of the Chinese professional manager market, and draws unusual conclusions. In general, the analysis of this book is comprehensive but not complicated, subtle but not verbose, stick to tradition but not fall into convention. It is recommended for people in academia and management circles.

Chapter 1

Introduction

Small and medium-sized enterprises occupy a prominent position in China's private economy, which are playing an increasingly significant role in the economic system in terms of value contribution, job creation and technological innovation etc. At present stage, however, such enterprises are faced with problems of low production level and low management ability, which makes most of them break down in less than 3 years (Huang, 2007). Reasons are various for causing the short-life of small and medium-sized private enterprises, such as the external environment constraints, narrow market space, uneconomical running scale and entrepreneur's ability-limitation etc. But low level of overall management ability is one of the main reasons, which Penrose (1995) considered as the decisive factor. In Penrose's view, the limit of an enterprise's development is determined by its internal management ability. Companies need to constantly recruit management resources from the outside to improve their own management capabilities, to achieve sustained growth and "rebirth" by breaking through the running period limit. It is difficult for small and medium-sized private enterprises to attract excellent managerial talents and retain them. As a result, the closed family governance model is becoming increasingly common, which directly affects the business time (Xiao, 2015).

Research Problem

How to absorb and retain the internal management resources, to realize the long-term sustainable growth of small and medium-sized private enterprises, has become a major task facing academia, policy makers and businesses. Related research at home and abroad has been focused on the essence, cause, process and consequences of employee turnover as well as the countermeasures etc. For the problem of professional managers' turnover in small and medium-sized private enterprises in our country, the given theoretical explanation and management suggestions are insufficient. For the two core questions, why do the managers resign and how does the turnover intention come into being, answers are generally weak.

Most researchers take general employees as the research objects. First, the turnover of professional managers bears mainly two sides of particularities, one is the small and medium-sized enterprise, and the other is the managers. In order to give suitable explanation and put forward reasonable suggestions to related issues, it is necessary to go deep into its particular characteristics. Second, based on the background of western culture, the existing research models consider the influencing factors of objective variables, such as the job, the organization and the environment etc. few studies have specifically considered the employers' personal factors. In the context of eastern culture, emphasizing authority consciousness and focusing on relationship management, the employers' personal factors cannot be ignored. This is especially true for small and medium-sized private enterprises. Third, the decision-making of professional managers' turnover in small and medium-sized enterprise may not conform to the predictions of existing process model. For instance, the turnover caused by the shock of entrepreneurial opportunities is difficult to be categorizes into any kind of process proposed by Lee and Mitchell (1994). Fourth, the existing research on the consequence of professional managers' turnover is not completely suitable for managers who have a special impact on the company. And most of these researches are based on the assumptions of perfect legal system and market mechanism. Whether it is applicable to examine current situation in small and medium-sized enterprises remains to be verified. Fifth, existing treatment suggestions can hardly really solve the manage resources problems in small and medium-sized enterprises, such as the problem of ignoring the employer personal factors and information asymmetry etc. Finally, using the process model and factors model obtained by empirical tests, to put forward systematic management measures, is not quite available in present ways of research.

This research combines theoretical and empirical methods. It considers the Chinese particularity of the problem of managers' turnover in small and medium-sized private enterprises. Based on survey data, it uses the structural equation model, the Logit model and the variance analysis to identify the key process and influencing factors of professional managers' turnover. It aims to establish and validate process model and factors model with stronger prediction ability, to find out the interrelations between different factors, different paths and different phases in the same path, and the functioning mechanism. It analyzes the empirical research results in fields of management, psychology, economics and other relevant disciplines, integrate them to the current study and put forward targeted governance recommendations on the problem of professional managers' turnover in small and medium-sized private enterprises in China.

Innovations of this study can be categorized into six aspects. First, it makes up for the gap of incomplete explanation in the problem of professional managers' turnover in China, especially of small and medium-sized private enterprises. Based on existing influencing factors, this research introduces new variables considering cultural background difference, particularity small and medium-sized enterprises and professional managers group. Second, it enriches the literature on managers' turnover by cross-cultural comparison. In the context of Chinese culture, this research examines the mature models in western countries, compares its resemblance and differences with Chinese model, and identifies the commonness and particularities on influencing factors of managers' turnover. Third, it clears up the relationship between different paths and stages in varied existing process models. This study makes qualitative research with full consideration on Chinese managers' personal characteristics like career goals, achievement motivation, commitment tendency, object of commitment, and job involvement etc. it comes up with process model on manages' turnover by looking into the clue from the perception of related factors, the change of job attitude, the intention to search for a new job, and to final turnover. Fourth, it promotes the development of private enterprises research to some extent. This study investigates the long-term development problems from the perspective of absorbing and retaining management resources, to improve the management ability of enterprises. Fifth, it offers proposals from aspects of recruitment, employment contract, employee training, job design and so on. In point of managing managers' turnover, this study can improve the existing human resources management theory. Sixth, it deepens people's understanding on family private enterprises. Adverse selection and dynamic matching model are utilized, to discuss the problem of manager turnover and the familization of private enterprises. The essential difference of family business between western countries and China are emphasized.

In terms of management practice, this research provides targeted countermeasures for managers' turnover of small and medium-sized private enterprises, to achieve sustainable development. Meanwhile, a set of assessment tools are offered, considering staff perception, job attitude, working status, and career goals etc., which would help researchers to understand employees' psychological state and predict the future intention, to better manage and make full use of existing human resources. Referring the assessment of managers and proposed governance mechanism, small and medium-sized enterprises owners can design specific human resource management measures, and finally to retain management resources and achieve sustainable management.

Research Background

1. China's small and medium-sized private enterprises and the significance of its continuous growth

The latest statistics show that China's private economy has accounted for about two-thirds of GDP, and the main force is small and medium-sized private enterprises (Huang, 2007). In the year of 2015, Imports and exports of private enterprises reached $ 1.03 trillion, accounted for 45.2% of total imports and exports of China, which made private enterprises the largest export market of China. Outward foreign direct investment by private enterprises has accounted for one half of gross, and been the main force in this field (Wang, 2017). Private enterprises have a large share in employment creation, fixed asset investment, taxation, research and development and so on. It can be said that the rapid development of private enterprises in the past 20 years is the reflection of China's rapid economic growth in the same period. Private enterprises have been acting as an indispensable and important role in China's economy.

As for the private enterprises, 20 years of developing has already marked the history, since private enterprise in China is comparatively a new industry. Due to the limitations of various internal and external conditions, the clear majority of private enterprises remain in small and medium size. Tracing back to its history, private enterprises was originally created in the late 1970s by government, to address the employment problem of educated youths. At that time, state policy of China allowed some of them to start their own businesses. But they had very small amount of primitive capital, furthermore, the state had limitations on the size of private individual economy, which made them have to start from small business and operate on small scale. After the year of 1987, private enterprises could be officially registered in the industrial and commercial departments. Since then, private enterprises became the official subject of China's economy and started to develop gradually (Dai, 2005). Later, the southeast coastal areas, such as Guangdong, Zhejiang and Shanghai, became the main positions for the development of private enterprises. The rapid growth of these regions was closely related to the contribution of small and medium-sized enterprises. It can be said that the development of small and medium-sized enterprises has led to the economic development of the whole region.

I can be indicated that small and medium-sized private enterprises have incredible influence on the overall performance of the national economy, and its own growth is of great significance. Although the survival of enterprises usually follows the market's law of survival of the fittest, it is normal for enterprises of low efficiency to be eliminated by those of high efficiency, it is also important to note that principle of survival of the fittest doesn't mean to reshuffle and update all businesses periodically. An appropriate proportion of long-term sustainable growth is critical to the stability and sustained growth of the economic entity. The best condition should be that a certain percentage of enterprises grow with long and lasting develop, while another certain proportion appear and die out according to its periodic cycle rule, so as to maintain the dynamic balance of enterprises. In view of the small and medium-sized private enterprises in China, it's commonly being presented with weak body, slim shape and short life. Its extreme short life cycle has exceeded the scope of the normal economic system. Problems of how to enhance its strength and prolong its running life, to realize the continuous and healthy growth of small and medium-sized private enterprises have become major issues faced by academia, decision-making institutions, and business communities.

2. Management specialization and professionalization are essential for the growth of small and medium-sized private enterprises

Research shows that the important condition for enterprise growth is the synchronous expansion of management ability (Penrose, 1995). As the enterprise grows, its original management ability will gradually fail to meet the needs of resource coordination and internal functions. The further expansion of enterprises needs to continuously supplement the management resources from the outside, to overcome the development obstacles caused by insufficient management ability. Enterprise's capacity to absorb and retain new management resources become a necessary condition for continued growth for a long time, and the limits of an enterprise's expansion are determined by the managerial capabilities inherent in the present and potential managers of the enterprise (Penrose, 1995).

The development history of western companies shows that the power source of modern industrial and commercial enterprises is a pioneering career management coordination work carried out by a group of paid managers. Chandler (1978) regards the modern enterprise as a multi-unit enterprise managed by a set of paid senior managers. His analysis shows that the emergence of professional manager class is the inevitable development of modern industrial and commercial enterprises. Market expansion and technological progress have led to the expansion of enterprises. Therefore, the management is complicated and specialized. It makes the owners cannot undertake the management work in person. So, it is necessary to entrust the specific management functions other than important strategic decisions to paid managers. These managers have the knowledge and ability of enterprise management, and receive the employer's mandate and authorization in a paid way. On this basis, the group that performs its management functions has gradually grown up and become a special class of modern society. They have promoted the emergence of manager-type capitalism and achieved the manager revolution. Modern industrial and commercial enterprises have also realized the specialization and professionalization of management functions.

Although the origin and development path of private enterprises in China are different from that of western enterprises, all enterprises have the commonality of economic organization's pursuit of profit. The professionalization and professionalization of enterprise management, which accord with the inherent law of social division of labor, are still the necessary condition for the small and medium-sized private enterprises to grow to modern enterprises. Domestic research shows that one of the important contents of the development of private enterprises in China is the continuous integration of social human capital (Huang, 2007). An enterprise must constantly absorb and integrate new management resources in the process of growing up. With the expansion of enterprise scale, the increase of business, and the increase of technical content etc., the supply of human capital, especially of management resources, is inevitably insufficient (Chu,

2004). Absorbing external management resources becomes an inevitable choice for enterprises to achieve sustainable growth (Ji and Zhang, 2007).

For small and medium-sized private enterprises, professional managers not only help to supply manage resources and enhance management skills, but also contribute to the institutionalization and standardization of enterprise management. Small and medium-sized private enterprises are mostly entrepreneurial enterprises (Li, 2002). The main characteristic of this kind of enterprise is that the decision-making and execution belong to the same person. The strategic decision-making and daily management, however, have great randomness, making it difficult to standardize management activities. In addition, small and medium-sized private enterprises are not mature enough, with unique characteristics of entrepreneurship (Bhide, 1999). This leads to the need of adapting to the external environment flexibly. If the daily management is not institutionalized and standardized, the long-term strategic planning is difficult to be carried out.

The biggest problem for small and medium-sized enterprises is that how to find a foothold in the market and generate cash flow as soon as possible, to ensure that the enterprises can survive temporarily (Bhide, 1999). These enterprises pay more attention to the market instead of its management. As a result, they mostly lack perfect enterprise management system. They focus more on developing markets, capturing markets and establishing reputations rather than on the internal management procedures, management rules and control systems etc.

Professional managers, however, can help solve these problems. Most of them have received professional education, and their careers also determine the need for human capital investment in management knowledge and skills improvement. So, they have enough professional expertise, to realize the institutionalization and standardization of enterprise management, to reduce the arbitrariness and partiality of enterprise management, and to promote the democracy and feasibility of enterprise strategic decision-making. Business owners can also get out of day-to-day management and focus on the long-term development.

In addition, the growth barriers brought by the lack of entrepreneurial ability can be alleviated by the introduction of professional managers. Research indicates that the insufficient supply of private entrepreneurs in China is one of the fundamental reasons for the difficulty in growth and sustainable development of enterprises (Zhang and Zhao, 2007). While this can be partially improved through the entrepreneur's own learning, there is no denying that the self-quality of the entrepreneur's pre-entrepreneurial determines that there is very limited room for improvement (Zhou, 2014). Being busy all day long in searching market, entrepreneurs hardly have enough time and energy to make systematic learning, which makes it hard for them to achieve self-ability improvement. While professional managers are systematically trained in business administration, and most have sufficient practical experience, they are competent enough for daily management. So professional managers can make up for the lack of entrepreneurs' own ability and remove the obstacles to the growth of enterprises to a large extent.

3. Small and medium-sized private enterprises have difficulty in attracting senior professional managers

As mentioned above, introducing professional managers to realize the professionalization and professionalization of enterprise management is the only way for small and medium-sized private enterprises to achieve long-term continuous growth. However, compared with foreign and state-owned enterprises, small and medium-sized enterprises are less attractive to professional managers, due to the gap in business scale, capital, and management level etc. what's more, the carefully accumulated management resources are usually in a massive loss. Management resources, the most important human capital, have become the bottleneck of the growth of many private enterprises in China (Chu, 2002), which will undoubtedly affect its survival and development. How to absorb and retain excellent managers is a major problem for private enterprises.

Many studies have begun to focus on the attractiveness of private enterprises to career managers. Attracting managers into the private enterprise is the most important influencing factors, followed by the career development opportunities and space, salary and welfare level, employer's integrity to the manager, organizational justice, scale and the image of the enterprise. The first four factors have a significant effect on the willingness of professional managers to enter the private enterprise (Zhang and Huang, 2003), with career development ranked first, organizational justice the second, salary and welfare level the third, and employer's integrity to the manager the fourth. Apart from these factors, the matching status between professional managers and private enterprises, career development, organizational fairness and salary also have an impact on organizational attractiveness (Pi, 2013).

The four most important influential factors were further influenced by the enterprise developing prospect, salary level, distributive equity, the employer's personal character and so on (Huang, 2007). The organizational career management (OCM) of private enterprises will also affect the attractiveness of private enterprises. However, professional managers' perception on the OCM is generally low, which means that the attractiveness of private enterprises in China is indeed inadequate (Zhang, 2007). Research on the attractiveness of private enterprises to professional managers is also carried out in aspects of trust, family system, information characteristics and relational contract etc. The main conclusion remains to its lack of attractiveness (Li, 2002; Chu, 2002; Chen, 1998). Findings reveal that the management ability of small and medium-sized private enterprises is low, and corporate operations have deteriorated to a closed family model (Ji and Zhang, 2007). The long-term survival and development of enterprises are seriously threatened.

4. The essence and main consequences professional manager turnover in small and medium-sized private enterprises

The lack of corporate appeal may lead to double-sides consequences. On one hand, it is usually difficult for professional managers to enter the enterprises, and it is also not easy for enterprises to absorb professional managers from outside to supplement the scarce management resources. On the other hand, it is easy for enterprises to lose outstanding managers on-the-job (Dai, 2005). According to Wen's research, more than 80 percent of the 10,302 people under investigation wanted to jump to other companies (Wen, 2005). Countries with mature market economy are also lack of professional managers (Holt et al., 2007), relatively speaking, the reasons for the loss of professional managers of small and medium-sized private enterprises in China are more complicated and the consequences are more serious (Li, 2003; Yang and Zhou, 2017). It results in a lack of management talents, low management level and serious obstacles to long-term survival and development of enterprises (Shaw et al., 2005, Qian, 1978). At the same time, with the turnover of professional managers, defection has also occurred (Zhang, 2002; Chu and Liu, 2005), which could be a fatal blow to small and medium-sized enterprises.

Professional manager turnover of small and medium-sized private enterprises not only means that they leave the enterprise voluntarily, but also means that the loss of company management capacity resulting from their turnover is difficult to be supplemented through the market. The turnover of excellent managers in such companies results in lower management ability of the enterprise, which cannot be compensated for attracting talent in the market. This loss is largely due to the company's own factors, and is persistent.

Looking from the normal flow of labor markets, the voluntary turnover of a career manager is not all bad. Existing research shows that appropriate rate of turnover is beneficial to the enterprise (Glebbeek and Erik, 2004, Shaw et al., 2005). The appropriate flow of professional managers in small and medium-sized enterprises has certain advantages to the company's reform, management innovation and process optimization. And, most importantly, the flowing pressure within the organization is conducive to the removal of managers who are at the edge of their ability, and to maintain the efficiency of the organization. As a result, business owners are happy to see a reasonable rate of turnover within the organization.

However, high rates of turnover are surely harmful to enterprises. The professional managers' turnover of middle and high-level will cause great damage to normal running of the enterprises. Managers' turnover not only brings direct cost loss to the enterprise, such as recruitment cost, training cost, replacement cost and so on. Indirect costs are incurred by affecting the normal running of the enterprise, like disrupted business processes, reduced customer service quality, reduced contract performance, and so on (Ramlall, 2003). The total cost of an employee's turnover is roughly 1.5 times to his annual income.

In the United States, the average loss in a company is about $1 million caused by every 10-professional staff's turnover (Fitz-enz, 1997). It is also worth noting that the turnover of professional managers will also affect the morale of the staff, the working atmosphere and the informal network within the organization (Karsan, 2010). The turnover of those managers in elevated position will largely affect the subordinates' work attitude and habits, sometimes even cause the "earthquake" of human resources, lead to continuous turnover of other managers. In the end, the turnover of professional managers may lead to the loss of customer resources, the imitation of core technology and business model, and the leakage of confidential information. In this case, the resulting loss is even huger.

5. Research Gaps

It is necessary and urgent to further study the process and influencing factors of the turnover of professional managers of small and medium-sized private enterprises, and to put forward the overall coordinated governance mechanism. Foreign research on employee turnover is comparatively more mature (Posthuma et al., 2007). It structures a systematic turnover process and factor model (Maertz and Griffeth, 2004). However, the main research object is the general staff, and the empirical analysis of the influence factors of the turnover of professional managers is relatively rare, and it pays little attention to the influence of the employer's self-factors. At the same time, due to the differences in cultural environment and the growth stage of professional managers, the proposed governance measures may lack pertinence and practicality for Chinese enterprises (Farh et al., 2007). Its conclusions and countermeasures are still to be verified in China. Most studies in China also apply the foreign theoretical framework, lack of sufficient investigation into local factors (Zhang, 2006). There is a lack of empirical analysis on professional manager turnover in small and medium-sized private enterprises.

On this account, this study tries to find out the key factors influencing manager turnover, reveal the process of its action, and to probe the internal mechanism related to individual motivation, decision-making process and relationship maintenance. It analyzes literature on employee turnover, enterprise growth, and human resource management both at home and abroad. Through practical investigation and theoretical analysis, the key factors that influence manager turnover are found from individuals, jobs, enterprises and employers themselves. It preliminarily establishes a process model for professional manager turnover of small and medium-sized private enterprises. Further, it gives economic interpretation on manager turnover theoretically. On basis of this, it puts forward methods to keep professional managers in enterprises under current condition.

Research Methods

The technical route of this research is as follows:

Literature review – field work – qualitative research – questionnaire survey – empirical analysis – establishing theoretical model – giving economic explanation – putting forward practical management mechanism

This is an empirical and normative study. Preliminary interview and pre-survey were done to set the main variables and related assumptions required for formal empirical analysis. It tests the influencing factors of professional manager turnover in small and medium-sized private enterprises, based on which a theoretical model was established. On one hand, it ensures the scientific and reliability of the research conclusions. On the other hand, it gives a new theoretical explanation for the turnover of the professional managers of private enterprises in China based on empirical findings. Then the theoretical results are applied in practice. This research raises a systematic governance mechanism to guarantee the practical value of the research results (see Figure 1-1).

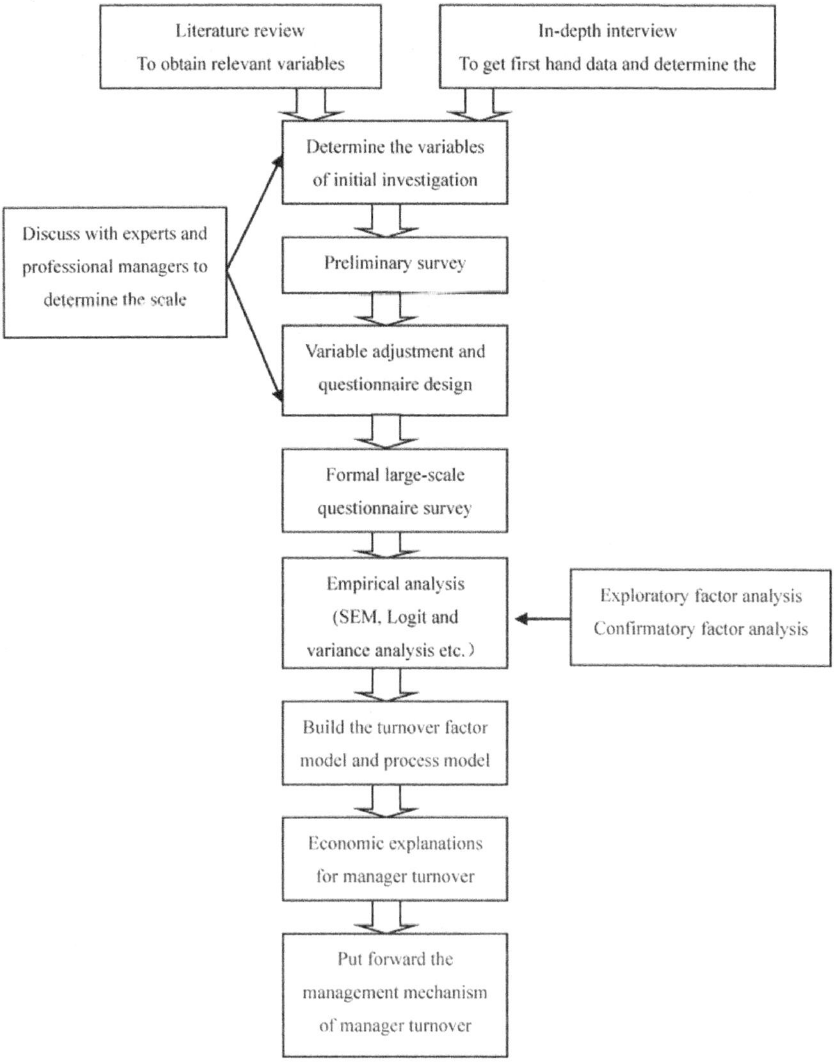

Figure 1-1 Research line

1. Preliminary investigation and selection of influence variables

Screen related variables that affect the turnover of professional managers combined with domestic and foreign research results – Conduct field survey and in-depth interview with no less than 5 small private enterprises in order to obtain first-hand materials and perceptual knowledge related to this study to modify and expand the scale – Make a small preliminary survey of professional managers to improve the scale – Use correlated measurement method to set the primary dependent variables and intermediate variables that affect manager turnover according to results of the survey – Establish hypothesis of the turnover of professional managers based on relevant research results.

2. Formal questionnaire and second survey

Step 1: Set variables

Set individual variables, organizational variables, employer variables, work-related variables, and control variables as the independent variables, according to the actual situation of relevant research and investigation. The personal attitude variable is the intermediate variable. The turnover intention and the turnover behavior are the dependent variables. And the necessary moderating variables are considered.

Step 2: Measure the data

a. Data of the second condition variables such as the position, to leave or not, gender are assigned 0 or 1 according to the situation.
b. The degree variables such as Job satisfaction degree, turnover intention, organizational condition perception, job autonomy, employer leadership, organizational commitment is measured by the Likert-type seven rating scale. 1, 2, 3, 4, 5, 6 and 7 are assigned according to the degree of investigation.
c. The counting variables such as the age and scale of the company are assigned the corresponding numerical value.

3. Use SPSS, Eviews, LISREL software package etc. to conduct the empirical test

Correlation Analysis: Use SPSS16.0 multivariate statistical method to investigate the relationship between the variables, to analyze the correlativity between independent variables, between the independent variables and the mediation variables, and between the independent variables and the dependent variables, finally to identify the important variables that affect the willingness of manager turnover.

Structural Equation Model (SEM) Analysis: By using LISREL8.72 software package and SPSS16.0 reliability test program, based on the large-scale survey data, the test items and data for further analysis are preliminarily set by exploratory factor analysis. It uses confirmatory factor analysis to confirm the relevant data. It tests the reliability of the confirmed latent variables, to ensure that the formal data meet the validity and reliability requirements. At last, it uses these data to make the whole model test of structural equation, finally to find out the optimal turnover process model of fitting index.

Robustness test and regulatory effect test: Based on different measures on intentions of manager turnover[1], we constructs an influencing factors model, and uses the Eviews5.0 package to estimate the corresponding OLS and Logit, compares the relative parameters of the two models to determine whether the estimates are reliable enough, and tests the moderating effect of individual factors on related attitude variables and the moderating effect of employer factors on organizational factors on basis of Logit model.

Consistency test of turnover intention and turnover behavior:

a. Establish Logit Discrete Dependent Variable Test Model. Respectively take the turnover intention and turnover behavior as the dependent variable. It is difficult to get the longitudinal data to directly study the influencing factors of the turnover behavior. And the literature has shown that the turnover behavior is not identical with the intention. Therefore, it is necessary to investigate whether the prediction of turnover intention is consistent with the actual occurrence of the behavior. This study investigates managers who had turnover experience and who are on-the-job now. It mainly studies their perceptions on the company. It tries to test the influencing factors of the manager turnover by using the discrete dependent variable model. Specifically, Managers who have

[1] One is Likert-type seven rating scale, and another is dichotomy variable.

stayed in the company for at least 4 years are set as the variable of "on duty"[2]. Related apperceive variables on current companies are to be measured. Managers who have the experience of turnover are set as the variable of "out of duty". Related perception variables on current companies are to be measured as well. In these samples, the influence factors of the behavior of manager turnover can be tested. Even though this would cause recall biases (Kammeyer-Mueller et al., 2005), under current conditions, comparing the results of this research to the related results of structural equation model has some reference value, based on which the coherence between turnover behavior and turnover intention can be investigated.

b. ANOVA. Variance analysis on managers' perception is used respectively to those who bear turnover intention and who already have turnover experience. In this way, the coherence between turnover behavior and turnover intention of professional managers can be investigated, which can be contrasted to the results of test a.

4. Establish a process model for professional manager turnover

Based on empirical study, this research considers the special institutional environment of private enterprises, explains the way, the process, the path, and the mechanism of professional manager turnover, and establishes a process model for professional manager turnover.

5. Theoretical explanation for professional manager turnover in small and medium-sized private enterprises

Reverse selection and dynamic matching model are used to investigate the process of introducing professional managers into private

[2] This setup is arbitrary to some degree. Despite all this, some studies show that the employees staying in company longer are less possible to leave (Jovanovic, 1979; Boswell et al., 2017; Chen and Francesco, 2000; Mitchell et al., 2001). Consequently, it is somewhat reasonable to set 4 years as threshold.

enterprises. This research tries to deliver a theoretical explanation for professional manager turnover from an economic perspective.

6. **Put forward the management mechanism and corresponding countermeasures regarding professional manager turnover**

Based on the process model and factors model, and the theoretical explanation, this research further explains the influence of different governance mechanisms on the way, the path and the process of professional manager turnover in the real world. It analyses the interaction between various governance mechanisms, and then systematically put forward the management mechanism of the overall coordination of professional manager turnover.

Research Framework

1. SEM method

This part of analysis is mainly done under the frame of Figure 1-2. The preliminarily influence path is as follows:

1. Conception variable of X_1 ......X_{19} affect attitude variable of Y_1......Y_3.
2. Conception variable of X_{20} ......X_{23} and attitude variable of Y_1......Y_3 jointly affect attitude variable of Z_1 and Z_2.
3. Attitude variable of Z_1 and Z_2 affect turnover intention T_1.

This set of process model is to be tested by SEM method. By comparing theoretical research and fitting index, and constantly moderate the path between related variables, the process model which has the highest fitting degree with actual survey data and which obeys theoretical deduction is to be found. This would lay the foundation for further research.

2. Moderating effect

Based on the further empirical research on the factors, the personal variables such as concept consciousness, risk aversion degree and the moderating function of employer factors are to be investigated.

3. Consistency of fore-assessment efficacy between turnover behavior and turnover intention

By using Logit model and ANOVA analysis, it can be tested that whether the fore-assessment of turnover behavior is consistent with turnover intention.

4. Hypotheses

Based on the summarization and collation of relevant literature at home and abroad, the previous in-depth interview and trial investigation, the following research hypotheses can be preliminarily given, on the factors affecting the professional manager turnover of small and medium-sized private enterprises. (See chapter 4 for related theoretical basis)

H1a: The work engagement of professional manager will affect their turnover intention, and the higher the participation degree, the lower the intention to leave the job.

H1b: The work engagement of professional manager will moderate the effect of dependent variables on turnover intention, and the higher the engagement, the weaker the effect of dependent variables on turnover intention.

H2a: The commitment tendency of the professional manager will affect his turnover intention and the higher the commitment tendency, the lower the intention to leave the job.

H2b: The commitment tendency of the professional manager will moderate the influence effect of the dependent variable on resignation intention, and the higher the commitment tendency, the weaker the influence.

H3a: The entrepreneurial motivation of the professional manager will affect the intention to leave, and the stronger the motivation, the higher the turnover intention.

H3b: The entrepreneurial motivation of the professional manager will moderate the influence effect of the previous dependent variable on the resignation intention, and the stronger the entrepreneurial motivation, the stronger the effect.

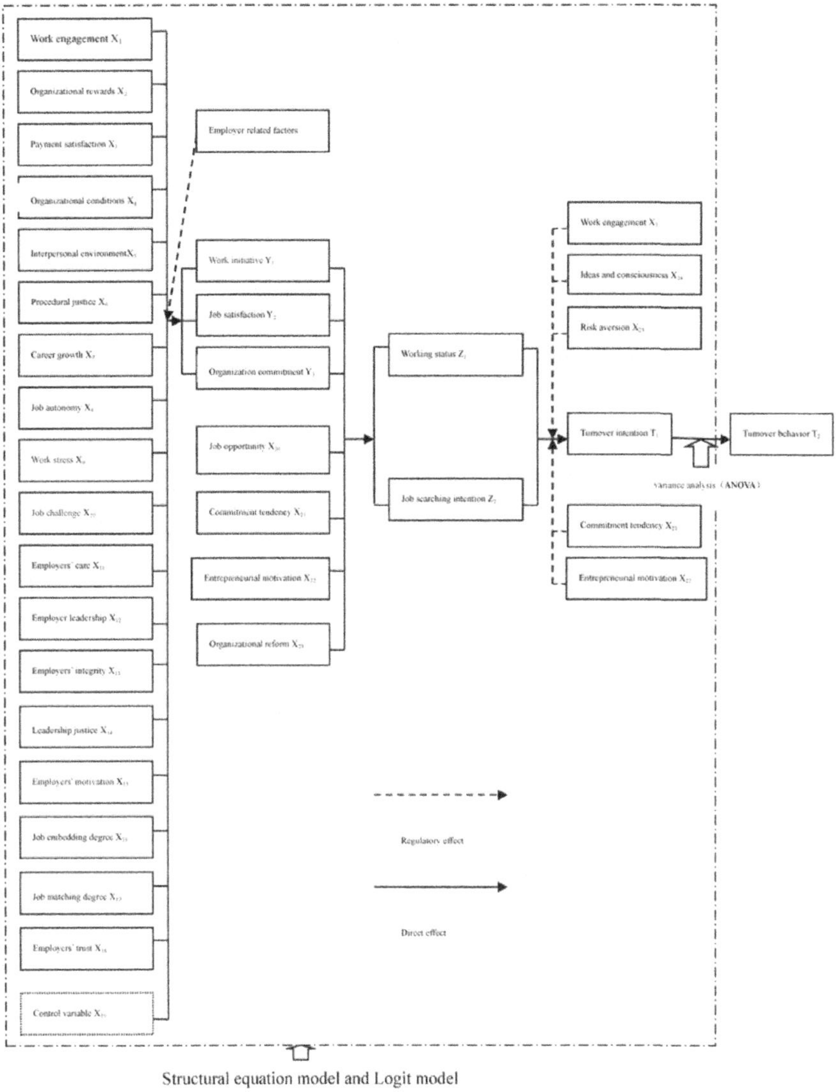

Figure 1-2 Analysis

H4: The organizational rewards that the company provides to the professional manager will influence the manager's turnover intention, and the more satisfied the professional manager is with the perception of the organization's rewards, the lower his intention to leave the job.

H5: The salary that the company provides to the professional manager will affect the manager's turnover intention, and the more satisfied the professional manager is with the salary perception, the lower his intention to leave the job.

H6: The organizational condition of the company will affect the turnover intention of the professional manager, and the more satisfied the professional manager is with the perception of organizational conditions, the lower his intention to leave the job.

H6b: The organizational attractiveness of the company can affect the turnover intention of the professional manager, and the more satisfied the professional manager is with the perception of organizational attraction, the lower his intention to leave the job.

H7: The interpersonal atmosphere of the company will affect the turnover intention of the professional manager, and the more satisfied the professional manager is with the interpersonal atmosphere, the lower his intention to leave the job.

H8: The fairness of the company will affect the turnover intention of the professional manager, and the more satisfied the professional manager is with the perception of fairness, the lower his intention to leave the job.

H9: The career growth opportunity offered by the company to the professional manager will influence the turnover intention of the manager, and the more satisfied the professional manager is with the perception o career growth opportunities, the lower his intention to leave the job.

H10: The organizational change that the company is undergoing or about to go through will affect the turnover intention of the professional manager. If the professional manager perceives this change, the likelihood of his turnover will be higher.

H11: The job autonomy will affect the turnover intention of the professional manager, and the more satisfied the professional manager is with the perception of the job autonomy, the lower the intention of his turnover.

H12: Job stress can affect the turnover intention of the professional manager, and the higher the job pressure perceived by the professional manager, the higher the intention to leave the job.

H13: Job challenges can affect the turnover intention of professional managers, and the more challenging the job managers perceive, the lower the intention to leave the job.

H14: The employer's attention will affect the turnover intention of the professional manager, and the more satisfied the professional manager is with the perceived perception of the employer, the lower his intention to leave the job.

H15: The employer's leadership will affect the turnover intention of the professional manager, and the more satisfied the professional manager is with the perception of the employer's leadership, the lower his intention to leave the job.

H16: The employer's achievement motivation can affect the turnover intention of the professional manager, and the more satisfied the professional manager is with the perception of the employer's achievement motivation, the lower his intention to leave the job.

H17: The integrity of the employer will affect the turnover intention of the professional manager, and the more satisfied the professional manager is with the perception of the employer's integrity, the lower his intention to leave the job.

H18: Leadership fairness will affect the turnover intention of the professional manager, and the more satisfied the professional manager is with the perception of the leadership, the lower his intention to leave the job.

H19: The employer's trust will affect the turnover intention of the professional manager, and the more satisfied the professional manager is with the perception of the employer's trust, the lower his intention to resign.

H20: Job embedding degree will affect the turnover intention of the professional manager, and the higher the degree of job embedding perceived by the career manager, the lower the willingness to resign.

H21: The matching degree will affect the turnover intention of the professional manager, and the higher the matching degree between the professional manager and the organization or the employer, the lower the intention of his resignation.

H22: Other job opportunities will affect career managers' turnover intention, and the more job opportunities the manager perceive, the higher their willingness to leave the current job.

H23: Job satisfaction will affect the turnover intention of the professional manager, and the higher the job satisfaction perceived by the career manager, the lower the intention of leaving the job. In addition, job satisfaction mediates the relationship between the dependent variables and the turnover intention.

H24: The organizational commitment will affect the turnover intention of professional manager, and the higher the organizational commitment of the professional manager, the lower the willingness to leave the job. In addition, the organizational commitment mediates between the dependent variables and the turnover intention.

H25: The work initiative has the ability to predict the turnover intention of the professional manager, and the higher the work initiative of the professional manager, the lower the willingness to resign. In addition, the work initiative plays a mediating role between the related antecedent variables and the turnover intention.

H26: The job status has the ability to predict the turnover intention of the professional manager, and the worse the job status of the career manager, the higher the intention of leaving the job. In addition, the working state mediates between the dependent variables and the turnover intention.

H27: The job searching intention has the ability to predict the turnover intention of the professional manager, and the higher the job search intention of the manager, the higher the willingness to resign. In addition, job searching intention mediates between the relevant attitude variables (e.g., job satisfaction, employer commitment, etc.) and the turnover intention.

H28: The idea and consciousness of professional manager plays a role of regulating the relationship between the dependent variable and turnover intention, and the stronger the traditional consciousness, the weaker the correlation between them.

H29: The degree of risk aversion of the professional manager plays an important role in regulating the relationship between the dependent variables and the turnover intention, and the greater the risk aversion, the weaker the correlation between them.

H30: The employer related factors play a role of regulating the relationship between the organizational factors and turnover intention, and the higher the degree of satisfaction perceived by the professional manager, the weaker the correlation between them.]

H31: The turnover intention is related to the actual turnover behavior, and the higher the turnover intention of the professional manager, the higher the probability of his actual resignation.

Main Contents and Structure

The first chapter introduces the research purpose and significance of this book, gives the relevant research background and research methods, and summarizes the analytical framework and main contents.

Chapter 2 refers to literature review. In order to reveal the shortcomings of existing studies, to support the research hypotheses, the empirical test, theoretical explanation of this research, and to provide preliminary framework of governance mechanisms, this research probes into literature about the effects of the manager turnover to the company, the turnover process and the mechanism, and the influencing factors etc. Comprehensive review of existing literature is made.

Qualitative research based on preliminary field investigation and in-depth interviews with entrepreneurs is conducted in chapter 3, in order to put forward correct relevant research hypotheses and to deliver rational explanation to empirical results. This contributes to building a suitable research framework, which is more in line with manager turnover process and influencing factors of small and medium-sized private enterprises in China.

Chapter 4 stretches into the influencing factors that may cause manager turnover, based on literature review and the qualitative research results from chapter 3. Then specific research hypotheses are put forward respectively, according to the previous dependent variables, mediation variables, moderating variables, interpreted variables and the order of control variables.

Chapter 5 is the core of this book. Based on the actual survey data from Guangdong province, the research hypotheses are empirically tested. First, it gives concrete testing methods and steps, and then it reports the test results of the structural equation model, finally it discusses on the relevant direct and indirect effects, in order to build the process and factors model which are more in line with the particular manager turnover problems of small and medium-sized private enterprises.

Chapter 6 probes into the reliability of the structural equation model by empirical study. The stability of manager turnover factors is tested in this chapter. The moderating effect of manager characteristics and employer factors are tested, and the significance of each variable is investigated according to the characteristics of managers and the company. What's more, it tries to test if the antecedent variables, which can predict turnover intention, can also predict the actual turnover behavior.

Chapter 7 illustrates the process of introducing professional managers into private enterprises in China. Reverse selection and dynamic matching model are used. It tries to find out a theoretical explanation for the manager turnover and the family ownership of private enterprises from the perspective of economics. This explanation also provides several important management implications.

The main conclusions are put forward in the last part. Related management methods of manager turnover are suggested based on the previous research. At last, the innovation of this book is emphasized, and the shortcomings and further research direction are expounded.

Chapter 2

Literature reviews

Manager turnover is caused by the professional manager's voluntary turnover. This book defines it directly as a non-malicious voluntary turnover in order to facilitate the analysis. Existing domestic and international literature on turnover takes general employees as the research objects, and professional managers also belong to this group in the extension. Therefore, the two forms of managers and employees are used in the literature review.

The main reason why people attach so much importance to the issue of turnover is that the turnover will have many important influences on the company. This influence has been found to include two opposite aspects: the pros and the cons, depending on the degree and nature. According to the logical sequence in theory, before studying the process of employee turnover and influencing factors, it should be clear about its impact on company performance and long-term development, but the existing literature is relatively weak in this respect (Hancock et al., 2013; Glebbeek and Bax, 2004).

Impacts of Manager Turnover on The Company

The existing literature gives four types of relationship between voluntary turnover and organizational performance (Shaw et al., 2005): 1. Turnover is detrimental to organizational performance (Batt and Colvin, 2011; Ferreira et al., 2015); 2. At least to a certain extent, voluntary turnover contributes to improving performance (Park and Shaw, 2013); 3. The negative impact of voluntary resignation on performance gradually decreases as the turnover rate increases (Price, 1977); 4. The relationship between turnover and performance depends on the organization's human capital investment and compensation system (Shaw and Shi, 2017; Guthrie, 2001). Abelson and Baysinger

(1984) proposed an "optimal turnover" decision model, which argues that proper employee turnover may be good for the company, but excessively high turnover rates are by no means a good thing (Ekrot et al., 2016). In order to avoid administrative staffing costs resulting from employee turnover, "companies need to find a balance between the losses that may result from employee turnover and the costs of avoiding turnover" (Glebbeek and Bax, 2004, p278).

Conventional views generally hold that leaving a job without doubt is not conducive to organizational efficiency and long-term development (Ferreira et al., 2015). For example, Castro-Casal et al. (2013) pointed out that employee turnover has a strong negative impact on organizational performance. Shaw et al. (2005) conducted an empirical study of the relationship between employee turnover, social capital losses, and store performance with data from 38 stores in a chain of restaurants. The results verified a negative correlation between turnover and store performance. McElroy et al. (2001) divided the turnover into three types: voluntary turnover, involuntary turnover and layoffs, and then examined the effect of different turnover behaviors on the performance of the organizational subordinates. Results found that each form of turnover has a negative impact on the performance of subordinate units. Relatively speaking, layoffs have greater and more widespread negative effects.

In recent years, a large number of theoretical and empirical studies have found that there is no simple negative linear relationship between turnover and corporate performance, and the inverted U-curve hypothesis has been proposed to test it. Based on previous research, Glebbeek and Bax (2004) first examined the hypothesis of this curve relationship between employee turnover and company performance[3]. The results show that higher turnover rate is harmful to the company and the inverted U curve hypothesis is slightly supported. The study by Shaw et al. (2005) also showed that the relationship between voluntary turnover and labor performance has a negative relationship, but with the further increase in turnover, the negative relationship has been

[3] Their research covered both voluntary and involuntary turnovers.

eased. The study also found labor performance as a mediator between voluntary turnover and organizational financial performance. The explanation given by Shaw et al. is that, at a lower level, appropriate voluntary turnover will promote organizational renewal, and the resulting organizational dynamism will help improve employee performance by promoting innovation, work flexibility, and adaptation (Abelson and Baysinger, 1984).

It is worth noting that whether the voluntary turnover of employees is beneficial to the company not only depends on the severity of the separation, but also depends to a considerable extent on other contingencies (Shaw and Shi, 2017; Guthrie, 2001). Shaw and Shi (2017) pointed out that differently oriented human resource management systems[4] have a regulatory effect on the relationship between turnover and labor performance. For those organizations that are characterized by high rewards and high investment-oriented HRM measures (high commitment systems), the relationship is more intense, and for those organizations that with low-investment, low-paying (control systems), the relationship does not perform strongly. In the latter type of HR management system, employees are regarded as easily replaceable products. The vacant positions of former employees can be quickly replaced by other employees. Voluntary turnover does not usually have a significant impact on organizational performance (Shaw et Al., 2005). Guthrie's (2001) interaction effects tests found that when companies use high-involvement work practices (HIWP) too much, employee turnover can reduce productivity. Conversely, when HIWP is used infrequently, turnover increases. In addition, Salamin and Hom's (2005) study found that when leaving employees are highly profitable, and the employees have valuable knowledge and many customer networks, the turnover is more harmful to the company (Wang et al., 2016; Lazear, 1998).

---

[4] In the literatures on strategic human resource management, scholars suggested two sorts of human resource management measures (HRM). One was thought as *investment*, which could ensure high quality of human capital. Another was helpful for retaining human capital and named *inducements* (Pittino et al., 2016).

Regardless of the overall relationship between turnover and organizational performance, the negative impact of employee turnover on the company is unquestionable, especially in the case of higher turnover rate. Studies have shown that the total cost of an employee's turnover is roughly equivalent to 150% of an employee's annual income (Ramlall, 2003). The data presented by Holt et al. (2007) also show that the cost of employees' turnover in private institutions is between 50% and 200% of employees' annual salary (Mitchell et al., 2001). According to estimates by Fitz-enz (1997), in the United States, every 10 managers or professional employees leave, the company will lose an average of about 1 million US dollars. The turnover of top managers is more damaging and sometimes devastating (Wendy et al., 2005).

Because of the many direct costs and indirect costs associated with active turnover, it is very difficult to attempt to give an accurate estimate of the total turnover cost. Kevin et al. (2004) believes that it is difficult to make a comprehensive assessment of the financial impact of turnover because it is not easy to measure the effect of resignation on corporate culture, employee morality, organizational social capital, and organizational memory (Dess and Shaw, 2001). Possible calculable costs include: recruitment, selection, on-boarding education, training, job rotation, job placement, learning costs, possible impact of production and service quality, management time, costs for short-term induction, cost of agency or temporary employees and many more. Even these calculable costs are hard to estimate (Cheng and Brown, 1998).

Mohamad and Nasurdin (2006) pointed out that leaving a job will have a lot of indirect and direct costs, and it will affect the organizational ethical norms, productivity, reputation of the corporation, and the survival of the organization (Mathieu, 2016). Rudy (2007) summed up four direct costs of turnover, respectively separation costs, job vacancy costs, job replacement costs and training costs. In addition, there are indirect costs, such as the reduction of productivity, the destruction of moral and ethical atmosphere, the loss of knowledge and experience, the loss of opportunities, the decrease of customer satisfaction, and the loss of innovation opportunities. Further, Morrell et al. (2001) believe that the employee turnover not only affects the organization, but also affects the employees themselves and the society. The total cost of turnover needs to consider these additional effects.

These studies mainly examine the consequences of ordinary employee turnover in Western organizations. It is easy to see that the harmful effects of professional manager turnover in small and medium-sized private enterprises in China may not stop there. Professional managers are the core resources in an enterprise, and the dependence of small and medium-sized private enterprises on certain individuals is relatively large. The behavior of managers at elevated levels has a significant influence on the organization. Its turnover not only directly leads to the chaos of the normal operation of the company, but also drives its subordinates or other colleagues to "leave". The results are sometimes fatal. A survey of private enterprises in Zhongshan by Li (2003) reveals that private entrepreneurs' primary concern for the introduction of professional managers is trust and loyalty (accounting for nearly 50%). Related to this, the main obstacles for hiring managers come from doubts about their "leaving", such as the leakage or loss of important business private information (corporate tax avoidance information etc.). Professional managers' betrayal activities, such as abusing power, taking away core resources, jumping to competitors etc., may result in interest loss of private entrepreneurs (Ji and Zhang, 2010). Most of the results were confirmed by our field survey.

Concerns about the professional manager turnover have led private entrepreneurs to dare not easily open important management positions to them. Studies by Penrose (1995), Chandler (1978), Zhang (2001), Chu and Li (2003), Zhang and Huang (2003) have shown that private companies must introduce professional managers after they have reached a certain stage, so as to break through the bottleneck of growth and achieve professionalization of management. Therefore, the current problem is that there is a difficult trade-off between the benefits of introducing professional managers for professional management and the agency costs that professional managers may leave (Zhuo et al., 2004). Zhuo et al. (2004) believe that the employment of external professional managers depends on the size of the company. We believe that judging whether to introduce external management resources by size seems too far-fetched, because many theoretical studies have proved that the income generated by employment of external professional managers is greater than the agency cost after considering the risk of turnover.

In fact, in mature market economy countries, the phenomenon of frequent turnover of professional managers is also very common. There is such a warning language in western countries that "Do not let your employees do what you have done to your boss" (Tang, 2003). However, the question here is why betrayal has not always seemed to be a severe problem for employers and managers in these countries. Although the relationship between private entrepreneurs and professional managers in China has its own characteristics, such as the trust based on specialism, it is difficult to establish a true mutual trust relationship between entrepreneurs and professional managers (Liang, 2003; Fukuyama, 1998; Zheng, 1995; Fei, 2005); Civil law system weakens the sense of fiduciary responsibility of professional managers (Lang, 2004), but any similar answers are much too simple by being lack of adequate theoretical and empirical basis.

The existing studies on the consequences of the turnover are mostly based on the assumption that there are sound legal system and market mechanism. Whether the analysis is applicable to test the grave consequences of manager turnover at the present stage in SMEs in China remains to be verified. Therefore, a more in-depth discussion of this should be a very significant topic. Such research will not only help us find the real root cause of professional manager turnover in private enterprises in China, but also help draw lessons from the experiences and solutions of developed market economies in solving similar problems. This book will make effort for this purpose.

Processes and Mechanism of Manager Turnover

The study of the turnover process and mechanism has always been the focus of the voluntary turnover literature. The main purpose of this kind of research is to construct a turnover process model with good explanation, and use it to predict the real-time turnover behavior, and then put forward corresponding governance measures. In addition, this kind of study provides an overall analysis framework for the investigation of the antecedent, mediation, and moderating variables that affect the turnover. In recent years, studies have attempted to combine the process model with the factor model to perform comprehensive tests, and the interpretation result is quite satisfactory (Maertz and Campion, 2004). Relevant studies have shown that it is difficult to clearly separate the research on employee turnover process and influencing factors, and the empirical analysis of this book is based on this understanding. We must not only find the in-depth reasons that affect professional manager turnover, but also build on this basis the entire process model of manager turnover. Aiming at the various stages and paths of the manager turnover, the corresponding operational governance suggestions are proposed.

1. The classic process model of employee turnover

Based on the contributions of Barnard (1938) and Simon (1945), a groundbreaking study by March and Simon (1958) pointed out that employees' actual turnover behavior depends on their perceived desirability and the ease level with which they leave. The former is often equated with job satisfaction in research (Sun and Wang, 2011) and it is influenced by other variables such as work environment, personal values, work relationships, organizational characteristics etc. (Ertürk and Vurgun, 2015; Maertz and Campion, 2004; Mossholder et al., 2005); while the latter is often measured by the number of other job opportunities or the difficulty level of getting a job (for example unemployment etc.) (Griffeth et al., 2000). Both have gradually become the common pillars of turnover studies (Zimmerman et al., 2016).

Morrell et al. (2001) pointed out that although the voluntary resignation literature has made a lot of progress, most studies are still decisively influenced by theorists such as March and Simon. Most of the later progress was only based on these pioneering researches, and real breakthroughs have not yet emerged. Modern research is still based on March and Simon (1958). Steel (2002) also acknowledged that most of the recent resignations have been expanded based on the core model previously proposed, and that the truly fundamental progress has not yet been seen.

As far as the impact of the turnover study itself is concerned, no single research area can be compared to attitude theory. The core model of turnover has been using behavioral attitude variables such as exit/turnover intention. Mobley's (1977) original model first incorporated behavioral willingness into the turnover framework. Other major core models also included similar or related constructs (Waldman et al., 2015; Ertürk and Vurgun, 2015).

The ease level of actual turnover has also been valued by later research institutes, and scholars generally measure the impact of this factor by the number of other job opportunities or the difficulty level of getting a job (Griffeth et al., 2000; Mai et al., 2016). Steel and Griffeth (1989) reported that the average corrected correlation coefficient between perceived other employment opportunities and turnovers reached 0.13. Hom and Kinicki (2001) found that the unemployment rate will directly affect the turnover. In a recent study, Kammeyer-Mueller et al. (2005) used two-year tracking measurement data at five different time points to study the employee's turnover process, and found that the actual turnover was affected by the turnover cost. When repeated measurements were taken along different times, the industry's unemployment rate, job satisfaction, and search for other job opportunities also had a significant effect.

The classical process model of voluntary turnover and the subsequent major developments are based on the two core variables proposed by March and Simon (1958), and most of the later studies centered on these two variables. However, as pointed out by Maertz and Campion (2004), it is not enough to focus solely on the research on the turnover issue. As early as 1986, Cotton and Tuttle (1986) showed that there were at least 26 independent variables, including economic, organizational, work, and personal characteristics, are related to employee turnover. Later studies have gradually expanded the scope of this variable.

2. Mobley intermediary linkage model and its extension

The first major advance in March and Simon's (1958) classical turnover model came from Mobley's (1977) model of mediation. This model deeply investigates the specific process and mechanism of action that employee satisfaction level leading to voluntary turnover of employees. This process includes: status assessment, perception of satisfaction, consideration of turnover, evaluation of expected utility and cost of search behavior, generate search intention, conduct search activities, evaluate other job opportunities, compare with the status quo, generate turnover intentions, and turnover. The greatest value of this model is that it gives a description of the relevant psychological process (Lee and Mitchell, 1994).

Further, Mobley et al. (1979) extended the model of Mobley (1977) further in the framework of the earlier study of March and Simon (1958). This model includes more factors such as organization, environment and personal variables. The model believes that there are four main factors that affect the employee's turnover decision process, namely job satisfaction, expected utility of other work within the organization, expected utility of other work outside the organization, and non-work value and role needs (Morrell et al., 2001). The extended model also makes a meaningful distinction between turnover intention and actual turnover behavior.

Mitchel's (1981) empirical research from the sample of professional managers supports the Mobley model. However, it is worth noting that studies have also found that the relationship between job satisfaction and turnover intention is not as close as expected (as pointed out by Hom and Griffeth, 1991). This may be due to the large difference between the employee loyalty and employee satisfaction. Compared to employee satisfaction, employee loyalty (directly determining the turnover decision) is a more holistic and persistent evaluation response, while job satisfaction is only a short-term emotional response to a job (Dickter et al., 1996).

Because the empirical tests of the early literature on the Mobley model yielded quite inconsistent conclusions, the later resignation studies were very cautious when it came to the relationship between work attitude and turnover. Harrison et al. (2006) recently proposed a concept that is broader than job satisfaction and more explanatory about turnover: the total work attitude. This comprehensive concept includes job satisfaction and organizational commitment (Meyer and Allen, 1991), which has higher explanatory power than any single variable. Harrison et al. applied the principle of compatibility in attitude theory in this study. They believe that the overall work attitude, including job satisfaction and organizational commitment, has strong predictive power on integrated standard of behavior for employees, which combines job performance, non-working contextual performance, late rate, absenteeism rate, and turnover status. And the empirical results support this hypothesis.

There are also many literatures that extend Mobley's (1977) model and other models related to job satisfaction and voluntary turnover. Steers and Mowday (1981) proposed a model that describes the general process of employee turnover behavior. Unlike the aforementioned Mobley model, they considered the role of personal values and job expectations in employee turnover decision-making. The authors believe that personal values and job expectations will affect the employee's emotional attitude toward work, and the latter manifested as job satisfaction, organizational integration and job integration. This emotional attitude is considered to be a decisive factor in the employee's turnover intention. It is also affected by other non-work factors. Finally, this tendency will eventually lead to actual turnover. However, like Mobley's (1977) study, in the comprehensive test of the model by Lee and Mowday (1987), the actual data provided only a very weak support. Hom and Kinicki (2001), based on Hom and Griffeth's (1991) work on the study of how job satisfaction leads to resignation, applied structural equation modeling and survival analysis methods to more closely examine the relevant models. This study increased the influence of job avoidance, role conflict, and employment conditions. Empirical results show that role conflict and work avoidance will indirectly affect the turnover, which is consistent with the view of Hom and Griffeth (1991), and the unemployment rate also plays an important role in the process of turnover.

The labor economic model proposed by Hulin (1985) contains more turnover behavior variables than the Mobley model, such as: psychological retreat of employees (for example: reduction of intentions for work input) and special behavior changes (such as the behavior of wanting to change jobs). Chen et al. (1998) attempted to explain the employee's actual separation behavior by considering the employee's extra-role behavior (i.e., the behavior outside the employee's own job scope). Chen et al. pointed out that the reduction of organizational citizenship means that employees will reduce their work efforts and reduce their work participation. If a series of extra-personal behaviors including morale establishment, relationship promotion, etc. is an employee's upfront payment for the employer's ultimate return (Aryee et al., 2017), then the decrease in performance is the signal of turnover. Similarly, in the work-embedding model of Mitchell et al. (2001), the author believes that a major factor in reducing employee turnover intentions is interpersonal relationships developed through out-of-person mutual assistance behavior. Mossholder et al. (2005) also provide evidence that employees who have fewer interpersonal connections in the company are more likely to leave. In addition, empirical study of Chen et al. (2007) on Chinese samples has taken note of the impact of traditional values on employee turnover decision-making. These studies mainly increase other influence variables in the turnover process given by the Mobley model, to improve the explanatory power of the intermediary relationship model.

3. **Unfolding model of voluntary turnover**

It is generally believed that the aforementioned variants of the Mobley (1977) mediation model occupy the mainstream of early turnover process research. However, Lee and Mitchell (1994) pointed out that this type of model implies a linear rational decision-making process and does not include all possible types of separation process. Based on the concepts and constructs of multiple decision theory, statistics, and social psychology studies, Lee and Mitchell (1994) proposed an unfolding model of voluntary turnover from the perspective of psycho-ethics. This model extends the breadth and depth of the turnover process study. They borrowed concepts from "image theory" to analyze the process of employees' generating exit ideas, searching for job opportunities, and eventually conducting turnover behavior. Based on the concept of "impact", Lee and Mitchell proposed five different turnover decision paths. One typical path (path 3) is that: "impact" generation, personal-organization matching assessment, job satisfaction perception, other job search, other job evaluation, comparison of other job expectations and status, turnover intention, and actual turnover.

Lee et al. (1996) conducted an empirical test on the expansion model. The results show that people will experience different psychological processes when they leave a certain organization. It is difficult for the existing turnover theory to reveal some of the turnover processes and paths. Expanding the model provides a useful framework for analyzing multiple exit decision paths, which can help explain employees' multiple and complex psychological processes. In the sample of Lee et al. (1996), 63% of the turnover can be classified into the four special turnover decision paths.

In fact, before Lee and Mitchell (1994), it had already been pointed out that the specific employee turnover process may be varied, but these studies did not propose a systematic theoretical framework.

There was also no study for the psychological reasons behind the different processes. For example, Steers and Mowday (1981) has proposed that voluntary employee turnover follows a general order. First, personal values and job expectations affect the employee's emotional response to work (which is often embodied in job satisfaction, organizational commitment, job engagement, etc.). Second, this emotional reaction affects employees' willingness to leave. Third, this willingness may eventually lead to actual turnover behavior. Steers and Mowday pointed out that this sequence may vary from person to person, so the specific process of turnover has certain characteristics. This model is partially empirically supported by Lee and Mowday (1987). As an important advance in the aforementioned study, Hulin et al. (1985) recognized that other job opportunities and job satisfaction may have different effects for different people. Therefore, in fact, the cognitive process leading to the final turnover behavior may also be different for different people (Zimmerman et al., 2016; Price and Mueller, 1986). Of course, these studies do not clearly indicate how these differences affect the entire employee turnover decision-making process.

Expanding the model has recently aroused people's interest. Here are three important studies briefly introduced. In order to compensate for the shortcomings of using turnover intention as the turnover behavior variables, Kevin et al. (2004) used actual turnover behavior variables to study how "impact" leads to certain types of turnover decision paths for employees. The authors pointed out profoundly that for the turnover studies, the fundamental problem lies not in why employees leave their jobs but in how they make this decision. Therefore, it is more important to examine the "process" of the turnover decision. As the habit has a major influence on the decision-making of employees, the essence of the resignation decision lies in the decision of "what not to do". Kevin et al. also pointed out that there are multiple impacts may lead to turnover. These impacts may come from personal reasons. They may also be work-related or unrelated, or positive, or just an expectation etc. In short, distinct types of impacts have different effects on the turnover decision process.

Kammeyer Mueller et al. (2005) measured the impact variables of turnover at five different points in 2 years, and attempted to arrive at a dynamic model that better understood the turnover process. The authors used a survival regression method to predict whether employees would leave or not, and predict when they would leave. The empirical results show that the turnover behavior is affected by the perceived turnover costs, organizational commitments, and key events that occur soon after entering the organization. When repeated measurements are taken along various times, industry unemployment, job satisfaction, and the search for other job opportunities significantly affect the turnover behavior. The study also found that key events affect turnover in a way that is different from the concept variable, which is consistent with the interpretation of the unfolding model (Lee and Mitchell, 1994). Unfolding model shows that the main reason why most people continue to engage in a job is not the choice but the habit. However, the key events will shock individuals and make them reassess their status. A study by Kammeyer Mueller et al. found that 26.5% of the departed employees experienced discontinuous key events before leaving the job. It can be roughly estimated that the same proportion of employees in this sample was resigned after being attacked by extraordinary events. Thus, the reported key events are indeed related to higher risk of turnover. Another noteworthy aspect of the study is that it examines the dynamic process of turnover by repeatedly measuring certain turnover predictors, which can help identify important inter-relationships. For example, previous studies did not find a meaningful relationship between job search and turnover, but according to Kammeyer Mueller et al. (2005), this may be due to previous studies using static data.

The research aim of Holt et al. (2007) is also to test the Lee and Mitchell (1994) model. The survey data for this study comes from 182 US Air Force officers who have resigned. The results showed that 47% of the respondents left the organization in the way of the five different turnover paths proposed by Lee and Mitchell (1994). In order to reflect the unique nature of military services (for example, some military officers have previously planned to leave the army after a certain period of time or when an incident occurs), the revised deployment model can explain 83% of the turnover decision.

4. The "embeddedness" model

Mitchell et al. (2001) borrowed the concept of "embeddedness" in socioeconomics (Granovetter, 1985) in his study on employee turnover, and proposed to use job "embeddedness" to explain employee turnover intention and turnover behavior. Here, the work embeddedness is used to reflect the status of the employee's contact with a social network (community or organization, etc.). It consists of three important aspects: 1. The extent to which employees maintain links with other people and activities; 2. The degree of fit of work and work-based communication circles with other aspects of the "life space"; 3. The ease level of the contact being broken (i.e. the sacrifice if they leave the current company).

Lee et al. (2004) empirically tested the "embeddedness" model. The author divides the structure of "embeddedness" degree into two dimensions: the on-the-job and off-the-job degrees of embeddedness, which are then introduced into the econometric model. Relevant empirical results show that the degree of off-the-job "embeddedness" is significantly related to voluntary turnover and automatic absence, while the degree of has no corresponding explanatory power; the degree of on-the-job "embeddedness" is significantly related to organizational citizenship behavior and work performance, and off-the-job "embeddedness" has no forecast effect on it. In addition, the degree of "embeddedness" also moderates the effects of absenteeism, organizational citizenship behavior, and work performance on employee turnover.

The greatest contribution of the "embeddedness" model is the emphasis on the impact of employee-relative social networks on their turnover decisions. Previous studies either completely ignored this factor or treated it as an accessory variable and lacked the theoretical basis for introducing this crucial factor. Mitchell et al. (2001) keenly perceive that individuals are deeply trapped in the social network. They borrowed the concept of "embeddedness" from the research results of economic sociology, and provided a theoretical basis for people to formally examine the influence of social networks in the turnover process model.

Under the guidance of Mitchell et al. (2001) and Maertz and Campion (2004), the latest study by Mossholder et al. (2005) examines the ability of relational variables to predict turnover behavior. The article finds that the relationship variables of individual's network centrality and interpersonal citizenship behavior significantly influence employee's turnover intention within 5 years. This study to some extent supports the "embeddeness" model.

5. Other extensions of the turnover process model and the latest developments

The aforementioned four types of models occupy the mainstream of research on the turnover process. Now there is an endless stream of literature that continues to enrich relevant theoretical and empirical research. This section continues with a brief review of the other aspects of the process model's expansion and recent developments around the subject of turnover decision-making process.

Some scholars have reminded that the reason why the turnover problem is still far from being fully understood is mainly due to the openness of methodological problems (Steel, 2002) and that the psychological process behind turnover has not yet been fully understood (Dick et al. (2004). Although the above-mentioned expansion model and intermediary linkage model have made some work on this, it must be admitted that we are still far from the complete understanding of the psychological process behind the turnover and the corresponding turnover decision-making process.

There are several studies in the literature that focus on the personal history and experience of employees before they enter the company and their impact on the subsequent decision-making process. Murray and Zimmerman (2005) pointed out that although the existing resignation study has been "sweeping," most of the research focuses on the process and reasons why employees leave the organization, and few studies have examined whether employers can reduce their turnover rate during the recruitment selection phase. Most of the researchers are concerned that before the applicant accepts a job, the organization provides a clear perception and expectation at the beginning of the job by providing it with favorable or unfavorable information about the job, thereby reducing the turnover intention afterwards. Therefore, it is of great significance to examine the history of employees before they enter.

Wendy et al. (2005) focused on the aforementioned traditional turnover process models (March and Simon, 1958; Mobley, 1977, etc.) by studying the dynamic mechanisms and processes of interactions and interactions between job conversion and job satisfaction. Wendy et al. pointed out that low job satisfaction can lead to job conversion, which in turn can temporarily increase job satisfaction (honeymoon effect), and then reduce job satisfaction (hysteresis). This study models job satisfaction as a function of individual job conversions, which will determine whether the work attitude changes systematically with the turnover process. The practical significance lies in reminding managers that the previous turnover experience of new employees has a dynamic impact on their current job satisfaction and turnover intention. Susanna and Aryee (2003) noted that the history of the collapse of psychological contract experienced by an individual is related to the collapse of the current psychological contract. The latter is also related to their turnover intention, psychological turnover behavior, and organizational citizenship. Samples of the study were taken from Hong Kong of the Chinese employees (N=152). Its conclusion has direct and inspirational significance for us to study the issue of manager turnover in the context of China.

To understand the mechanism of the "outbreak" of the employee turnover, Sheridan and Abelson (1983) proposed a so-called spike catastrophe model. The dynamic model points out that before the final decision of turnover, the employee's sense of work tension and commitment to the organization will cross a certain threshold levels. Only when the combination of the two-dimensional variables accumulated to a certain extent, actual turnover behavior will occur.

In addition, the latest research by Maertz and Campion (2004) attempts to combine the process model and the factor model of turnover to conduct comprehensive tests. According to their understanding, the process model focuses on the process of how employees leave, while the factor model focuses on the reasons that affect employee turnover. As the turnover intention leads to the turnover decision-making process (Mobley, 1977), a certain type of intention may lead to the occurrence of a particular type of turnover more frequently than other types (eg, the temptation of other job opportunities may lead to rational turnover after employee's deliberate consideration, and dissatisfaction and resentment with bosses may easily lead to a confrontational irrational turnover process). Therefore, it is necessary to combine the turnover intention and turnover process to conduct a comprehensive study, so as to provide a more accurate description, and more specifically propose corresponding governance measures. In empirical studies, Maertz and Campion (2004) summarized the sample of 159 actual demobilized employees into four diverse types of turnover processes, and measured the size of each of the eight intentions leading to their turnover. It was found that those who did not have other job opportunities were worse off than other job leavers, which meant they might be emotionally driven. Maertz and Campion suggested that combining these two types of models would be a promising direction for future turnover studies.

6. Related domestic research

Zhang (2003) studied the importance and mechanism of mutual trust in maintaining professional manager loyalty. He pointed out that the mechanism for the realization of this trust includes three types, namely legal mechanisms, emotional mechanisms, and reputation mechanisms. As for how to establish mutual trust between entrepreneurs and professional managers, the author believes that it can start with the internal system and the external environment. The former includes the accumulation of trust resources, proper separation of control rights, information communication, the construction of corporate culture, formal rules and non-formal rules; the latter include the legal environment, the role of intermediary agencies (such as accounting firms), managers' markets, education for professional managers, and so on. Zheng (1995), Chu and Li (2003), and Li (2003) also studied the influence of the trust mechanism on the decision-making process of employees and managers in the Chinese organizations and Chinese private enterprises.

Zhang (2002) emphasized the influence of employer honesty on manager's betrayal decision. The model given in this paper analyzes in depth how the gaming relationship between entrepreneur and manager leads the manager to make a betrayal decision. Xie et al. (2006) proposed an employee turnover early warning mechanism based on the analysis of the relationship between employee loyalty and actual turnover. Liang et al. (2005) studied the impact of job embeddedness, employee organizational performance, and personal relationship networks on employee turnover behavior. Zhao et al. (2005) proposed that whether employee's turnover intention can be converted into actual turnover behaviors is affected by the difficulty degree in getting other jobs. The latter is generally determined by the supply and demand conditions in the labor market.

7. Brief review

The above research can provide some theoretical basis and research framework for us to analyze the process and mechanism of manager turnover. The turnover decision of the special group of professional managers, however, does not necessarily conform to the prediction of the existing process model. For example, the turnover process caused by the "shock" brought about by entrepreneurial opportunities cannot be classified as any of the paths proposed by Lee and Mitchell (1994). The turnover decision caused by the deterioration of the "relationship" with employers is difficult to examine under the framework of the mediation model proposed by Mobley (1977) and its extension.

In addition, due to the particularity of the turnover process of professional managers in private enterprises in China, and the great differences between cultural background and institutional environment, many local factors that have important impact on the turnover process and mechanism are difficult to examine under the framework of foreign research. For example, SME managers often equate the organization with the employer itself, and its perception of employer characteristics and behavior plays a key role in the decision-making process (Zhang, 2002), but the existing process model does not pay attention to it. At the current stage, when the legal system and market environment are not so perfect, the external lack of binding force on the behavior of managers will inevitably affect the calculation of turnover costs and benefits of professional managers. Differences in this external environment are difficult to be analyzed under the existing framework.

Therefore, it is not appropriate to copy the existing conclusions of foreign research and propose relevant governance proposals. The domestic literature on the employee turnover process is relatively inadequate (Zhang, 2006), and the empirical research on the turnover of professional managers is even rare, which makes it difficult for us to put forward a practical governance mechanism for the turnover of managers of small and medium-sized enterprises based on the existing literature.

Based on China's reality, this book analyzes the intrinsic characteristics of small and medium-sized private enterprises and entrepreneurs in depth using qualitative research method. It combines with the uniqueness of Chinese managers' career goals, achievement motivation, commitments propensity, and job involvement etc., proposes and verify the turnover decision model from the process of related factors perception, work attitude change, job search intention and final turnover behavior, and clarify the chaotic relationship between different paths and phases given by different existing process models. A new process model is proposed based on adequate consideration of sufficient local factors.

Influencing Factors of Turnover Intention and Turnover Behavior

1. Overview

The turnover intention and turnover behavior of professional managers are determined in a series of processes, any factors that contribute to this process will have an impact on professional managers' decisions (Tews et al., 2013). There are many papers in the literature studying these influencing factors (Posthuma et al., 2007; Glebbeek and Bax, 2004; Griffeth et al., 2000). Based on these studies and the information obtained from the previous field interviews, this book will fully consider the specificity of the turnover of professional managers in small and medium-sized private enterprises, and design scales suitable for the study of this book to conduct large-scale surveys and empirical analysis, and finally find out the deep reasons that affect the turnover of professional managers in small and medium-sized private enterprises.

Based on the pioneering contributions of Barnard (1938) and Simon (1945), March and Simon (1958) identified two main reasons that affect employee voluntary turnover, namely: desirability and easy degree, which later became the main constructs and cornerstones of the turnover study (Zimmerman et al., 2016). Lee and Mitchell (1994), after reviewing previous relevant literature, pointed out that research on the factors affecting the voluntary turnover can be divided into two categories: 1. Factors other than individuals lead to turnover, that is, pull theory; 2. Individual internal factors lead to turnover, that is, push theory. Russ and Mcneilly (1995) believe that in theory, the variables that affect turnover behavior and turnover intention mainly include organizational commitment, job satisfaction, role pressure, supervisory variables, and environmental variables etc.

Mobley (1982) also gives a classification of the factors affecting turnover, namely: economic environment (such as unemployment level and inflation, etc.); organizational variables (such as company size, job design, etc.); personal non-work variables (such as spouse occupation, family responsibility etc.); individual work-related variables (such as expectations, abilities etc.). Tews et al.'s (2013) classification is similar: individual variables (eg, age, gender); work-related variables (eg, role conflict, peer support); environmental variables (eg, job opportunities); employee orientation (eg, organizational commitment, turnover intention) (Du et al., 2006). The study by Holt et al. (2007) concluded that the antecedent variables mentioned in the voluntary resignation literature can usually be classified into three categories, namely: personal characteristics, organizational characteristics, and environmental characteristics.

Traditionally, people generally believe that attitude theory dominates the major t turnover studies (Steel, 2002; Wendy et al., 2005). However, later studies have shown that working attitudes play only a minor role in employee retention and turnover (Griffeth et al., 2000), and other factors are also very important for understanding employee turnover (Mai et al., 2016; Mitchell et al., 2001). For example, the motivation model of Price and Mueller (1986) emphasizes structural antecedent variables. This more complete factor model gives a causal path between the influencing factors and the final turnover behavior (Price, 2001).

In general, foreign literature mainly involves influencing factors of: personal variables, such as values, job participation, achievement motivation, etc. (Chen et al., 2007; Trevor, 2001; Maertz and Campion, 2004); work-related variables, such as job autonomy, work stress, etc. (Posthuma et al., 2007; Judge et al., 2010; Lee et al., 2004); relational variables, such as commitment propensity, family responsibility, etc. (Price and Mueller, 1986; Tews et al., 2013; Maertz and Campion, 2004); organizational factors, such as compensation system, promotion space, procedural fairness, etc. (Payne and Huffman, 2005; Benson et al., 2004; Farh et al, 2007); external environment, such as unemployment, other job opportunities, etc. (Griffeth et al., 2005).

As mentioned above, many studies have been carried out around factors affecting turnover (Glebbeek and Bax, 2004; Griffeth, et al., 2000). But so far, it is surprising there is not a general explanation accepted by most people why the staff conduct turnover (Lee and Mitchell, 1994). Maertz and Campion (2004) reminded that even though the existing substantial number of turnover studies has verified many factors that lead to turnover, but even the most massive models may ignore some important variables (Mai et al., 2016; Mitchell et al., 2001). Griffeth et al. (2000) pointed out more worryingly that although many factor models have certain validity in the measurement test, in general, most of the articles are based on independent variables set for their research purposes and research conditions. Few models have explained more than 10% of the variance of turnover variable.

In order to change this situation, Maertz and Campion (2004) gave an analysis framework based on predecessors' research that included most of the influencing factors of employee turnover. The framework summarizes numerous factors into the eight motivational forces. Maertz and Campion pointed out that previous studies ignored or underestimated the influence of relationships, embeddedness, family and friend expectations, psychological contracts, and other factors, and only studied the "surface" relationships between influencing factors and turnover, and did not give precise motivational process of turnover intention and turnover behavior. This should be the main reason for the poor explanatory power of existing factor models. The author therefore proposes a more complete system of influencing factors, including eight possible motives for employee turnover, namely: affective forces, calculative forces, contractual forces, behavioral forces, alternative forces, normative forces, moral/ethical forces, and constituent forces etc. These turnover motivations can enter in empirical models in the form of intermediary variables (Posthuma et al., 2007). This large system can integrate most of the turnover-influence factors involved in the previous study into a comprehensive framework, enriching the existing detachment literature in several ways: 1. To confirm the psychological mechanism of turnover caused by initial pre-variable variables; 2. To provide theoretical components for the analysis of the effects of related factors on turnover; 3. To supplement the turnover procedure theory and the further development of a comprehensive measure of turnover motivation (Maertz and Griffeth, 2004).

2. Main influencing factors of turnover

Personal factors

It is generally believed that employees' personal factors have a significant impact on their turnover intention and behavior. And as Waldman et al. (2015) pointed out, the turnover caused by personal reasons is very likely to be unavoidable. What the organization can do is to extend the turnover management to the starting point of the human resources management system, and from the recruitment process, it begins to pay attention to the issue of turnover. Of course, Campion's statement is too negative. In fact, some factors are unique to employees and have existed before entering the company, which cannot be changed by current organization. However, there are many personal characteristics that are formed after employees entering the company, which are within the control of the organization.

There are some probable personal variables that have an impact on turnover, namely: job involvement (Price, 2001; Lance, 1991), commitment propensity(Lee and Mitchell, 1994; Zhang, 2006), education level (Trevor, 2001), age and position (Cohen, 1999), specificity degree of human capital investment, personality adaptability (Barrick and Mount, 1996), personal values orientation (Hom and Griffeth, 1995), family responsibility (Iverson, 1992; Maertz and Campion, 2004), work experience (Griffeth et al., 2000; Meyer and Allen, 1991), emotional variables (Price, 2001; Zhang, 2006) and so on. Following are some brief reviews about selective ones.

Job involvement

Job involvement refers to the willingness of employees to work hard. It differs from the general concept of involvement, which also refers to the willingness to work, but does not specifically target a job (Price, 2001). It is pointed out that job involvement has a direct effect on organizational commitments because highly involved employees have a higher degree of commitment to organizations that can provide him with opportunities to perform work activities (Ravichandan, 2015; Lance, 1991). Therefore, it is very necessary to consider this variable in the turnover test model.

Commitment propensity

This is a personal characteristic that individuals have before entering the organization. In general, employees who have a lower commitment propensity before entering the organization are unlikely to have a high commitment propensity to the organization (Lee and Mitchell, 1994). The reason is that the employees with lower commitment propensity sometimes regard "job-hopping" as an important means to increase professional experience and qualifications. Therefore, it can be expected that employees who have had multiple turnover experiences are more likely to leave their jobs (Zhang, 2006).

Family responsibility

Price (2001) places emphasis on the relationship between family responsibilities and the turnover. He pointed out that since economists and psychologists occupy a decisive position in this field, the turnover study seldom considers the variable of family responsibility. Economists are interested in variables such as opportunities, general training, salary, and search behavior. Psychologists mainly examine attitude variables such as job involvement, positive/negative emotions, job satisfaction, and organizational commitment. Therefore, family responsibilities are rarely mentioned by these researchers. Price believes that family responsibility will reduce the probability of turnover. Iverson (1992) and Maertz and Campion (2004) also pointed out that the sense of responsibility for the family does affect the employee's turnover decision.

Work experience

The influence of past work experience on employee turnover decisions has also attracted the attention of many scholars (Meyer and Allen, 1991; Griffeth et al., 2000). An empirical study carried out by Susanna and Aryee (2003) based on the Hong Kong sample found that the history of psychological contract ruptures that employees have experienced in other companies in the past may affect the degree of psychological contract stability in current organization. The reason is that employees with a history of psychological contract rupture will weaken the trust of similar employers. He would think that he is not in relational contract relationship with current employer, but in transactional contract relationship. He would leave once this trading relationship breaks down. Griffeth et al. (2005) applied managerial studies to examine the dynamics and processes of interactions between job conversion and job satisfaction, and to challenge the traditional turnover model's focus on the recursive relationship between job satisfaction and turnover. The study pointed out that a low level of job satisfaction can lead to job conversions, which in turn can temporarily increase job satisfaction (honeymoon effects), and then reduce job satisfaction (hysteresis). This means that employees with experience in job conversion will have more satisfaction when they first enter the company, but as time passes, this satisfaction will return to normal levels. Therefore, the satisfaction survey of recent employees has been investigated. It is difficult to obtain a true estimate of the turnover intention.

Emotional variables

Positive/negative emotions refer to the dispositional tendencies of an individual's pleasant/unpleasant emotional state. This variable seems to be like job satisfaction, but it is different. It is an individual's own orientation of temperament, and has nothing to do with work, organization or even other personal factors. According to the study of Brief et al. (1988), positive and negative emotions not only directly affect job satisfaction, but also modulate the relationship between other exogenous variables and turnover. For example, the study of

Eisenberger et al. (2001) found that emotional factors can moderate the relationship between POS and emotional commitment and organizational self-distribution. Therefore, the study on turnover must control the influence of such emotional variables in the turnover model. Otherwise the results obtained by the model will be biased. The literature shows that emotional variables often affect job satisfaction through selective perception. Highly positive employees selectively perceive good aspects of their work and thus increase their job satisfaction. At the same time, he will look at those ambiguous stimuli and shocks in a positive manner and attitude to improve satisfaction. Conversely, employees with negative emotions often perceive the bad side of work or organization, thereby reducing their job satisfaction (Price, 2001). Zhang's (2006) research from the employee sample of the Chinese IT industry supports the significant effect of emotional variables on job satisfaction and thus on turnover intention.

Other personal factors include the specificity degree of human capital investment (Becker, 1964), general training (Price, 2001; Zhang, 2006), some personal key events (Kammeyer-Mueller et al., 2005; Kevin et al., 2004; Lee and Mitchell, 1994), demographic background (Griffeth et al., 2000) etc.

Organizational factors

Organizational factors are the focus of our research. From the perspective of private enterprises themselves, the factors that they can control have more important significance. Enterprises can take relevant measures according to the actual situation to enhance their attractiveness and retain excellent professional managers.

By summarizing, the organizational factors involved in the existing literature mainly include: the degree of organizational integration (Hom et al., 2017); the organizational socialization process after employees enter the company (Griffeth et al. (2000), such as the company's mentoring of new employees (Paynea and Huffman, 2005; Park et al., 2016); the company's human capital investment (Benson et al., 2004; Becker, 1964), such as on-the-job and off-the-job training funding (Trevor, 2001; Johnson, 2007); organizational structure, such as the degree of decentralization of decisions (Korff et al., 2017) and the development of policy measures and related procedures (Meyer and Allen, 1991); development potential provided by company (Rubel and Kee, 2015; Morrow, 2011; Trevor et al., 1997; Lyness and Judiesch, 2001); demographic background and degree of social integration of groups (Dulebohn et al., 2016); teamwork; Leadership; pay satisfaction; fairness; promotion opportunities; company location; working atmosphere and so on (Griffeth et al., 2000; Ramlall, 2003).

The primary purpose of most of the turnover studies is to find the organization's own controllable factors, and then take corresponding management measures accordingly, to achieve the goal of reducing turnover. Therefore, research on organizational factors is a major part of the relevant literature. Almost all literature on employee attitudes, job performance, and turnover intentions consider the effects of organizational factors (Lee and Mitchell, 1994; McElroy et al., 2001; Ramlall, 2003; Krishnan et al., 2006).

The theoretical basis for analyzing organizational factors in human resource management research includes labor market theory, social exchange theory, and social identity theory. Certainly, not all relevant studies have explicitly pointed out the theoretical framework, but it is not difficult to find from the literature that the research on the turnover of organizational factors actually implies these theoretical foundations. Labor market theory should apply the standard economic analysis methods to study labor supply and demand, so as to determine what organizations need to do for employees. Since the main conclusions in this regard have been written into textbooks, the book will not repeat them. Here we mainly review the main points of social exchange theory and social identity theory.

Blau (1964) first made a distinction between the two concepts of social exchange and economic exchange. According to his point of view, social exchange refers to the existence of some undefined future obligations. Although like the economic exchange, the social exchange relationship also has the expectation that the contributor will give a certain future return. However, unlike the economic exchange, the exact nature of this future return is not clearly defined in advance. Moreover, social exchange is not based on compensation or calculation basis. In general, economic exchanges are based on transactions, which are embodied in the form of transactional contracts. Social exchanges are based on personal trust and are embodied in the form of relational contracts (Prooijen, 2015). In social exchange relations, the parties believe that the other party in the relationship will fulfill their obligations fairly and reasonably in the long term (Frazier et al., 2016).

According to Blau (1964) and other scholars such as Porter and Sang, (2015) and Prooijen (2015), trust and other "macro motives" such as loyalty, commitment, etc. can provide the basis for relationship contracts and social exchange relationships. Macro motive is a collection of attributes that portray individuals' feelings and beliefs about their trading partners, such as the belief that "My supervisor is trustworthy". Under such macro-motivated support, the relationship contract between the organization and the employees will motivate the latter to act in a desirable way that is not specifically requested by the boss (Prooijen, 2015).

Social identity theory is often used to explain individual behavior in organizations (van Dick et al., 2004). Organizational identification is a self-defining concept which refers to the sense of the overlap between the self and the group, as well as the internalization of the organization's core values and identity characteristics. Existing research points out that social identity within an organization can explain individual performance, satisfaction, and willingness of turnover (van Dick et al., 2004). According to the theory, identity is a general, extended-out feeling of the common destiny of individuals and organizations. Therefore, an employee with a high degree of recognition will not easily leave the organization. Similar identity theory and self-verification theory (Burke, 1991; Bench et al., 2015) also pointed out that subordinates' needs should be met, to establish, confirm, and maintain its role identity. For individuals, the importance of a given identity is determined by the fact that they no longer maintain this role or abandon the social and personal costs of the role expectations (Brown, 2015). Therefore, an organization can reduce employees' turnover intention by increasing the cost of employees' abandonment of organizational roles (Farmer and Aguinis, 2005).

Van Dick et al. (2004) used the social identity approach framework to study individual behavior. They point out that individuals will think and act in the direction of the interests of their respective groups, because the identity of being a member in this group increases his social identity, which will partly determine his self-esteem. The theory of social identity and self-categorization points out that stronger organizational identity is associated with lower turnover intention. Van Dick et al. found that since identity is a more general perception of the common destiny of employees and organizations, the relationship between identification and turnover will be indirect, with job satisfaction in between playing an intermediary role. The four samples of this study all support this hypothesis.

Work factors

The meta-analysis results of Griffeth et al. (2000) show that the factors related to the work itself have an important influence on employees' turnover intention and behavior. Three of the seven structural variables given by Price (2001) are related to job characteristics, respectively: job autonomy, job stress, and job monotony. The work pressure here includes insufficient resources, ambiguous roles, conflicting roles, and workload (Zhang, 2006).

Rusbult and Farrell (1983) defined two important types of work variables that are significantly related to turnover: job benefits and work costs. The former includes autonomy, impartiality, support from superiors and partners (Tews et al., 2013; Judge et al., 2010), pay and performance (Hom et al., 2017). The latter includes job routilization, role confusion, role conflicts, work risks, etc. (Kahn et al., 1964; Roof, 2015). Employees tend to conduct turnover when job gains fall or work costs rise (Rusbult and Farrell, 1983). In addition, job embeddedness (Lee et al., 2004; Mitchell et al. 2001), job matching and job content itself (Griffeth et al., 2000) also affect turnover intentions and actual turnover behavior. According to the literature, combined with previous field surveys, this book considers three important work factors, namely: work autonomy, work pressure and job challenges.

Relational variables

Since March and Simon (1958), most of the studies on turnover believe that employees' perceived satisfaction is the main predictor for employee turnover. For instance, the review by Griffeth et al. (2000) and Mai et al. (2016) shows that the perceived sense of desirability of employees measured by job satisfaction or other work-related attitudes is negatively related to turnover. The results strongly support the main conclusions of this classic study from March and Simon. On this basis, people gradually noticed that relational variables have a significant impact on employee turnover beyond job attitudes and other job opportunity variables (Price, 2001). Cohen (1999) pointed out that some non-working areas of variables (such as relationships with peers, etc.) can affect the actual turnover decision (which is different from the turnover intention). Dess and Shaw (2001) also noted the importance of relational variables for interpreting turnover behavior. Low quality of relationships can lead to high organization costs, which resulting in higher turnover rates.

Systematic studies of relational variables are from Mitchell et al. (2001), which examined the impact of relationships on employee turnover intentions and behaviors based on an important concept in economic sociology— "embeddedness". Mitchell et al. use the concept of job embeddedness to reflect the employee's connection to a social network (community or organization, etc.). In this framework, work embeddedness includes three important dimensions: 1. The extent to which employees maintain links with other people and activities; 2. The fit degree of employees' work and social circle and other aspects of "life space"; 3. The ease of the connection being broken - that is, the sacrifice if they leave the present company. These three dimensions are named by Mitchell et al. as links, fit and sacrifice.

In addition, under the guidance of Maertz and Campion (2004), the study by Mossholder et al. (2005) examines the predictive power of relational variables on turnover behavior. It finds that the relationship variables of network centrality and interpersonal citizenship behavior significantly affect the actual employee turnover behavior after 5 years, while the other two previous theoretical and empirical studies found that the very important relationship variables, namely: perceived coworker support and the felt obligation toward coworkers, did not receive empirical support from the sample. The authors pointed out that this may be because the five-year forecast period is too long for such concept variables. But in general, relational variables do play a very important role in employees' turnover decisions.

Employer factors

As the third chapter of this book will point out, the employer-side factors play a key role in the decision-making process of professional managers of small and medium-sized private enterprises. However, in the context of western culture, the employer's own influence on the personal attitudes and results within the organization is less important. Related to this, the existing literature rarely directly studies the employer's influence on employee turnover intention. This section mainly reviews the research related to the relevant factors of superiors, and combines some documents based on oriental cultural background to clarify the reasons for our focus on employer factors.

Scholars have noticed that research organizations in the context of Chinese culture must consider the influence of certain important individuals. The reason for this difference is very complicated. The first reason is of course cultural differences. Since many studies originate in English-speaking countries, many widely-dissemination theories and findings of circulation do not necessarily apply to other cultural environments (Hom and Xiao, 2006; Farh et al., 2007). Some people think that the importance of superiors is rooted in Chinese traditional culture and is influenced by Confucianism (Farh and Cheng, 2000). In the Confucian ethical order, there is a five-state theory. In the five-in-one relationship, individuals with lower status have the obligation to obey and be loyal to their respected superior figures. On the other hand, high-ranking individuals are considered to show kindness and affection for the lower-status people. Chen et al. (2002) mentioned that in the United States, individualism and independence are the main values, and the promises to the superiors are based on common values and goals. Their respect is also treated as a person who is the same as himself. In China, however, the main value orientation is collectivism and authoritative dependence, and subordinates' commitments to superiors are mainly based on personal sacrifice (self-sacrifice), responsibilities, and respect for their boss role as an authority figure (Chen and Aryee, 2007). "In a relationship-oriented society, employers are more important than non-personalized organizations in influencing employee behavior and attitudes" (Chen et al., 2002, p353).

Another study pointed out that this may be related to the fact that Chinese society still retains a degree of human governance rather than the rule of law (Chen and Francesco, 2000). The main characteristic of the rule of society is that the influence of important people in social groups is greater than that of groups and institutions, and the distribution of resources depends mainly on the will of certain individuals. China is a society characterized by "personalism" (Redding, 1990), where rules from people, rather than rules from the law, regulate the internal behavior of organizations. The leader of organization dominates everything. Chinese company leaders are often seen as signs and symbols of organizations. For individuals in an organization, showing respect and loyalty to superiors helps them gain opportunities for promotion or more resources (Selmer, 2001). Therefore, Chinese people are more loyal to individuals to organizations and systems (Redding, 1990). In Chinese organizations, the organizational commitment of employees is highly relevant to their loyalty to the top boss (Chen and Francesco, 2000). A study from Chen et al. (1998) gave strong empirical support for this. They found that in China, organizational commitments are significantly positively correlated with the five dimensions of loyalty to their superiors. Therefore, research on Chinese organizations needs to emphasize the core position of employers.

There are also many studies examining the influence of boss factors on employee attitudes and work results in the context of China. Using samples taken from Chinese joint ventures, Wong et al. (2002) studied the reasons and results of employees' loyalty to superiors. They found that interaction fairness affects subordinates' loyalty to their superiors, and employees' trust in their superiors plays a mediating role. Further, Wong et al. also showed that loyalty has a significant impact on employee performance and organizational citizenship behavior. Therefore, the commitment to superiors is particularly critical to understanding the behavior and attitudes of Chinese employees (Wong and Kung, 1999; Wong and Wong, 2013).

To examine the role of power distance and traditional Chinese culture in regulating the relationship between organizational support and work outcomes, Farh et al. (2007) obtained 163 pairs of superior-subordinate relationships from mainland China. The study pointed out that due to the obedience and respect of authority, employees who have a high degree of recognition of power distances are rarely based on reciprocity norms when considering their own contributions to the company. Conversely, employees who have low recognition of power distance are more likely to use reciprocal norms as the main principle. The premise of such research is the relational model of authority (Vogel et al., 2015). The model states that when people have personal connections with authority figures, they will care very much about how the authority figures treat themselves. Subordinates in Chinese organizations generally consider themselves to be at a large distance from their superiors. Therefore, they usually do not "bargain" with their superiors in accordance with the reciprocity norms, but unilaterally expect their superiors to give themselves appropriate returns.

Although in western society, the influence of business leaders on employees is not as large as that of Chinese society, its influence on employees' work attitudes or other outcome variables has been examined by many studies. Based on the theory of identity and resource dependence, Farmer and Aguinis (2005) proposes that when a supervisor controls the resources the subordinates need to establish and maintain their presently desired identities, the superior has an influence on their subordinates. In this situation, the behavior and attitude of employees cannot be influenced by their superiors. George (2000) shows that leaders can influence the emotions of subordinates in many ways. There is also a lot of evidence supporting the influence of leaders on subordinate emotions. Hogan et al. (1990) pointed out that 60%-70% of staff reported that their most important work pressure comes from their immediate superiors. This shows that, in general, the superior's attitude towards subordinates has a very large influence.

The models used to explain the influence of superiors on employees mainly include social exchange theory, leadership theory, and leadership-member exchange model (LMX). The framework of modern exchange theory tends to give two types of interpersonal relationships (Blau, 1964; Mo and Shi, 2017), namely: economic transaction relations and social transaction relations. The former emphasizes economic interests while the latter includes social emotional interests (socio- emotion benefits). Since social exchange theory emphasizes employee perceptions of the boss's responsibilities, dependencies, and approvals, past research suggests that the concept of organizational commitment is applied to make social transactional relationships between employees and their organizations operational (Cropanzano et al., 2017; Ertürk and Vurgun, 2015). There is empirical evidence from researchers of social exchange theory that the lack of social transaction relationships can lead to higher turnover intention, poorer performance (Rupp and Cropanzano, 2002), less citizenship behaviors for organization and superiors (Takeuchi et al., 2015).

In the framework of social exchange theory, Cropanzano et al. (2003) examined the consequences of emotional exhaustion of employees and employers. Studies have found that emotionally exhausted employees exhibit a lower level of commitment and a higher probability of searching for other employment opportunities (Liu et al., 2015). Results confirm that emotional exhaustion is indeed related to turnover intentions. Eisenberger et al. (2002) conducted three studies based on social exchange theory to examine the relationships of perception of superior support (PSS), perceived organizational support (POS) and employee turnover. It was found that PSS and POS are positively related, and the PSS-POS relationship will be strengthened as the positional awareness of superiors in the organization increases. Study also found that POS plays a complete mediating role in the negative relationship between PSS and turnover. The study pointed out that since superiors act as organizational agents, they are responsible for guiding and evaluating the performance of subordinates. Therefore, employees will regard their attitude towards them as a sign of organizational support. Behavior of the organizational agent is often seen as an expression of the will of the organization rather than the behavior and willingness of a specific individual (Rhoades et al., 2001). Bosses are considered to be equivalent to the organization to some extent. Their support for subordinates' work affects the latter's perception of organizational support (POS), while POS is often attributed to the personification of the organization (Eisenberger and Stinglhamber, 2011), which will ultimately affect turnover intention. Obviously, this finding by Eisenberger et al. is also applicable to Chinese private enterprises.

The leadership theory in the management literature has long sought to find individual characteristics related to effective leadership. Studies have found that leadership's five-dimensional personality characteristics are highly correlated with successful leadership behavior (Judge et al., 2002). Other studies have noted the role of leaders in key employee retention (Harris and Brannick, 1999). Mark and Canger (2004) used a five-factor model of leadership personality to examine the relationship between boss personality and the overall work attitude of his subordinates. The results show that the personality characteristics of the boss are indeed related to the work attitude of subordinates. In general, the superior's agreeableness, emotional stability, extraversion, and conscientiousness are related to the subordinates' satisfaction degree, total satisfaction degree, emotional commitment degree with the superior, and the turnover intention.

In the aspect of the Leadership-member Exchange Model (LMX), Sparrowe et al. (2006) proposed a combination of LMX theory and a group engagement model, in which the relationship between leader-affecting skills and members' helping behavior depends on the quality of LMX. The results of the study support the interaction effects of the three impact techniques and LMX quality. This study shows that the leader's leadership behavior will affect the subordinate's work behavior, and this relationship is also affected by the quality of LMX. We expect that this conclusion is also true for the turnover intention.

This book will introduce employer variables in specific model settings. Chen et al. (2002) once suggested that future studies should test the determinants of employer loyalty. Such possible variables include the trust of the employer, the relationship with the employer, the understanding of the employer, communication with the employer, employer's competence, quality, honesty and integrity, and relationships with demographic variables. Through many literature reviews, inductions, and screenings, combined with previous field surveys and in-depth interviews with entrepreneurs, this book introduces employers' attention, employer leadership, employer honesty, fairness in leadership, employer's achievement motivation, and employer's trust into the model, to examine the effect of these factors on the turnover intention of professional managers of small and medium-sized private enterprises.

Other factors

Other factors that have been examined in the current literature include job embeddedness (Mitchell et al., 2001), matching (Lee and Mitchell, 1994; Kammeyer-Mueller et al., 2005), and other job opportunities (March and Simon, 1958; Griffeth et al., 2005) etc. The book will also try to test the effects of these factors on a theoretical basis.

3. Brief review

Foreign studies involve most of the possible influencing factors of employee's turnover, but as Maertz and Campion (2004) stated, almost all factor models inevitably lack some important variables. Most models only test certain types of factors according to their research purpose. Complete system models were not commonly seen. In addition, the existing literature mainly focuses on general employees. The turnover of professional managers, however involves the specificities of both SMEs and managers. Thus, to give appropriate explanations of relevant issues and make reasonable recommendations, it is necessary to conduct in-depth analysis of this special nature. Based on the western cultural background, the influencing factors of the existing research model for the turnover mainly include objective variables such as work, organization, and environment. Few studies specifically consider the important influence of the employer's own factors. However, in the context of the eastern culture that emphasizes "authority" awareness and pays attention to relationship governance, the employer factor cannot be ignored. This is especially true for small and medium-sized private enterprises. Therefore, the huge differences in social, cultural, and institutional environments make factor models based on western scenarios not entirely applicable to China (Farh et al, 2007).

Domestic empirical research has progressed up to now. For example, Zhang and Li (2001) found that job satisfaction affects the employee's turnover intention; Xie et al. (2006) showed that the education level, career, and average monthly income of employees will affect the turnover intention. Zhang and Wang (2003) confirmed that the development prospects, wages and benefits, fairness, career development opportunities, and employer honesty have a significant impact on the turnover intention of professional managers in private enterprises in Guangdong. Self-realization, employee organizational performance, job embeddedness, external compensation associated with personal social networks, and family responsibilities are also found having a significant effect on the turnover (Liang et al., 2005).

However, most of these studies apply foreign existing theoretical frameworks and lack the introduction and investigation of local factors (Zhang, 2006). They also use general employees as the main research object. Professional managers of small and medium-sized private enterprises are a special group. Research on the turnover of ordinary employees may not necessarily provide useful governance advice. For example, in small and medium-sized private enterprises, due to the small scale of the organization, the employees and employers have more frequent contacts. Professional managers often equate enterprise organizations with their own employers. This makes the employer factor very important. However, this has not been the focus of investigation in existing domestic research.

Therefore, this book will examine the mature model of turnover factors of Western countries in the context of Chinese culture, compare the differences and similarities between them, determine the commonality and specificity of related models, and draw new factor models that meet Chinese characteristics through cross-cultural comparisons. This model aims to find the root cause of the turnover of professional managers in small and medium-sized private enterprises, and to put forward a more realistic governance mechanism. It enriches and refines the existing turnover theory from the perspective of distinct cultures and special employees.

Governance Mechanism of Manager Turnover

As mentioned above, high rate of employee turnover is very unfavorable for the company, not only in reducing visible business performance such as profitability and productivity (Shaw et al., 2005), but also potentially affects employees' morale and the company's attractiveness to outstanding employees. The nature of professional manager determines that it has a greater impact on the company than the average employee, thus the negative impact of the turnover on the company is even more severe (Li, 2003). Therefore, it is very necessary and urgent to put forward the system of turnover governance mechanism. In fact, the main research purpose of the decision-making mechanism and influencing factors of employee turnover at home and abroad is to provide corresponding countermeasures and suggestions for management practices, so as to retain outstanding talents. Therefore, the above-mentioned related studies have correspondingly proposed some useful countermeasures. This section provides an overview of this issue, with a view to providing reference for the management of the turnover of professional managers.

There are two aspects of governance measures related to turnover. On the one hand, if the voluntary turnover of all employees is unavoidable, the focus of resource use must be repositioned. Organizations and managers need to find ways to minimize the damage and inconvenience caused by this unavoidable phenomenon. The corresponding governance model mentioned in the literature is called the "control model", emphasizing the control of the loss caused by the turnover. On the other hand, if the turnover is to a certain extent avoidable, then there is the possibility that managers actively intervene in this process, and the corresponding "a prevention model" is proposed in the literature, emphasizing the measures to prevent the turnover intention and behavior (Morrell et al., 2001).

1. Human resources management measures of preventing turnover

Research shows that employee turnover is largely predictable and controllable. Therefore, many companies deliberately consider adopting measures to help reduce the turnover of employees when building human resource management systems. This "active" governance mechanism has been found to have a good preventive effect on the turnover.

The human resources management literature distinguishes two different human resource management systems: commitment vs. control (Shaw et al., 2005; Shaw and Shi, 2017). The former is characterized by high compensation and high investment-oriented HRM measures, while the latter is characterized by low-investment and low-paying HRM measures. High-commitment human resources practices, which may also be referred to as high-involvement work practices (HIWP), are generally considered to include concrete measures such as improving employee skill levels, motivation for work, providing relevant information, and authorizing and so on (Laroche and Salesina, 2017; Fu et al., 2017; Pfeffer, 1998). Guthrie's (2001) study found that there is a positive correlation between HIWP and employee retention and company productivity. Further tests of interaction effects found that when HIWP is used excessively, employee turnover will reduce productivity, whereas, when HIWP is used infrequently, the turnover will improve productivity. There are two opposite effects of HIWP on turnover and its impact on the company. The reason lies in the fact that the use of HIWP in large-scale companies means investing in human capital, which will bring about two kinds of results. On the one hand, HIWP helps retain employees (Shaw and Shi, 2017; Shaw et al.,1998); On the other hand, the use of HIWP can easily lead companies to run into trouble when employees resign, because the use of HIWP makes the company rely too much on "intangible assets". Guthrie (2001) summarizes that the HIWP projects include: internal promotion, performance-based/premium-based promotion, skills-based compensation, team-based compensation, employee share ownership, employee participation planning, information sharing, attitude survey, team orientation, cross-training or cross-use training centered on future skill needs. It is easy to see that these measures can indeed prevent turnover in advance.

Mohamad and Nasurdin (2006) pointed out that the existing studies neglected the influence of employees on the perception of organizational variables, especially human resource management measures (Momani, 2017; Waldman et al., 2015). Mohamad and Nasurdin conducted an empirical study on the influencing factors of turnover intention. This study introduced the trust of the organization as a medium variable of the corresponding relationship. As a result, it was found that to increase employees' trust in the organization and reduce their turnover intention, managers need to continuously provide training and development plans for employees, use fair and formal reward and punishment systems, provide rich and clear career development space, and other human resources management measures. Delery and Doty (1996) systematically conceptualized HRM measures as a set of internally consistent policies and measures that were designed and implemented by the organization to ensure that the company's human capital contributed to the company's achievement of its commercial purpose. From an employee's point of view, HRM measures are seen as the efforts of organizations to bring benefits to them and promote their professional development. Although there is still much debate on the specific content of HRM measures, such as work presentations, mentoring programs, compensation systems, job security, performance evaluation, training and development, and professional growth are often identified as important (Park et al., 2016; Delery and Dotty, 1996). A research conducted by the Gallup Organization in industries such as retail, hospitals, healthcare, and manufacturing confirms that proper human resource management practices can help employees form a motivated team (Suzanne and Luthans, 2006). Participation is, however, negatively related to turnover intention (Price, 2001).

Sun et al. (2007) examined the relationship between high-performance human resource management measures and productivity and turnover for samples taken from the Chinese mainland (PRC). Samples were taken from hotels located in 12 cities in the eastern coastal provinces of China. The results show that service-oriented organizational citizenship behavior plays a part in mediating the relationship between high-performance human resource management measures and turnover. The unemployment rate plays a regulatory role in the relationship between OCB and turnover. The high-performance human resource management measures considered in the study include: improving employee skills, participating in decision-making, and encouraging self-directed work etc. (Aryee et al., 2016). Although many studies have found that high-performance measures are related to resignation or employee retention (Shaw and Shi, 2017; Batt, 2002;

Guthrie, 2001), the mechanism behind this relationship has so far been speculative. According to Sun's view of social exchange, especially reciprocal normative theory, Sun expects high-performance human resource management measures to be negatively related to turnover. Batt (2002) also pointed out that trust-based HR incentives such as training, job security, and relatively high treatment may promote employee attachment and commitment, thus reducing the turnover rate.

Another important contribution of Sun et al. (2007) is to show that the positive effects of high-performance human resource management measures on company performance have also been verified in non-Western cultural environments, which generalizes the close relationship between human resources management measures and the turnover. China's reform and opening up and the large number of foreign companies that came with it have made Western-style human resource management measures popular in China, such as employment contracts, performance management systems, and high-performance human resources measures (Wang, 2003; Zhu and Warner, 2011). Sun's research provides empirical support for the effectiveness of these human resources management measures implemented in the Chinese environment.

Human capital investment is an important HRM measure that is often mentioned in the literature. It plays a key role in actively preventing employees from turnover. In the highly competitive and volatile modern economy, the stability of work is becoming more and more difficult. The phenomena of layoffs, restructuring, and unemployment have become commonplace, and the job security commitments provided by the company have become increasingly difficult to deliver. As a result, many companies have found that if human capital investment can improve employee's employability in the market, then the company's ability to attract and retain outstanding employees will be greatly enhanced (Craig et al., 2002). It is estimated that US companies spend about 160 to 55 billion U.S. dollars on employee training. A nationwide survey in 1996 showed that 75% of U.S. employees provide more than 20 organizations and almost all larger employers with several types of tuition funding programs. The related investigations of Hewitt Associates in 1998 also reached the corresponding conclusion (Benson et al., 2004). The main reason for U.S. companies to make such investments is that employee training and development helps to improve employee satisfaction and retention (Cappelli, 2000; Craig et al., 2002).

But the theory of human capital originating from Becker (1964) pointed out that if the company invests in the employees' general skills, the probability of latter's turnover may increase. Because generic skills increase employees' competitiveness in the labor market, employees are confident that they will face better employers after leaving the company. The relationship between the positive effects of employee development on retention intentions and the negative effects of human capital theory, as well as the direction of the overall effect, are pointed out in a large number of resignations. Benson et al. (2004) empirically analyzed the impact of employee tuition funding on their turnover probability from this perspective.

Many studies have pointed out the possible impact of tuition funding on turnover intention. March and Simon (1958) pointed out that the ease of work flow is a very important factor affecting employee turnover. Tuition subsidy to help employees improve their skill level helps to increase the ease of their work flow. Trevor (2001) found that previous education and vocational training played a role in regulating the relationship between local unemployment and job satisfaction and turnover. If job satisfaction, unemployment, and the pay remain unchanged, more highly educated employees may voluntarily resign (Trevor, 2001). The unfolding model of Mitchell and Lee (2001) pointed out that employee development could reduce the "shock" that may lead to their turnover. This model predicts that the primary effect of tuition funding is to improve the matching of employees with the company and reduce their turnover probability. Johnson (2007) found that employees participating in some form of off-site learning classes funded by companies are more likely to leave. Loewenstein and Speltzer (1997), on the other hand, points out that there is no connection between participation in university-sponsored classes and the turnover.

In addition, studies have found that promotion is negatively related to turnover in a company (e.g., Rubel and Kee, 2015; Morrow, 2011). Other studies have argued that promotion is positively related to voluntary resignation when it comes to controlling the increase in salary that may increase with promotion (Trevor et al., 1997). Here, the promotion serves as a signal to the outside potential employer that the promoted employee has a higher ability (Razir, 2000). However, another study did not find evidence of that promotion ncreases the probability of turnover after controlling for salaries (Lyness and Judiesch, 2001).

Benson (2004) combined some of the views of human capital theory into the resignation model to test the relationship between employees' general skill improvement, promotion and voluntary turnover, to clarify the aforementioned confusion. This empirical study from 9439 samples shows that getting tuition fees can reduce the turnover probability of the students in the school. However, when employees obtain a diploma through tuition subsidy, the probability of their leaving is higher than those who get subsidized but do not have a degree or do not receive tuition at all. When employees receive education through subsidization and are later promoted, the probability of their separation is greatly reduced. The management significance of this article is that when the company finances the skill development of its employees, it needs to carefully measure the positive and negative effects of this investment on the turnover probability, and it is necessary to consider the use of supporting measures such as promotion and adjustment work. The company must not only provide training and education grants for employees, but also promotes them to the right positions according to their newly acquired skills. Otherwise, company funding will most likely become "fighting for others", which will on the contrary increase their turnover probability.

In domestic research, Zhang and Wang (2003) proposed several human resources measures to help retain professional managers, such as: improving manager's income and benefits, adopting multiple distribution methods for various levels of managers, providing more learning and development opportunities, improving the trust and credibility on managers under the premise of improving the supervision system. Yi (2004) believes that establishing a complementary relationship between corporate material assets, intellectual assets and human capital can help form the enterprise's talent specificity. By increasing the opportunity cost of this specific talent turnover, employees can increase their loyalty and make the excellent professional managers stay in the company for a long time.

2. Management mechanism of professional managers in the early stage of employment

Relevant research on the turnover process shows that employees will go through a series of stages and procedures in the turnover decision process. The governance of the turnover requires different measures to be taken in various stages. The truly effective governance mechanism must be a multi-level and multi-angle system framework. As pointed out by Maertz and Campion (2004), there is a need to integrate process models and factor models for the study of the turnover problem. The important revelation of the "comprehensive model" they propose to the relevant governance mechanisms is that management authorities can determine their specific exit decision-making process according to the employees' different turnover motives, and then propose corresponding governance mechanisms for various stages of the process. The process models and factor models that have been reviewed in detail already provide a theoretical basis for us to propose a system's overall governance mechanism. The following discussion concerns some of the organizational governance measures that may be useful at the early stage of the employee's staying in the company.

As mentioned, most of the turnover studies focus on the process and impact factors of employee turnover (Murray and Zimmerman, 2005). Few people are looking to see whether it's possible to reduce the turnover probability in the recruitment selection period. In fact, employers have something to do with the management of turnover. Some personal factors related to active separation can be identified now. The meta-analysis of Griffeth et al. (2000) shows that the applicant's bio data is a good predictor of his future turnover probability (=0.31). Based on theory of work embeddedness perspective, Mitchell et al. (2001) pointed out that applicants who have friends or relatives in the company before entering will have a higher degree of commitment to the company after entering, and their probability of turnover is also lower. In addition, the duration of previous work is also a very important predictor of future turnover intentions (Fleishman, 2010; Joseph et al., 2015). If a person has the habit of "job-hopping", this can be reflected by the length of his working time in the previous working place, the lower duration means that he lacks professional ethics, and the latter is closely related to organizational commitment and turnover (Hom et al., 2017). Cascio (1976) found that the applicant's length of service in the previous company can predict its current rate of turnover. Wendy et al. (2005) pointed out that the excellent work attitude of new employees of some companies may have originated from the previous work change process itself, and has nothing to do with the relevant organizational and environmental factors of the company. Therefore, we should not give too optimistic responses to the higher job satisfaction of this type of new employee. It can be expected that the satisfaction of employees who have achieved high satisfaction due to previous job conversions is difficult to maintain over time.

Murray and Zimmerman (2005) examine in detail the power of several variables that can be used early to predict the probability of future turnover. It was found that the personal resume data, the clear-purpose attitudes and intentions, and the disguised-purpose dispositional retention scales are predictive of turnover. The results also found that the resume information and purposeful camouflage retention measure significantly increased the explanatory power of the model for the departure variance. These variables can be observed even before employees are hired. Employers can use this information before entering to identify applicants with higher turnover tendencies and, to a certain extent, make the departure an organizational precaution.

In order to confirm which personal factors had the ability to predict the turnover probability in advance while at the early stage the employee's staying in the company, Kammeyer-Mueller and Wanberg (2003) conducted four stages of longitudinal sampling of seven organizations. Corresponding empirical studies have found that the knowledge, proactive personality, and the social influence from the organization, superiors, and working partner before entering will affect the moderating variables of new employees, such as job proficiency, role clarity, work team integration, and political knowledge etc. These variables, in turn, have a mediating effect on the relationship between other variables and organizational commitments and turnover. Employees in the early stages of entering the company will form the impression of the organization and decide if they match this. Such early attitudes have a great influence on the attitudes and behaviors of later work (Zimmerman et al., 2016; Holtom et al., 2017).

Literature in the fields of personality, personal and environmental matching, and socialization show that new recruits have their own unique concept and commitment tendencies when they enter the organization. They may form preconceptions based on their first impression of the organization after entering the organization. (Judge and Larsen, 2001; Lee et al., 1992; Holtom et al., 2017). Kammeyer Mueller et al. (2005) found that employees who left their employment within the first few years of their careers would soon show significant differences from those who stayed in the company.

In the initial stages of employment, the initial perception of employees on the organization, work, and self-adaptation often determines their future work attitude (Kammeyer-Mueller and Wanberg, 2003; Kammeyer-Mueller et al., 2005), while the attitude further influences their turnover intention. The company can adopt certain human resources management measures to "proactively" improve this kind of initial perception of employees to increase their organizational commitment degree. An important measure often cited in the literature is organizational socialization. Through the socialization process of the organization, employees can obtain relevant work skills, have a certain understanding of the organization, and get the opportunity to support communication with working peers, and accept some existing rules and methods of specific organizations (Connie and Kammeyer-Mueller, 2000). Organizations can exercise some sort of control in this process to achieve the goal of reducing turnover intentions.

Harrison et al. (2006) pointed out that organizational commitment can be improved through the organizational socialization process of employees. Through this process, new employees can acquire the ideas, behavioral orientation, and knowledge which are necessary to become members of the organization. This helps Reduce their turnover intention (Griffeth et al., 2000). Based on a two-year survey of more than 1,000 officers, Payne and Huffman (2005) found that mentoring can significantly improve the organizational commitment of newly recruited officers, and is negatively related to turnover behavior. This relationship is subject to supervisory versus nonsupervisory. Payne and Huffman's research shows that mentoring is essential to improve the organization's socialization of employees. It can provide support, direction, and advice on careers and personal development for new junior employees. A key element of organizational socialization is the understanding and acceptance of organizational goals and values. Research shows that employees who can share organizational goals and values will have a higher degree of emotional commitment to the organization, which will reduce their turnover intention (Griffeth et al., 2000). Therefore, it is necessary for the organization to establish a certain kind of mentoring relationship between the superiors and the subordinates, and it is necessary to define the counselor as the official role of the manager and require him to assume the corresponding duties.

3. Other measures and mechanisms

In addition to formal human resource management measures, organizations have many other options that can be used to reduce employee turnover. An empirical study based on Mitchell et al. (2001) by Lee et al. (2004) shows that the degree of work embeddedness (internal/external) can moderate the relationship between related factors and turnover, that is, it will magnify or mitigate the effect of related independent variables on the role of turnover. Therefore, managers can influence the employee's turnover decision-making process by improving the degree of embeddedness, and ultimately affect their turnover behavior. The degree of work embeddedness can be improved by establishing social circles, enhancing sense of belonging, establishing close links among employees, and increasing social capital. Among them, employees' links[5] with the organization can be strengthened through teamwork and long-term projects; sacrifice can be increased through long-term work and organizational returns; and fit can be gained by linking employees' knowledge, skills, abilities and attitudes to job requirements. It is worth noting that managers can also increase the degree of out-of-work embeddedness to reduce turnover intention, such as providing employees with information on the communities where their workplaces are located, and providing social support for local activities and affairs. Dess and Shaw (2001) also pointed out that social capital in corporate development organizations can not only reduce the turnover rate, but also help improve the organization-wide production efficiency.

4. Brief review

The above research provides us with a certain theoretical basis and analytical ideas for the turnover management of professional managers in small and medium-sized enterprises. However, the turnover management advice given in the existing literature is difficult to really solve the reservation problem of SME management resources. For example, they are ignoring the employer factor and not considering

[5] Embeddedness includes 3 dimensions: links, sacrifice and fit (Mitchell et al., 2001).

information asymmetry etc. Moreover, using the process model and factor model obtained through empirical testing to present the system's governance mechanism in stages and in all directions, is still rare in existing research.

In this book, different governance proposals are proposed for various stages to build an overall coordinated loss management mechanism, based on the new turnover process model verified by the structural equation model, and according to the manager's decision-making process, such as the perception of relevant factors, changes in satisfaction and commitment, changes in job initiative, decline in work status, and job search intentions. At the same time, relevant governance measures are put forward considering recruitment, employment contracts, training, work design and other aspects. A turnover governance mechanism that runs through the entire human resources management system is formed.

Finally, issues of the manager turnover and the family business of private enterprises are studied by using the reverse selection and dynamic matching model. The essential difference between Chinese family-owned companies and western family-owned enterprises is emphasized. On this basis, this book proposes to improve the inefficient information asymmetry equilibrium and break through the "familyism dilemma". A series of countermeasures are put forward. Together with the above-mentioned overall governance mechanism, these proposals form an important guarantee for small and medium-sized private enterprises to absorb and retain the human capital of professional managers.

The Major Academic Schools for Turnover Studies

The issue of turnover has always been the subject of organizational theory keen to study. According to the preliminary statistics of Shaw et al. (1998), as of 1998, more than 1,500 articles on the subject were studied (Kevin et al., 2004). Despite this, a general explanation of employee turnover accepted by most people has not yet appeared in the literature. Van Dick et al. (2004) believe that the issue of turnover has so far not been fully understood, mainly because of the openness of methodologies (Steel, 2002), and the psychological processes behind turnover have not yet been clarified.

This raises the question that people put forward their own analytical framework according to their own understanding, and used this framework to conduct corresponding empirical research, and then give inconsistent explanations to those plausible conclusions. No framework can be accepted by most researchers, and no theory can internally give a variety of contradictory empirical findings to interpret reasonably (Lee and Mitchell, 1994). In this section, we briefly introduce the main schools in the turnover study according to the classification methods in the literature, and provide some reference for the theoretical framework of the book.

Under the guidance of the classic model of March and Simon (1958), turnover studies can be broadly divided into two schools: the economic school (or labor market) and the psychology school (Morrell et al., 2001; Kevin et al., 2004). The former emphasizes the influence of external factors (such as the temptation of other job opportunities, etc.), so it is also known as pull theory; the latter emphasizes internal personal factors (such as work-related perceptions and attitudes, etc.), also known as push theory (Lee and Mitchell, 1994).

The research scope of labor market school includes: other job opportunities (Gerhart, 1990; Zimmerman et al., 2016), labor market opportunities (Kirschenbaum and Mano-Negrin, 1999), job search (Boswell et al., 2017), performance (Jackofsky, 1984; Waldman et al., 2015), investment or the "sunken" cost (Morrell et al., 2001) and the role of expected utility (Weng and Mcelroy, 2012) and so on.

The research scope of psychology faction mainly includes: job satisfaction (Hom and Kinicki, 2001; Mobley, 1977), organization or other forms of commitment (Mercurio, 2015; Meyer and Allen, 1991; Hom et al., 2017; Somers, 1995), job involvement (Korff et al., 2017a), fairness perception (Aquino et al., 1997), and psychological contract (Robinson, 1996) and so on.

In contrast, the psychology faction deals more with issues of affect and attitude. Its research focuses on job satisfaction, organizational commitment, job involvement, career development, role pressure, organizational climate, fairness, psychological contract, professionalism, etc. And its analysis of employee turnover is more likely to explain or predict individual turnover decisions. The labor market school emphasizes more on the decision-making dimension of turnover, and its research focuses on the impact of external determinants such as opportunities on turnover. Steel (2002) has pointed out that there is no single type of research area that can surpass the attitude theory that belongs to the branch of psychology in terms of the studies on the impact of turnover, even the labor market school is with no exception.

According to Morrell et al. (2001), the turnover study of the psychology school, on the basis of March and Simon (1958), developed in three directions: the causal model of Price and Mueller (1986); the expanded model of Mobley et al. (1979); and the catastrophe model of Sheridan and Abelson (1983). These models have already been introduced in the second section of this chapter. The core framework of this book is based on the psychological school, but we will also introduce some of the constructs of the labor market school, and try to give a complete explanation of the turnover of professional managers.

Chapter 3

Qualitative Research

As mentioned earlier, the studies on foreign turnover issues have been relatively complete, but due to the distinct cultural backgrounds, our research objects are quite specific. Simply applying the ready-made analysis framework will incur deviations. At the same time, most of the domestic literature on the exit of employees and the growth of professional managers are also insufficient for the introduction and investigation of local factors, and it is difficult to integrate the research topics of this book in many aspects. Therefore, in order to provide relevant research hypotheses in the next chapter and make reasonable explanations and extensions after giving empirical results, this chapter is based on the previous private enterprise on-site investigations and in-depth interviews with entrepreneurs, and the relevant literature for exploratory analysis, in order to obtain a more consistent research framework of turnover process and influencing factors of professional managers in China's small and medium-sized private enterprises .

This chapter examines the specificity of the turnover of managers of small and medium-sized enterprises using qualitative research methods. Specifically, based on research on employee turnover, business growth, and family businesses at home and abroad, we conducted on-site surveys of 5 small and medium-sized private enterprises in Guangzhou, and conducted in-depth interviews with business owners on related topics. Based on the existing literature and these interview materials, the following section will first analyze the impact of professional manager turnover on small and medium-sized private enterprises in China; then focus on the main characteristics of small and medium-sized private enterprises and professional managers in China, in order to provide a snapshot of the turnover of professional managers in SMEs; finally briefly point out the meaning and contribution of this exploratory analysis to the later text.

Impact of Professional Manager Turnover on Small and Medium-sized Private Enterprises

In fact, from the perspective of the normal flow of the labor market, the professional manager's voluntary turnover is not without any benefit. However, as mentioned above, the excessive turnover of professional managers not only hinders the improvement of enterprise management capabilities, but also "familyizes" the operation of private enterprises and exacerbates the difficulties of the survival of small and medium-sized private enterprises.

Existing studies have shown that a proper turnover rate is beneficial to firms (Glebbeek and Erik, 2004; Shaw et al., 2005). The proper flow of professional managers in small and medium-sized enterprises can help the company's metabolism, and it has certain benefits for company changes, management innovation, and process optimization. And most importantly, the flow of pressures within the corporate organization is conducive to clearing out those managers whose capabilities and performance are marginal, and maintaining the organization's high efficiency. This was partially verified during the interview of our entrepreneurs. The owners of the five companies believe that the over-stability of the professional manager team is not a good thing for the organization. One of the entrepreneurs also worried that the company's human resources are stable so that he feels terrible. The main reason is that the marginal figures in terms of work performance and capabilities remain in the organization for an extended period of time, which may lead to decreased efficiency. Correspondingly, the employer may also feel that the reward paid to the manager may far exceed the market average in relation to his ability, otherwise why not resign? In addition, managers who do not match the organization are not necessarily advantageous even if they are reluctant to stay in the organization. Another entrepreneur who is engaged in machinery manufacturing mentioned that managers are inevitably inactive for long-term employment, and that the development of young people also needs the "giving way" of the older generations. Therefore, entrepreneurs are happy to see a reasonable turnover rate within the organization.

However, it is obvious that excessive turnover rate is not a good thing for enterprises. The turnover of middle and high-level professional managers will cause great damage to the normal operation of the company. The turnover of managers not only brings direct cost loss to the company, such as recruitment costs, training costs, replacement costs, etc., but also incurs indirect costs by affecting the normal operations of the company, such as disrupting business processes, decreasing customer service quality, and contract performance. According to foreign research estimates (Ramlall, 2003), the total cost of employee turnover is roughly equivalent to 1.5 times of the annual income, while Fitz-enz (1997) pointed out that in the United States, every 10 management and professional employees leave, the company will lose on average about one million US dollars. It is also worth noting that the turnover of professional managers will also affect the morale, working atmosphere of the employees, and the informal network within the organization (Rudy, 2010). If the outgoing professional manager is in a key position, his subordinate's work attitude, work habits, and work performance will also be greatly affected. During our interviews, we discovered that most owners have noticed that the turnover of professional managers can result in poor business processes, loss of customer resources, imitation of core technologies and business models, and leakage of confidential information. One of the companies also revealed that the turnover of a certain manager will cause the turnover of his subordinates and other colleagues. Another company engaged in machinery manufacturing mentioned that the turnover of one or two executives has negligible impact on the company, but if they the turnover of a group of people happens, the consequences will be more serious.

The advantages and disadvantages of the manager turnover described above are related to the manager's voluntary turnover behavior. The declined managerial ability caused by the turnover of professional manager can be restored through the personnel supplementation. It is the same for any type of company. However, what needs to be emphasized is that, compared to large-scale private enterprises, state-owned enterprises, and foreign-funded enterprises, the turnover of professional managers of small and medium-sized private enterprises is to some degree continuous, and their overall management capabilities will be weakened. On the one hand, companies face the active turnover of professional managers; on the other hand, it is difficult for enterprises to attract outstanding managers. Overall, the result is the permanent loss of professional management capabilities of small and medium-sized private enterprises. Our interview verified this point. All the interviewed entrepreneurs complained to us that the company could not recruit outstanding managers. They are very confused that the company's conditions and benefits are not bad, why excellent managers are reluctant to come here to serve.

This is an important reason why we have focused our attention on small and medium-sized private enterprises. The reason why most of the current turnover studies do not focus on small and medium-sized private enterprises may not be aware of this issue. In order to realize the professionalization of small and medium-sized private enterprise management and promote its long-term sustainable growth, it is necessary for us to thoroughly study the root causes of the turnover of professional managers from such enterprises. Based on this, the relevant governance measures are proposed in a targeted manner. The following analysis starts around this issue.

The Uniqueness of Small and Medium-sized Private Enterprises and Its Impact on Manager Turnover

In China's private economy, SMEs account for the vast majority. Most of these companies are short-lived. The only successful companies that have grown from a small company to a company with a certain influence are only a few. According to statistics, 150,000 private enterprises are newly born every year in the country, and more than 100,000 insolvencies occur each year. 60% of private enterprises go bankrupt within 5 years, and 85% become insolvent within 10 years. Their average life span is only 2.9 years (Huang, 2007). As far as our survey respondents are concerned, only one of the five companies has a business life of more than 7 years. In addition to the number of employees in a machinery manufacturing company reaching 550, the number of employees in the other four companies is between 30 and 60, with small operating scale, and the boss is under the age of 40. As one of the entrepreneurs put it, the "smallness" of the company in all aspects may be the main reason for the turnover of professional managers. For us, this is the reason as well as the result. On the one hand, the turnover of professional managers leads to a low level of management ability which has affected the further growth of small and medium-sized private enterprises to a great extent. On the other hand, the lack of growth of enterprises has adversely affected the employment options of professional managers. The vicious circle thus formed became small and medium-sized. It is difficult for private enterprises to solve this "dead knot". Here we extend this judgment and comprehensively analyze the characteristics of small and medium-sized private enterprises in order to find some of the deeper causes that lead to the turnover of managers.

1. Personalization of the company

An important feature of small and medium-sized private enterprises is that entrepreneurs and enterprises are inseparable and integrated. This affects the perception of professional managers in several ways.

First, the opportunity for employers to do business directly affects the organization of the company and thus affects the manager's inaugural decision. Regardless of whether it is forced by passion or by life, the entrepreneurial opportunities create a deep imprint on companies. If managers find that the boss does not plan to pursue the enterprise as a long-term career, it is difficult to maintain loyalty. Moreover, the bosses of many SMEs are simply doing "home business". One of the entrepreneurs we met in the survey mentioned that due to family and other personal reasons, he could not devote all its energy in to business in the year of 2006, which caused the company's revenue to decline in the current year. This can have an impact on the psychological impact of professional managers.

Second, the personal relationship between professional managers and entrepreneurs will influence the decision of the former. Unlike big companies, most SME professional managers have frequent contact with their bosses. The quality of the relationship between them will directly affect the organizational commitment of the former. Due to inevitability of unfairness in terms of work arrangements, distribution of benefits, and even the closeness of contacts, personal attitudes toward employers will naturally evolve into attitudes towards organizations, leaving them as their last choice. In the interview, an entrepreneur who engaged in the sale of medicine told us that the only "old man" who had followed her since the company's start-up had recently left the company because the boss did not reuse him as he did before.

Third, the boss's own value concept, personal conduct, and entrepreneurial ability will also affect managers. In large companies, most managers are only part of the entire company's operating system. Naturally, they do not care too much about the employer's values, personal conduct, and capabilities. But for SMEs, this is crucial. Because the value concept of the boss is the company's value concept, and the latter directly stipulates the employee's rules of conduct. Personal conduct not only determines the business nature of the company, but also directly affects the manager's own interests. The level of entrepreneurial ability determines the survival of the company.

2. The "family-oriented" tendency of business operations

Most private enterprises in China adopt the family governance model (Chu, 2000; Li, 2002), while small and medium-sized private enterprises are almost all family businesses. Our "family business" here refers not only to full family ownership, but also to the full participation of family members in business management (Churchill and Hatten, 2010). As we all know, most of the western business forms are also family businesses. According to a 2004 survey by the Business Weekly, 177 of the constituent stock companies of the S&P 500 Index are family-owned companies. The Wal-Mart, according to the Fortune magazine's newest publication in 2007, is a typical family enterprise. However, it is necessary to pay close attention to the fact that the similarities between the eastern and western family businesses are only superficial, and the family business in China and even the entire Chinese community is fundamentally different from the family business in Western societies (Davis, 1983). China's family business is based on the "home culture". Scholars generally believe that the core of understanding Chinese society and culture lies in the family (Liang, 2005; Fei, 2005). As far as the theme of the book is concerned, on the one hand, the family has shaped and trained private entrepreneurs to manage their businesses and handle various internal and external relations. On the other hand, their sacred status constrains the behavior of enterprises and entrepreneurs.

Specifically, first of all, business owners often see companies as part of the "home" organization, and various management activities and rules within the organization often inevitably carry the color of "family ethics". An employer who is engaged in asset assessment tells us that in order to increase employee loyalty to the company, the company needs to intentionally create a family atmosphere in daily management. The entrepreneur clearly knows that western companies pay more attention to the contractual relationship between the company and its employees. It is also known that Chinese companies are different from this. The cold legal relationship is not conducive to the retention of professional managers. Another entrepreneur who is engaged in machinery manufacturing also emphasizes that managing Chinese employees needs to cultivate a family culture within the company and continuously strengthen the "parent-child relationship" between the boss and the manager. Once this kind of relationship with particularism is established, even if the professional manager is temporarily treated unfairly, turnover will not easily happen.

Second, family interests and family responsibilities override the interests and responsibilities of the company. The family has a unique position in eastern culture, and the decisions of private entrepreneurs are often influenced by this. Due to excessive consideration of family or family interests, many companies intentionally or unintentionally forget about the efficiency, which is the core requirements as an economic organization (Davis, 1983). The bosses are largely doing "home business". Similar phenomenon of sacrificing corporate interests to take care of family interests is common in private enterprises. In order to emphasize family responsibilities, the social responsibilities that they should shoulder (such as environmental protection, donations, community activities, etc.) are often ignored.

Third, they are not willing to share or give control rights to people easily. Studies related to economics and management demonstrated that it is very necessary to motivate high-level professional managers by using control rights or equity. However, in small and medium-sized private enterprises, ownership and control of absolute ownership of enterprises have symbolic significance for family success. Enterprise employers are naturally reluctant to give the rights to others. Wagner (1995) once pointed out that individuals in western society tend to be individualist and appear to define themselves as an entity formed by a single individual and defined by their own bodies. Individuals in eastern societies tend to be collectivistic. They define themselves as individuals that go beyond individuals to include certain other specific groups and are bounded by the social scope of specific groups. To a certain extent, the Chinese in the disparate pattern define the self-concept with a group close to him, so he has a sense of group responsibility. The main reason why the bosses of small and medium-sized private enterprises are not willing to give power easily may be that he fulfills his group responsibility in the family as the controller and serves as the leader's group responsibility for all employees of the organization. That is, Chinese business owners do not use their own personal boundaries. He wants to play his role in a specific group. This requires him to retain his corporate leadership.

We have been wondering during the interview that why the entrepreneurs are very sensitive when it comes to incentives such as equity, control, and partnership to motivate professional managers? In fact, self-employment, one of the reasons why entrepreneurs often refer to the turnover of managers, is related to this. Under this thinking mode of the bosses, it is not surprising that aspiring managers who cannot play an entrepreneurial spirit within the organization leave the company. Compared with the phenomenon that many western entrepreneurs are willing to resell their companies to other investors for cash after they succeed, in China, "home culture" has a tremendous influence on Chinese entrepreneurs.

Finally, the specialist tradition derived from "family culture" hinders employers' trust in professional managers. This issue has attracted the attention of many scholars (Fukuyama, 1998; Li, 2002; Huang, 2004, etc.). In terms of the theme of this book, professional managers have to assess their position when choosing a job. The truly competent manager does not necessarily have to be in a favorable position.

3. Failure to understand the operating rules of modern company systems

Due to the short development history of private enterprises in China, coupled with the influence of non-individualist cultural traditions that are slightly inconsistent with the modern corporate system (Fukuyama, 1998), most small and medium-sized private enterprises don't understand the operating rules of the modern company system, and certainly not put it into use. This is embodied in three aspects. First, management is too centralized. As mentioned earlier, due to the influence of "family culture", employers are reluctant to share control rights with managers. In fact, one reason is that they do not understand the modern company system. The modern company is an organic system based on the division of labor and cooperation. As business leaders, the key lies in how to maintain the virtuous operation of the system, rather than replacing system components. In our interviews, we found that all entrepreneurs felt that they were tired and uneasy, but on the other hand, professional managers felt that there was no room for freedom. One of the entrepreneurs said, "our managers think I occupied their places". The fundamental reason for not knowing right share is that they do not understand the operating rules of the modern company system.

Second, they are not aware of the special position of professional managers in the rise of modern companies and even modern society. The literature of corporate historiography and corporate governance shows that the evolution and development of enterprises require the professionalization of management, and the professional managers have acquired an increasingly important economic status (Chandler, 1978; Berle and Means, 1932). Western society even has a saying of "manager capitalism". However, the employers of most private enterprises in China have not yet realized the importance of this issue. Failure to respect the special status of managers, distrusting the professional ethics of managers, and neglecting the importance of managers are important reasons for the turnover of professional managers. Separation of powers, the professionalization of entrepreneurs and managers, and the division of entrepreneurship functions (Zhang, 1996) have been the inevitable laws of the development of modern company systems. Small and medium-sized private entrepreneurs need to change their traditional modes of thinking and regard professional managers as partners in their own business, other than subordinates. Rational division of labor, positive interaction can jointly promote the growth of the company.

Third, "rule of man" is more than "rule of law". The development of the modern company system has reached the stage of standardization, institutionalization and standardization. The concept of equality in rules is crucial to the long-term stability and sustainable development of the company. However, the subjectivity, arbitrariness, and human orientation of many small and medium private enterprises are still relatively strong. The management system is loose and lacks strategic thinking. This "rule of people" model gives people an extremely unstable feeling. Professional managers cannot form expectations of long-term returns to the company, let alone bright prospects for development. We learned from our survey that one of the important reasons for the turnover of managers is the inability to see the development prospects of themselves and the company. However, we also know from the introduction of the owners that, in fact, the industries in which these companies are located have very promising prospects. In this connection, the possibility that small and medium-sized enterprises developed into large enterprises exists. The reason why people do not see a good future may be caused by unsettling management models and strategic orientation.

4. Insufficient investment in the construction of human capital and corporate culture

The capital constraints of SMEs have forced the company's budget to reduce those not necessary expenses. Employers who are busy collecting capital and soliciting customers throughout the day do not have time to pay attention to the career growth of employees. They also do not have enough financial resources and energy to consider how to give employees spiritual rewards, how to build a good corporate culture, and how to improve employee morale. However, most professional managers with many options in the manager's market do not understand these difficulties of the company. Once they discover that a better platform can promote their career growth, they have better space to satisfy their reputation and mentality, they will inevitably have turnover intention.

As mentioned above, professional managers are a special class and they are gaining more and more important status in society. In addition, this group is mostly in high-level and with high-quality. They are mostly well-educated with long-term interests and spiritual satisfaction. Moreover, due to the rapidly changing economic environment, most companies today cannot provide employment protection to their employees (Benson et al., 2004). For employees, the "unchangeable" response to this "changing" is their own professional ability. And these are related to the human capital investment. Therefore, the temptation of salary may not be able to retain them. Moreover, the salaries of most small and medium-sized private enterprises are not too obvious competitiveness.

Four of the five business leaders we interviewed mentioned that insufficient human capital investment in training, on-the-job learning, funding, etc. is one of the reasons for the turnover of managers, but they also mentioned that the reason for the shortage is that the company has more important things to do, and they don't have time for consideration in this area. While the other entrepreneurs engaged in machinery manufacturing attach significant importance to the development of the company's human resources, he said that employees value their career growth in the company, and if they do not have the opportunities to improve their ability in this place, then it is inevitable that they will leave. Therefore, he specifically pointed out that he spent lots of time training employees. The company does not worry that the manager who is able to improve his ability will leave because he sees that training itself is also the process of shaping employee loyalty. In addition, two entrepreneurs pointed out that compared with large-scale enterprises, especially foreign-funded enterprises, it is difficult for small and medium-sized private enterprises to invest too much in employee spirit satisfaction, and the company's visibility, social image, and reputation are brought to employees. Pride and identity are even less. Under other conditions being equal, these factors will definitely have an impact on the job selection of professional managers.

5. Characteristics of the company's cycle stages

As mentioned earlier, most small and medium-sized private enterprises have been in business for a brief period and are always in the early stages of the life cycle. It thus determines that there are some unique entrepreneurial characteristics (Bhide, 1999). Our investigation has confirmed this point.

First, the flexibility to the external environment determines that the management of the enterprise is difficult to be institutionalized and standardized, and long-term strategic planning is also difficult to carry out, which lead to the arbitrariness and volatility of management, and makes it impossible for employees to see the company's future development. The five companies that we visited all admitted that it is very difficult to formulate long-term strategies and put them into practice as companies need to change their business direction and strategies at any time when the external environment changes. A company engaged in asset appraisal and a company engaged in pharmaceutical sales both stated that their business activities will be affected by the adjustment of national policies at any time. It is difficult to formulate long-term strategic plans based on the prevailing circumstances, and companies have to pay more attention to short-term benefits. In addition, it's also difficult to make day-to-day management activities institutionalized and standardized. Maintaining the flexibility of organization and management process is crucial to adapting to the changes.

Second, the boss is very productive and everything must be done in person. The ages of small and medium-sized private entrepreneurs are at the best stage of career development. For example, the entrepreneurs we visit are all under the age of 40, and even two are under the age of 35. The wealthy boss is naturally not likely to retreat to the second line at this stage. The enthusiasm for career development drives its participation in the company's all-around management. This is necessary for entrepreneurial companies. After all, the company's operations have not fully entered the track. However, the full involvement of the boss will reduce the free play of managers (especially senior managers), and professional managers with entrepreneurial spirit will find it difficult to find opportunities to display their talents within the organization. The result is that those managers who think they have good abilities and have great ambitions are going away. When we visited a teaching material planning and sales company, we learned that the company's deputy general who had just left in 2006 was running away with someone who provided him with 600,000 yuan of unpaid venture capital. After an in-depth interview, we learned that he had previously revealed his idea of entrepreneurship to the boss, but this entrepreneurial spirit could not be recognized and played within the organization. The CEO of a machinery manufacturing company told us that he now fully recognizes the importance of authorization and decentralization. The company is making internal adjustments and intends to give professional managers more power.

Third, small and medium-sized private enterprises have large-scale multiple markets and light management, and there is no perfect human resources management and organizational career management systems. The biggest problem faced by start-up companies is how to find a foothold in the market and generate cash flow as soon as possible (Bhide, 1999). Most of the company's energy has to focus on developing markets, occupying markets, establishing reputations, and lacking sufficient attention to internal management procedures, management rules, control systems, etc. The management system and human resource management system which are related to managerial career growth have yet to be established. As the company pays more attention to the market, employees often feel that they are not valued, and at the same time they find that the company's management is not formal, which will inevitably lead to turnover intention.

Main Characteristics of Chinese Professional Managers and Its Impact on Turnover

In addition to the organizational factors of small and medium-sized private enterprises, the personal factors of professional managers will also affect their turnover intention. This has been confirmed by a large number of domestic and foreign research institutes on employee turnover, and our interview has also verified on this. In the following, regarding professional managers in western countries, the special characteristics of Chinese professional managers are combined with their significance to the turnover.

1. The tendency of "rather a chicken head, not an phoenix tail" in pursuit of a high position

In addition to pursuing monetary gains, Chinese managers also value their position and position in the company. Of course, we are not saying that managers in western societies do not pursue positions of authority and status (Herriot and Pemberton, 1994), but that this is particularly evident in Chinese managers. This is a profound social and historical reason for this.

First, thousands of years of feudalism created the "official-level" consciousness in people's minds. Prominent position and power is a symbol of dignity, status, and reputation (Huang, 2004). This kind of consciousness in the enterprise manifested that the managers excessively pursue high positions. Second, the relational characteristics of Chinese society make professional managers from the "outside" find ways to enter the "internal", and it is better to be a family or a member of the Pan family. Being in a key position can bring them closer to the family core, and to a certain extent become the employer's confidant. Third, the incompleteness of the macro-micro system has led managers with certain real powers to gain direct control gains. Some managers believe that even if the nominal income is not high, as long as the position is high enough and the power is big enough, the hidden income is also very high.

In the survey, we found that an important reason for the turnover of professional managers was to start their own business. After an in-depth interview, they learned that these managers who left for business reasons were because they could not get higher positions or more control power within the company. Although we previously mentioned that entrepreneurship is the main reason, the tendency to pursue high positions has an important influence on the turnover.

2. Weak responsibility for organizations or individuals outside "home": lack of social responsibility

Although modern industrial civilization has influenced China's professional managers in many ways, the "home culture" that has been shaped by Chinese tradition for thousands of years still inevitably has an impact on their values and modes of action. The "benevolence" emphasized by Confucianism is about the "five human relations", so Mencius said, "Fathers and sons are relatives, monarchs and courtiers are righteous, couples are different, seniors and juniors are orderly, and friends have trust". This series of ethical standards is all of particularism. People's sense of responsibility toward others varies with the latter's position in their "disparity order pattern". Unlike the contract society based on individualism in western countries, the Chinese do not regard the personal relations defined by the contract as the target of "benevolence". Thus, except to the father, the king, the husband, the brother, and the friends, people can behave without "benevolence". People may probably not help each other unless there is some kind of relationship (Huang, 2004, p116). The lack of social responsibility should be said to be the main reason of that lots of Chinese professional managers conduct "job-hopping" easily when they are less satisfied. The owner of the company told us that the turnover of many professional managers was simply because other companies provided slightly better treatment, and they had no feeling of embarrassment when they left. Therefore, being lack of the sense of responsibility and commitment is another important reason for manager turnover.

3. Analogous expectation to the employer as to the parents

Still due to the influence of "family culture", Chinese professional managers often generalize the rules that deal with family relations to the outside. They think that superiors should treat their subordinates as elders do to juniors, fulfilling with kindness and care. Correspondingly, employee's own commitment to the organization is also translated into the loyalty to one specific boss. If an individual has lost confidence in his superior, then his commitment to the organization will also be lost (Wong et al., 2002; Chen et. al., 2002). In small and medium-sized private enterprises, the direct leader of most professional managers is the boss. Therefore, whether the boss plays the role of the "parent" well in the company is an important factor that influences the professional managers' loyalty. An entrepreneur in an interview who was engaged in asset assessment tells us that the relationship between companies and employees in the context of China and even eastern cultures is different from that of western societies. If the boss only maintains a fixed contractual relationship with employees, it is very difficult to retain them and make them work hard. Therefore, business leaders need to create a certain family atmosphere within the company, so that employees feel the company's warmth and the boss's care. Another entrepreneur who engaged in machinery manufacturing mentioned the role of family relationships in maintaining manager loyalty. He pointed out that the company should develop the relationship between the boss and its subordinates to a level like that of father-son relationship. This kind of "quasi-blood" relationship helps stabilize the psychological contract between professional managers and companies (Robinson, 1993).

4. Desire of being trustable friend of the boss

As mentioned above, the main object of the Chinese to maintain "benevolence" is members of the "pan-family" who have special relations with them such as father, king, husband, brother, and friends. And thus we can in turn say that in order to make others carry out "benevolence" to you, it is the best way to turn yourself into the other's trustable personal friend. For people in the workplace, being the trustable friend of the boss can not only receive special care but also get a better return. There are two ways to achieve this goal. One is to choose a company that has a "relationship" between the boss and himself; the other is to increase his close relationship with the boss after entering the company. Therefore, we expect that managers who have close relationship with employers before/after entering their employers would have lower turnover intention. And those professional managers who think they can't enter the boss's "relationship circle" are looking for another "circle" to be their best choice.

Summary

The problem of the turnover of professional managers in small and medium-sized private enterprises in China is very special, and this particularity comes from both companies and professional managers. The characteristics of the enterprise include: the characteristics of the company's personality; the "family-oriented" tendency of the operation; the business owner's lack of understanding of the operating rules of modern company system; the insufficient investment in the construction of human capital and corporate culture; and the company's life cycle stage determines that it has some unique entrepreneurial features.

Chinese professional managers also have some characteristics that influence their turnover decision, such as the tendency of "rather a chicken head, not a phoenix tail" in pursuit of a high position; weak responsibility for organizations or individuals outside "home"; analogous expectation to the employer as to the parents; and the desire of being trustable personal friend of the boss.

In this connection, a conclusion can be drawn that: based on the background of western society, the employee's voluntary turnover research and domestic research on general enterprises should not be completely used to explain the turnover of professional managers in small and medium-sized private enterprises. In order to propose a targeted governance mechanism, it is necessary to fully consider the particularities of SMEs and professional managers in the context of China, and to propose and validate relevant turnover process models and factor models. In order to more accurately find the root causes of manager turnover of small and medium-sized enterprises, and to construct related research hypotheses, it is necessary to conduct more rigorous empirical analysis based on the characteristics of these small and medium-sized private enterprises and professional managers that are roughly involved in the exploratory research in this chapter. This book works on this in later chapters.

Chapter 4

Influence Factors Analysis and Research Hypotheses

Figure 4-1 duplicates Figure 1-2, which gives the preliminary analysis framework of the book. The empirical analysis will be conducted under the guidance of the framework. This chapter presents all hypotheses about determinants, mediating and moderating variables. The dependent variables and control variables are also proposed here. Then we use appropriate methods to conduct the empirical tests, which include Scale validity and reliability test, Structural Equation Model analysis (SEM), Robustness and moderating effects test, Consistency analysis of the effects of turnover intention and turnover behavior, and so on. The final validated turnover process model and factors model will be given in the following related sections.

Influencing Factors of Manager Turnover

1. Personal factors

The impact of personal factors on their turnover intention has been confirmed by empirical studies (Holt et al., 2007). Although most of the variables in this area are beyond the control of the organization itself (Waldman et al., 2015), it is necessary to introduce it into the factors model. In this regard, individual variables that are not closely related to the organization can be controlled to accurately capture the effects of key organizational factors that affect the turnover of managers. On the other hand, it can provide suggestions for the organization to implement measures to prevent the turnover of managers during the recruitment phase, to improve the company's overall governance mechanism.

The study pointed out that the attitudes of employees who had just entered the organization had a profound influence on the attitudes and behaviors that followed (Zimmerman et al., 2016; Holtom et al., 2017).

Personal characteristics such as knowledge of the work (Ng and Dyne, 2015; Forrier et al., 2015; Holtom et al., 2017), desire and ability to adapt positively, aggressive personality (Prabhu, 2016; Kammeyer-Mueller and Wanberg, 2003), the unique personal concepts (Kammeyer-Mueller et al., 2005) etc. will also influence their future work attitude and behavior.

Susanna and Aryee (2003) use an empirical study from a sample of Chinese employees in Hong Kong (N=152) to show that the history of psychological contract ruptures that employees have previously experienced is related to the possibility of rupture of the current psychological contract, while the latter is also related to the turnover intention. This means that the work experience before the employee enters will affect his/her organizational commitment to the current company. Krishnan et al. (2006) studied the factors affecting the turnover of female members in top management teams (TMT) and pointed out that individual-level factors such as individual psychological and demographic characteristics are likely to affect female managers' turnover intentions. Since Krishnan et al. did not empirically test the relevant propositions and assumptions, the existence of this hypothesis remains to be further studied.

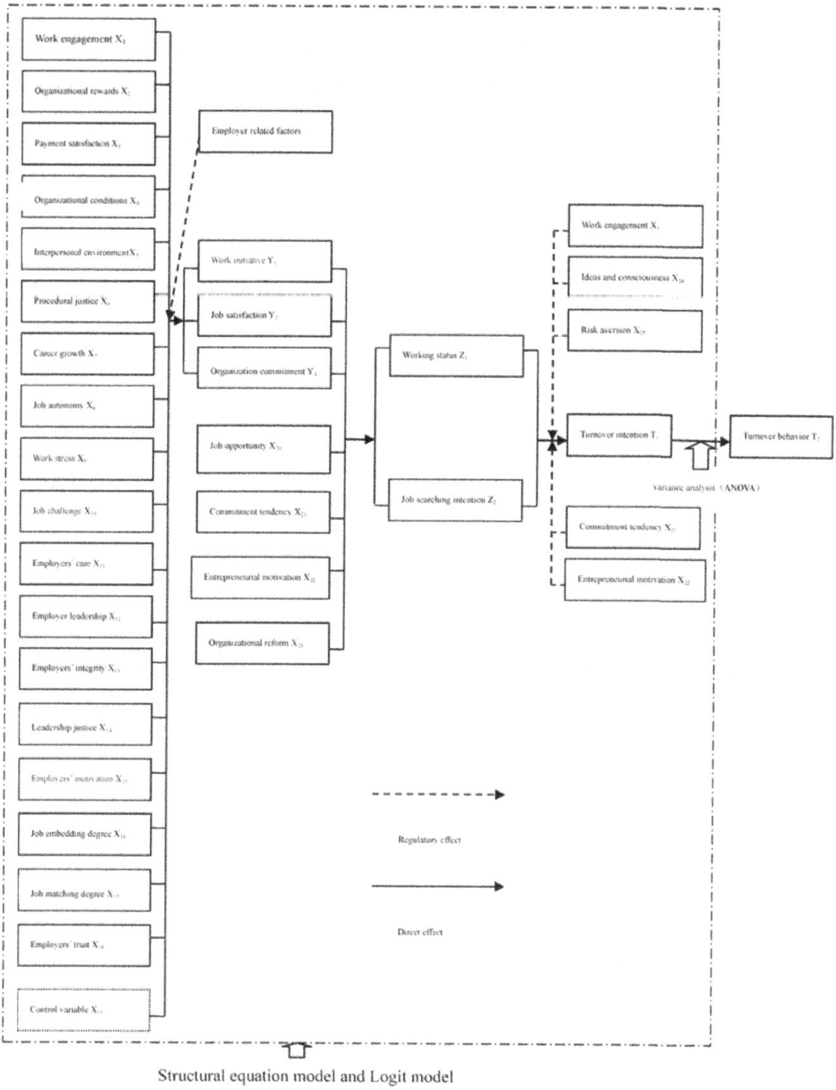

Figure 4-1 Analysis framework

The main purpose of studying personal factors is to prevent employees' turnover beforehand. If you can identify which personal variables will affect their turnover intentions, the organization can use the resume, interview, test, etc. to obtain the personal information to predict their turnover tendencies during the recruitment phase, and then distinguish those applicants who have a higher probability of turnover and avoid turnover happening (Murray and Zimmerman, 2005). Murray and Zimmerman's (2005) study found that personal resume data, clear-purpose attitudes and intentions, and disguised-purpose dispositional retention scales are predictive of turnover. The meta-analysis of Griffeth et al. (2000) also pointed out that bios can predict turnover well (ρ=0.31).

Personal factors have a great explanatory power for the manager's turnover intention, which not only means that it has a direct or indirect effect, but also means that this variable will moderate the effect of other antecedent variables on turnover intention. On the basis of literature, we selected five individual variables for empirical testing in combination with the previous survey data. These personal variables are job participation, commitment propensity, entrepreneurial motivation, Chinese traditional concept awareness, and risk aversion. The first three variables, as the direct and indirect effect variables and the moderating variables are introduced into the model, and the latter two are introduced into the model as the moderating variables. In this section, the hypotheses of the first three individual variables are given. The latter two research hypotheses will be given in the relevant chapters.

Job involvement

The most important variable of the personal factors is job involvement, which refers to the intention of employees to work hard (Price, 2001), and the extent to which employees are willing to complete a job role (Currivan, 1999). Empirical studies have pointed out that job involvement structure is not only different from job satisfaction but also different from organizational commitment (Currivan, 1999).

In general, employees with higher job involvemetn before entering the company have a relatively lower turnover intention (Latham and Leddy, 1987; Hom and Griffeth, 1995). Rusbult and Farrell (1983) found that organizational commitment can mediate the relationship between job involvement and turnover. Lance (1991) believes that the reason that work participation has a direct effect on organizational commitment is that highly involved employees are grateful to organizations that can provide him with opportunities to perform work activities, and therefore have a higher degree of commitment (Ravichandan, 2015). However, Mitchell et al. (2001) did not find this mediating role of organizational commitment.

In addition to this, we will also examine the role of this variable in regulating the effects of the relevant antecedent effects in this study. Hypotheses are made as follows:

H1a: *Job involvement of professional managers will affect their turnover intention, the higher the job involvement, the lower the turnover intention.*

H1b: *Professional manager's job participation will moderate the effect of the related antecedent variables on turnover intention, the higher the work participation, the weaker the latter's relationship.*

Commitment propensity

There are personal differences in managers' perceptions of the turnover behavior. Some consider turnover to be a major issue that needs careful consideration. It is considered irresponsible to rashly threaten to resign. Unless there are very good reasons, such managers generally do not leave the job. Some managers do not think that leaving a job is a major event involving responsibility. It is a matter of course when the job is not satisfactory. Some even use 'job hopping' as a strategy to stay competitive in their careers. They think that working in different companies helps improve their skills and qualifications (Parker et al., 2015; Connie and Kammeyer-Mueller, 2000). The literature introduces a commitment propensity construct to capture this difference. Obviously, the propensity to commit will affect the turnover of professional managers.

Commitment propensity is a characteristic that employees have when they enter the organization. It is the employee's values regarding the turnover behavior itself. Employees with a higher commitment propensity when enter the organization are more likely to have a high commitment to the organization, and thus have a lower turnover intention, but otherwise have a higher turnover intention (Kammeyer-Mueller et al., 2005). Since employees' past 'job-hopping' experience may reflect personal characteristics to a certain extent, it can be expected that employees who have had multiple resignations in the past are more likely to leave the company (Lee and Mitchell, 1994).

In relation to this, the duration of the work of the manager in the previous company is also an outward manifestation of commitment, and is thus a very important predictor of future turnover intention (Fleishman, 2010; Joseph et al., 2015). If a professional manager has a habit of 'job-hopping', this can be reflected in the length of time he worked in the previous workplace (Murray and Zimmerman, 2005). The lower duration means that it lacks professional ethics, and the latter is closely related to organizational commitment and separation (Hom et al., 2017). Cascio's (1976) study confirms this, and he found that applicants' length of service in the previous company could predict their subsequent turnover. Hypotheses are made as follows:

H2a: *The commitment propensity of professional managers tends to affect their turnover intention, the higher the commitment propensity, the lower the turnover intention.*

H2b: *The commitment propensity of professional managers tends to moderate the effect of related antecedent variables on turnover intention, the higher the commitment propensity, the weaker the latter's relationship.*

Entrepreneurial motivation

Although most of existing resignations have not officially introduced entrepreneurial motives into the model, the pioneering study of March and Simon (1958) did not rule out the possible impact of this factor on employee turnover intention. As professional managers are relatively high-caliber groups, their career pursuit is different from that of general employees. Having their own careers has become a career ideal for many on-the-job managers. In addition, many senior managers who work in small and medium-sized private enterprises often feel that their ability is not worse than their bosses (Dai, 2005). The idea of self-employment is very natural.

Based on the research of Barnard (1938) and Simon (1945), March and Simon (1958) identified two main reasons for voluntary turnover, namely: turnover desirability and ease of turnover. March and Simon (1958) understand the ease of turnover as the perceived function of the number of job opportunities offered by external organizations outside, the latter is sometimes a function of the level of business activity, the number of visible organizations, and the personal characteristics of employees. Later, this construct was relatively simple to measure in one dimension or less (Ravichandan, 2015), referred to as 'the availability of other opportunities' (Chen et al., 2016), 'Opportunity' (Waldman et al., 2015) 'Ease of Flow' (Sun and Wang, 2011) and so on (Griffeth et al., 2005). Entrepreneurial motivation can actually reflect the 'accessibility of other opportunities' in one aspect, because in a sense, self-employment can be understood as other job opportunities, and entrepreneurial motivation can be seen as the attractiveness of this job opportunity.

Kevin et al. (2004) pointed out that although people often act in accordance with inertia, and are unwilling to change easily. But if there are many other job opportunities, employees will not be motivated to overestimate the current job, which will lead to a decrease in job satisfaction and a desire to leave. A recent meta-analysis reported a correlation coefficient of 0.11 (Griffeth et al., 2000). Price (2001) pointed out that the impact of other job opportunities on turnover includes two aspects. One is the direct impact on their turnover intention, and the other is the indirect effect of job satisfaction on turnover intention. The study carried out by Sun et al. (2007) attempts to examine the moderating effects of other job opportunities on the relationship between related variables and turnover. The results were somewhat surprising. In short, professional managers' perceptions of other job opportunities have a direct or indirect impact on their turnover intention.

Therefore, if the professional manager's entrepreneurial motivation is large enough, his desire to grasp external opportunities is strong enough that he is willing to change the status quo and wants to take a chance, so his turnover intention will inevitably be higher. Therefore, hypotheses are made as follows:

H3a: *Professional managers' entrepreneurial opportunities affect their turnover intention, the stronger the entrepreneurial motivation, the higher the turnover intention.*

H3b: *Professional managers' entrepreneurial opportunities moderate the effect of related antecedent variables on turnover intention, the stronger the entrepreneurial motivation, the stronger the latter's relationship.*

2. Organizational factors

The primary purpose of most of the turnover studies is to find out the factors that the organization can control and influence employees' turnover, and then take corresponding management measures to achieve the goal of reducing turnover rate. Therefore, research on organizational factors is a major part of the relevant literature, and almost all literature on employee attitudes, job performance, and turnover intentions consider the role of the organization's own factors (Lee and Mitchell, 1994; McElroy et al., 2001; Ramlall, 2003; Krishnan et al., 2006). Based on a large number of literatures, combined with previous in-depth investigations, this book filters out the following organizational variables for further empirical testing.

Organizational rewards

Organization rewards involve the various tangible or intangible payments that organizations use to exchange employee labor services. They are the basis for organizations to attract employees, retain employees, and motivate them to work hard. Existing research shows that organization rewards are an important factor that employees consider during the turnover decision process. This book focuses on three dimensions: incentive systems, opportunities and sapce for development, and opportunities for higher rewards.

The incentive system is an important dimension of the organization's reward system, and is often valued by the analysis of employee performance. Simply put, the incentive system is about policies, measures, and institutions that link individual contributions with the rewards they receive. The study found that the incentive system plays a regulatory role in the relationship between employee's performance and the turnover. When the rewards are considered to have nothing to do with performance, those high-performing employees show higher turnover intention (Sturman and Trevor, 2001; Trevor et al., 1997; Suzanne and Luthans, 2006).

Existing research believes that job performance will affect turnover through multiple mechanisms. In some cases, high-performing employees have lower turnover intention, and in some cases, employees with superior performance are with higher turnover intention (Allen and Griffeth, 2001). An important hypothesis is that high performance leads to low turnover. The return on work is linked to performance. Therefore, the relationship between rewards and performance should be included as a moderator. Similarly, there is an important hypothesis that high-performance leads to a high turnover probability. That is, potential employers can observe that the employee is indeed with high-performance. Therefore, the observability of work performance should also be introduced as a moderator (Allen and Griffeth, 2001). A meta-analysis carried out by Williams and Livingstone (1994) shows that when the rewards are based more on performance, the negative relationship between performance and turnover is stronger. Harrison et al. (1996) found that when rewards are most dependent on performance, there is a strong positive correlation between performance and job satisfaction, so the employee with high-performance will have higher job satisfaction, and the turnover intention will be lower. Correspondingly, studies of such as Sturman and Trevor (2001), Becton et al. (2016), Wendy et al. (2005) also pointed out that when the rewards do not correspond to their contributions, those who perform well are likely to leave.

An empirical study of Trevor et al. (1997) found that monetary compensation moderates the linear relationship between performance and turnover. They also found that salary increase will change the curve between performance and turnover. Regardless of the turnover intention, if the employees are well-paid, the outstanding employees will not easily leave the job. Salamin and Hom (2005) also studied the relationship between job performance and turnover. They repeated and extended the work of Trevor et al. (1997) and applied more advanced survival regression measures. As a result, it has been found that the relationship between performance and turnover is in a curve, and that bonuses are more likely to prevent the performance of outstanding employees from turnover than the increase in salary. If high-performing employees do not receive enough bonuses for whatever reason (low position, in poorly profitable department, etc.), they will choose to leave. Since the bonus system is the most commonly used incentive system for many companies, this study also confirms the important impact of the incentive system on turnover.

Promotion and development space are also important organizational rewards. Trevor et al. (1997) pointed out that the traditional point of view is that promotion helps to increase employee loyalty. It is questionable because promotion will signal the market to the employee. This signal is a sign of higher employee productivity, which is observed by potential employers in the market (Lazear, 1998). External companies lack direct information on the productivity of other company employees. They need to extrapolate information from the behavior of other companies (Spence, 1973; Auriol et al., 2016). That is: the position of the employees of other companies became observable (Milgrom and Oster, 1987). It is worth noting that by promoting the ability to display information, low-energy people are also more likely to leave. Although they will get a certain promotion before their real capabilities are fully known by the boss in the early stages of their careers, with the continuous disclosure of information, it is difficult to continue to obtain further promotions, so the turnover intention will slowly arise. The findings of Trevor et al. (1997) are contrary to the generally accepted view in organizational psychology, which argues that promotions have reservations for employees with both high and low performances (Griffeth et al., 2000).

Meyer and Allen (1991) noted that work experience such as organization rewards, procedural fairness, and superior's support is more closely related to AC than organizational characteristics and employee personal characteristics. Eisenberger et al. (2002) found that the perception of supervisor support (PSS) influences turnover intention through the mediating role of POS. The reason is that the superiors are equivalent to the organization to a certain extent. Their support for subordinates' work affects the employee's perception of organizational support (POS), which ultimately affects employee retention. This point has important implications for our study of professional managers of small and medium-sized enterprises, because in small and medium-sized private enterprises, the managers also regard the boss and the organization as one. In addition, Rhoades et al. (2001) used three samples to examine the complex relationship between work experience, organizational support (POS), emotional commitment (AC), and employee turnover. The first study found that POS plays a mediating role in organizing returns, procedural fairness, and the relationship between superior support and AC. The second study examined changes in POS and AC after two years and three years respectively, and found that POS and AC are positively correlated, which means POS affects AC. The third study found that the negative relationship between POS and employee voluntary separation was played by AC in the intermediaries.

Taken together, these results show that good working conditions can help increase emotional commitment through organizational support perceptions, thereby reducing employee turnover behavior. Now we make the following hypotheses:

H4: *The company's organizational rewards to professional managers will affect the latter's turnover intention, the more satisfied* *the professional manager's perception of the organization's rewards, the lower the turnover intention.*

Salary satisfaction

Strictly speaking, the salary should be included in the scope of the organization's rewards, but since this variable is very important, we consider introducing it separately into the model. With few exceptions (Gaertner, 1999), almost all studies have shown that salary satisfaction is one of the most important organizational variables in turnover studies (Ramlall, 2003; Maertz and Griffeth, 2004). Its main dimensions include the salary level, internal fairness and external fairness (Zhang and Wang, 2003; Huang, 2007) and so on.

In order to examine the effects of salary incentives and non-salary incentives on employee turnover and other outcome variables, Suzanne and Luthans (2006) used longitudinal data to conduct empirical studies. The results found that salary incentives and non-salary incentives have a significant impact on employee turnover. However, the effect of salary incentives in both early and late periods is greater than non-salary incentives. This means that in general, salary satisfaction is the main factor that determines the employee's turnover. Suzanne and Luthans believe that equity theory can provide a possible explanation for this. Increasing the company's salary above the market reference level helps to reduce employee turnover (Sturman and Short, 2000; Trevor et al., 1997). This result also supports the relevant conclusions of the efficiency salary theory (Akerlof and Yellen, 1986).

In addition, Weiss et al. (1999) found that salary results have an important impact on employee well-being, and procedural fairness only plays a minor role, which suggesting that employees see outcomes as more important than the processes (Brief and Weiss, 2002). Therefore, salary satisfaction is an important determinant for employees to consider turnover or not. We make the following hypothesis:

H5: *The salary that the company provides to professional managers will affect the latter's turnover intention, the more satisfied* *the professional manager's perception of salary is, the lower the turnover intention.*

Organizational conditions and organizational attractiveness

The first two variables mainly examine organizational factors from the perspective of individuals. In the following, we examine the organization's two comprehensive variables: organizational conditions and organizational attractiveness. The next section examines the interpersonal climate variables related to this. Both constructs are complex variables and contain multiple dimensions. For example, Dess and Beard (1984) used munificence, dynamism, and complexity to describe organizational conditions (Krishnan et al., 2006). With reference to the definition of Dess and Beard and the research of Zhang and Wang (2003), this book considers the dimensions of the company's environment, development prospects, social image, and the extent of management. The study pointed out (Chen and Aryee, 2007) that organizational self-esteem has been found to correlate with job satisfaction, organizational commitment, job performance, and extra-role behavior (Bowling, 2010; Cai et al., 2015).

The relationship between organizational ethical values and turnover has been confirmed by some studies (Turan, 2015). Ostroff (1993) found that there is a strong correlation between organizational climate dimensions and organizational commitment. Organizational climate can explain the variance of employee organizational commitment by 21%. The organizational climate here has traditionally been described as a common perception of organizational returns and organizational support related policies, measures, and procedures (Davison et al., 2015). Hunt et al. (1989) also found that the value of corporate ethics has significant predictive power for organizational commitment. Schwepker (2001) found on this basis that employees' perception of a positive ethical and moral atmosphere is positively related to job satisfaction and organizational commitment. Here, the moral atmosphere is defined as 'a general concept of organizational behavior and procedures with moral content' (Victor and Cullen, 1988).

The empirical results of Sun et al. (2007) found that high-performing human resource measures increase service-oriented organizational citizenship behavior and create a supportive work environment to increase the psychological cost of employee turnover, thereby reducing their turnover probability. Based on these studies, we can make the following hypotheses:

H6a: *The organizational conditions of the company will affect the turnover intention of professional managers, the more satisfied the professional managers are with organizational conditions, the lower the turnover intention.*

H6b: *The attractiveness of the company's organization will affect the turnover intention of professional managers. The more satisfied professional managers are with the organization's attractiveness, the lower the turnover intention.*

Interpersonal atmosphere

In the organization, especially the Chinese society with special emphasis on 'relationships' (Xin and Pearce, 1996), the quality of interpersonal relationships between members and others is a crucial factor in the turnover decision. On one hand, this is because the degree of interpersonal harmony will directly affect the mutual support of employees. On the other hand, interpersonal relationship itself is the spiritual needs of people. In Maslach's (1982) research model of burnout, the second component of energy exhaustion is called depersonalization, which is a lack of interpersonal distance and contact with working peers and customers. It will directly lead to emotional exhaustion of employees (Cropanzano et al., 2003).

Existing turnover studies have also begun to emphasize the introduction of relational constructs to capture the effects of the quality and nature of work relationships (Chen et al, 1998; Maertz and Campion, 2004; Mitchell et al., 2001). Maertz and Campion (2004) found that a good relationship between employees and colleagues helps them stay in the company. Hom and Xiao (2006) examined how close networks can lead to strong loyalty connections based on the foregoing research. The empirical results show that a tight social network does help prevent employees from leaving the company. Sun et al. (2007) also pointed out that mutuality helps to establish trust and intention in relation to cooperative behavior (Simpson and Willer, 2015), and these contribute to employee retention (Mossholder et al., 2005).

Mossholder et al. (2005) systematically studied the predictive power of relational variables on turnover behavior. The article finds that two relationship variables significantly affect employee turnover behavior after 5 years, namely: the degree of individuals living in the network centrality and interpersonal citizenship behavior. Dess and Shaw (2001) also examined the importance of relational variables in interpreting turnover behavior. Low-quality relationships will lead to high organizational costs, leading to higher turnover rates. Organizational development and social capital can not only reduce the turnover rate, but also help improve organization-wide productivity.

It can be seen that the interpersonal atmosphere of professional managers of small and medium-sized private enterprises will affect their turnover intention. The hypothesis is given as follows:

H7: *The Company's interpersonal atmosphere will affect the turnover intention of professional managers, the more satisfied the professional manager's perception of the interpersonal atmosphere is, the lower the turnover intention.*

Fairness

The concept of fairness includes multiple dimensions, such as: fair distribution, fair information, fair procedures, interactive fairness, and fairness in leadership, etc. This book focuses on two dimensions: procedural fairness and leadership fairness. The reasons for this are as follows: 1. The level of managers is relatively high, and in the fairness of the organization, procedural fairness is the most important; 2. The secrecy system of remuneration (especially non-fixed bonuses) makes it difficult for managers to assess the fairness of the distribution of the treatment received; 3. External fairness in comparison with external peers has been characterized by the pay satisfaction variable

(DeConinck and Stilwell, 2004); 4. Interaction fairness and information fairness are sometimes viewed as fairness of procedural fairness (Wong et al., 2002; Zinta, 2005).

Thibaut and Walker's (1975) research on the individual's response to conflict resolution procedures led to the development of procedural fairness theory, which focuses on employees' judgment of the decision process and method. Researchers have provided different ideas and operational definitions for procedures fairness (Colquitt et al., 2015). Bies and Moag (1986) pointed out that the fairness in human relations processing is evaluated based on these factors: to what extent decision authority is trustworthy and respectable; full consideration of decision-making communication; interpretation and rationality of decision-making principles instructions. The procedural fairness perspective focuses on the process of making decisions (Khan et al., 2015; Yu et al., 2017). Since procedural fairness focuses on employees' perceptions of fairness in decision-making methods and procedures, these methods are used to determine the number of rewards and penalties, so how the results are decided is more important than the actual results (Cassar and Buttigieg, 2015). This type of study shows that the process of how results are determined is often influenced by the individual's superiority in the organization and the employee's influence on corporate governance trust (Khan et al., 2015).

Organizational fairness and employee turnover are among the most important research topics in the field of organizational research (Mai et al., 2016; Posthuma et al., 2007). Related research shows that perception of procedural fairness enhances employees' commitment to the entire organization (Greenberg, 1990). Some studies have provided empirical evidence that procedural fairness influences employee attitude toward the company through perceived organizational support. And the interaction fairness influences employees' attitudes toward superiors through the leadership-member exchange process (LMX) (Masterson et al., 2000). Tony and Roberson (2003) examine the impact of aggregate of justice perception on some outcome variables at the departmental and business unit level, and suggest that it is useful to distinguish procedural fairness from interpersonal equity at different levels. The empirical analysis from 4539 employee samples shows that the two diverse types of fairness will have an impact on employee organization and then on their turnover intention.

DeConinck and Stilwell (2004) found that procedural fairness is an important direct variable affecting employees' satisfaction with their superiors, while distributional fairness is predictive of salary satisfaction. Both fairness variables only indirectly affect organizational commitments. Erdogan et al. (2006) also showed that cross-referencing is strongly correlated with LMX, while the latter affects the employee's turnover intention. Of course, many studies have pointed out that the meaning of interpersonal justice can be included in the procedural fairness (Zinta, 2005).

Although many empirical studies have found a direct and significant negative relationship between procedural fairness and turnover intention (Aquino et al., 1997), but there is still much debate about whether this relationship really exists (Posthuma et al., 2007). Researchers have not been successful in establishing and confirming the relationship between fair procedures and actual turnover behavior (Aquino et al., 1997). There is no significant relationship between the general study report on the study of turnover behavior (Jones and Skarlicki, 2003). For example, Randall and Muller (1995) found that both distributional fairness and procedural fairness are related to turnover intentions, but the turnover behavior is not related. Spreitzer and Mishra (2002) found that allocation fairness and procedural fairness can predict organizational attachment, but they do not have such ability to turnover behavior. Some studies have also found a significant relationship between them, such as Yang (2014)、Jones and Skarlicki (2003) and so on.

One possible explanation for these confusing outcomes is the potential two-way effects of procedural fairness and turnover (Posthuma et al., 2007). Posthuma et al. (2007) divide the procedural fairness into four dimensions: advance notice, consistency, representativeness views, and decision-making participation opportunities. By examining the effect of these four dimensions on voluntary turnover behavior, we find that the two dimensions of advance notification and equal treatment are significantly negatively related to turnover behavior. In the logistic regression model, there are two dimensions that have different effects on the turnover behavior. The advance notice is negatively related to the turnover, while the representativeness views are positively related to the turnover. Posthuma et al. believe that the phenomenon of different procedural fairness dimensions having different or even opposite effects on turnover can be explained by using the theory of fairness, which states that procedural fairness conveys to employees that they are treated as members of organizations or teams (Lim and Loosemore, 2017). This recognition will increase its emotional connection to the organization (Bauer et al., 1998). Conversely, poor perception of procedural fairness leads to a negative emotional state of the organization (Cropanzano et al., 2017). As the different dimensions of procedural fairness may produce different signals, their action will be different accordingly.

In addition, studies have found the regulatory effect of procedural fairness. Such as Zinta (2005) found that procedural fairness will reduce the relationship between employee perception of covert self-serving political behaviors and turnover intention, but will not reduce the impact of blatant selfish behavior on turnover.

Based on the above analysis, we can make the following hypothesis:

H8: *The fairness of the company will affect the turnover intention of professional managers, the more satisfied the professional managers are about fairness, the lower the turnover intention.*

Career advancement opportunities

Career advancement reflects the role the organization plays in helping employees achieve their career goals. Fewer opportunities for promotion and career development can significantly increase employee turnover (Mohamad and Nasurdin, 2006).

High-performance measures related to the personal career development of employees are related to employee turnover or retention (Shaw and Shi, 2017; Batt, 2002; Guthrie, 2001). But so far, the mechanism behind this relationship is still in speculation. Batt (2002) believes that trust-based HR incentives such as training, employment protection, and relatively high treatment may promote employee attachment and commitment, and thus reduce turnover rate. Sun et al. (2007) conducted an empirical study of samples from mainland China based on social exchange, especially reciprocal normative theory, and found that high-performing human resource management measures were indeed negatively correlated with turnover.

Many studies examine the impact of career growth opportunities on employee turnover from the perspective of human capital investment. In the highly competitive and volatile modern economy, the stability of work is becoming more and more difficult. Downsizing, restructuring, and unemployment have become commonplace, and the job security commitments provided by the company have become increasingly difficult to achieve. Therefore, when employees choose to work, they pay more and more attention to the career growth opportunities provided by the company, which helps to improve their 'employability' in the market. If the company is willing to increase human capital investment in this area, its ability to attract and retain outstanding employees will be greatly enhanced (Craig et al., 2002). It is estimated that US companies spend about 160 to 55 billion U.S. dollars on employee training. A 1996 nationwide survey showed that 75% of U.S. employees provide more than 20 organizations and almost all larger employers with several types of tuition funding programs. The related investigations of Hewitt Associates in 1998 also reached similar conclusions. The main reason for U.S. companies to make such investments is that the training and development of employees can help improve employee satisfaction and retention (Cappelli, 2000; Craig et al., 2002). This is also the view held by many turnover literatures.

Based on the above analysis, the hypothesis is given as follows:

H9: *The career growth opportunities that the company provides to professional managers influence the latter's turnover intention, the more satisfied the professional manager's perception of career growth opportunities, the lower the turnover intention.*

Organizational change

Few studies have examined the impact of organizational change on turnover. However, based on the previous field surveys and in-depth interviews with entrepreneurs, we have found that the turnover of many professional managers is related to the major changes that the organization is undergoing or will undergo. These changes may include changes in scale, process reengineering, restructuring, strategic adjustments, and so on. Regardless of whether managers are out of their own occupational safety concerns or because they are worried that they will become the object of change for change, change as a real organizational factor does affect their turnover decision. This book attempts to introduce managers' perception variables of organizational change and examine its effect on turnover.

The voluntary turnover model initiated by Lee and Mitchell (1994) places particular emphasis on the effect of 'impact' on employee turnover decisions. One of the important impacts is the significant changes or fluctuations that organizations are undergoing or will undergo, such as equity changes, process reengineering, changes in management systems and major personnel changes. Some later development models and empirical studies also gave similar roles (Lee et al., 1996; Mueller et al., 2005; Holt et al., 2007).

Susanna and Aryee (2003) from an empirical study of a Chinese sample of employees in Hong Kong (N=152) found that organizational change is related to the breakdown of psychological contract, which in turn is related to turnover intention, psychological withdrawal behavior, and organizational citizenship (Alcover et al., 2017; Robinson, 1996; Turnley and Feldman, 2000). Psychological contract refers to an employee's belief that involves the responsibilities, terms, and conditions of the reciprocal transaction between the employee and the organization to which he belongs. Psychological contract breach refers to employees' perception that the organization has not fully fulfilled the implicit contractual obligations of the psychological contract. Organizational changes are often motivated by mediocre performance pressures. Therefore, an organization's inability to achieve its commitment to its employees will lead to the collapse of the psychological contract between the parties, thus prompting employees to leave the job. Therefore, the significant changes that the organization's managers are aware of or are going through will affect their turnover intention. The following hypothesis is made:

H10: *Organizational changes the company is undergoing or will experience will affect the turnover intention of professional managers, if professional managers perceive this change, they are more likely to leave the job.*

3. Job factors

Factors related to the job itself have a significant impact on turnover intentions and behavior (Lee and Mitchell, 1994; Griffeth et al., 2000). Three of the seven structural variables given by Price (2001) are related to job characteristics: job autonomy, job stress, and job monotony. The work pressure here includes four types: insufficient resources, ambiguous roles, conflicting roles, and workload (Zhang, 2006). According to the literatures, combined with previous field surveys, this book considers three important work factors that affect manager turnover, namely: work autonomy, work stress, and work challenges.

Work autonomy

Work autonomy is sometimes referred to as job control (de Einar et al., 2004), which means the degree of independence and freedom of employees to control their own work process. This concept plays a central role in many organizational pressure theories (Currivan, 1999). Hackman and Oldham (1975) defined the construct as "the degree of freedom, independence, and self-determination that a job provides to employees in work plans and procedural decisions" (p162). And Currivan (1999) gave similar definition to this.

The transformation of organizations from a bureaucratic structure to an organic one has become a global trend. This has brought more responsibilities to employees and more new work needs. These job demands have had an impact on the psychological and physical health of employees (Fairbrother and Warn, 2013). A well-managed organization recognizes that it is necessary to maximize the workforce's control to meet the needs of the workforce. Providing employees with freedom and initiative is becoming a basic goal of organizational design philosophy (Bosma et al., 2012). Many research suggests that those who have sufficient confidence in their ability to work should be given sufficient level of control over their power (Schaubroeck et al., 2000). Employees with higher work autonomy are more likely to face high demands of work, that is, he does not regard work requirements as high work pressure (de Einar et al., 2004). Price (2001) pointed out directly that autonomy moderates the relationship between job stress and satisfaction. In the case of high autonomy, high work pressure may not necessarily reduce satisfaction.

Some studies have begun to focus on the influence of cultural factors in the relationship between work autonomy and job needs. Schaubroeck et al. (2000) conducted a study of this. He examined job control in dealing with job demands, cultural factors, and the influence of different efficiency perceptions. It was found that in the United States, for those employees who reported a higher level of self-efficacy, a higher level of control can ease the impact of job demand on mental health symptoms and turnover intentions; but for those with lower levels of self-efficacy, the level of control will increase the effect of job demand. However, for a matching Hong Kong sample, the collective efficacy interacts with the level of control in the same way to influence the impact of work requirements. These differences can be attributed to different ego-centric tendencies and group-centered tendencies, which are linked to the social norms of individualism and collectivism.

As a form of employee participation in decision-making, the authorization dimension in work autonomy represents a kind of leadership behavior. It gives subordinates new responsibilities and additional authority to fulfill their responsibilities. That is, the superior grants part of his authority to subordinates to make him take responsibility for a specific activity. As a kind of leadership behavior, empowerment leads to a high level of self-esteem based on the organization. The reason is that empowerment provides employees with opportunities for self-direction and control. This means that the individual's ability and importance are recognized by the organization (Gardner et al., 2004).

Chen and Aryee (2007) found that in the Eastern context, organizational-based self-esteem and perceived insider status play a complete role in the relationship between empowerment and emotional commitment, and the relationship between authorization and job satisfaction play a partial media role. Further, traditionality moderates the relationship between authorization and these intermediary variables, the weaker the traditional concept, the stronger the relationship between authorization and intermediary variables, and the weaker the contrary. The explanation given by Chen and Aryee is that high-class employees are more willing to obey the guidelines of leaders and less inclined to play the role of leaders. Therefore, even when they are empowered, they may even feel uneasy. The reluctance of a high-class employee to accept job responsibilities arises from their sense of powerlessness or low sense of agency. Therefore, empowerment will not improve the self-concept of high-traditional employees. Kirkman and Shapiro (1997) pointed out that high-power-distance employees do not like the work of strong autonomy and responsibility, which is the main feature of high self-management. In order to test the effect of job autonomy in small and medium-sized private enterprises on turnover intention, we propose the following hypothesis:

***H11:** Work autonomy will affect the turnover intention of professional managers, the more satisfied the professional managers are with job autonomy, the lower the turnover intention.*

Work pressure

Work pressure refers to the difficulties and efforts that employees have to perform in carrying out their work (Currivan, 1999, p501). It mainly includes such dimensions: 1. role ambiguity, that is, unclear degree of role expectations; 2. Role conflicts, that is, inconsistencies in role expectations; 3. work burden, that is, too much work to be done; 5. lack of work support, that is, employees cannot obtain enough organizational support necessary to complete work (Currivan, 1999; Price, 2001). The study of the relationship between job stress, job satisfaction, and other relevant outcome variables is also a hot topic in organizational theory. Studies have pointed out that too much work-related stress is very common among managers, and the survey shows that 88% of managers think they are under too much pressure (Tillson, 1997).

The relationship between work pressures and outcome variables such as turnover is not yet clear (Cavanaugh et al., 2000). An empirical study by Balfour and Neff (1993) using a sample of nurses found that psychologically higher job demands are predictive for subsequent turnover. Spector and Michaels (1986) pointed out that stressful work does not necessarily lead to turnover. Leong et al. (1996) found no meaningful relationship between job stress and job satisfaction and turnover intention. Bogg and Cooper (1995) also concluded that perceived working pressure does not necessarily lead to poorer work outcomes. The recent survey even noted that not all work pressures are bad. Work stress can sometimes produce competitive advantages, and promote positive change, etc.

Cavanaugh et al. (2000) pointed out that the main reason for these confusion conclusions may lie in the different nature of stressors (based on employees' estimates). Their sample of research comes from 1886 professional managers in the United States. The study found that challenging-related self-reported stress is positively related to job satisfaction, negatively related to job search behavior and hindrance-related self-reported stress. The hindrance-related self-reported stress is negatively related to job satisfaction, and positively related to job search behavior and turnover. This means that distinct types of work pressure have different or even opposite effects on turnover intentions. In order to isolate the effect of negative working pressures on turnover intentions, this book considers the introduction of job-challenging variables alone to capture the different effects of different sources of stress pointed out by Cavanaugh et al. Price (2001) reminds us that we need to consider other factors (such as social support, etc.) to moderate the relationship between work pressure and turnover intention, otherwise it is difficult to draw a definite conclusion.

In spite of this, there are still many rigorous empirical studies that have drawn a positive relationship between work pressure and turnover intention. Empirical studies by De Einar et al. (2004) with two-year of longitudinal data samples from truck drivers show that job stress is significantly associated with voluntary turnover, and that the mentality of truck drivers plays an intermediary role. Other industries have similar findings, and employees with higher tension are relatively more likely to leave the company (Liu et al., 2015). A meta-analysis found that the correlation between emotional exhaustion and turnover intention reached 0.44 (Cropanzano et al., 2003). Other studies have also found a correlation between emotional exhaustion and actual turnover behavior (Liu et al., 2015). The main factors that lead to psychological tension and emotional exhaustion are the dimensions of job demand in work stress (Berkman et al., 2015).

The research of Farmer and Aguinis (2005) involves the work support dimension of work stress constructs. The correlative empirical results show that the work support related to the superior influences the employee turnover intention. In addition, many studies including three meta-analyses indicate that role conflict and role ambiguity are related to job satisfaction and organizational commitment (Hom et al., 2017). DeConinck and Stilwell (2004) found that role conflict has both immediate effects on organizational commitment and indirect effects through supervisor satisfaction. Role ambiguity only affects boss satisfaction, and there is no predictive power for organizational commitment.

Based on the above research, we can make the following hypothesis:

H12: *Work pressure affects the turnover intention of professional managers, the greater the work pressure perceived by professional managers, the higher the turnover intention.*

Job challenges

As mentioned above, existing research has drawn inconclusive conclusions about the relationship between working pressures and turnover intentions. According to Cavanaugh et al. (2000), this may be due to the different nature of the source of work stress. The challenging work pressure is positively related to job satisfaction, while the impedimental work stress is negatively related to job satisfaction. In order to separate out the different effects of these two different types of work pressures on turnover intentions, this book considers the introduction of job-challenging variables. This approach also helps us understand whether the exceptional group of professional managers actively responds to the work challenges.

In fact, the exploratory analysis conducted in the third chapter of the book has shown that professional managers of small and medium-sized private enterprises, especially senior professional managers, are motivated by entrepreneurship. If their entrepreneurial spirit is hard to be played in the enterprise, it seems natural to leave the job. Job challenges can, to some extent, reflect the space and platform that companies give managers potential to use, so we can make the following hypothesis:

H13: *Job challenges affect the turnover intention of professional managers. the greater the job managers' perception of job challenges, the lower the turnover intention.*

4. Employer factors

As mentioned above, the employer factors play a very important role in the decision-making process of professional managers' turnover in small and medium-sized private enterprises. This book will formally test the significance of this factor in the model. Redding (1990) once pointed out that employee loyalty to individuals under Chinese cultural environment is more important than loyalty to organizations. Chen et al. (2002) suggested that future research should examine the determinants of employer loyalty, which may include the trust of the employer, the relationship with the employer, the understanding of the employer, the communication with the employer, the employer's ability, quality, Integrity, honesty, and relationships with demographic variables. This book collates, summarizes, and screens through literature, and combines previous field investigations and in-depth interviews with entrepreneurs to determine the introduction of employers' attention, employer leadership, employer honesty, fairness in leadership, employer's achievement motivation, and employer's trust in the model. The employer's personal variables are relevant to examine the effect of these factors. The relevant research hypotheses are given below.

Employer attention

Whether the employee is concerned with the boss in the organization and whether this concern will translate into specific job support and personal benefits has an important impact on the employee's work attitude and turnover intention. Farmer and Aguinis (2005) pointed out that when a supervisor controls the resource that subordinates need to establish and maintain their presently desired identities, the superior has actual influence over subordinates. When the supervisor's strength is weak, and his emphasis on subordinates is insufficient, and the intention to provide resources is weak, employees' turnover intentions will increase. When the superiors are strong and their degree of attention and intention to provide resources are weak, employees will have strong incentives to search for other job opportunities. At the same time, there will be more psychological evacuation behaviors such as absenteeism and increased turnover intentions. Eisenberger et al. (2002) used the concept of 'perception of superior support' (PSS) to portray the importance of superiors to their subordinates. The authors found that PSS affects employee turnover, and POS plays a full mediating role in that employees are to some extent treating superiors and organizations equally (Eisenberger and Stinglhamber, 2011). When the boss gives himself enough attention, the staff will see this emphasis as a sign of organizational support. Although the causal relationship between PSS and POS has not been conclusive in the literature (Rhoades et al., 2001), the relationship between PSS and turnover is clear.

Social exchange theory points out that relational contracts based on personal trust motivate employees to take actions in favor of the organization that are not specifically requested by the boss (Blau, 1964; Prooijen, 2015). Since trust comes from the social interaction between the two parties and the history of mutual promises (Susanna and Aryee, 2003), the supervisor's emphasis on his subordinates helps to inspire the trust of the other person, thus stabilizing both parties. The psychological contract guarantees the long-term maintenance of the relationship (Eisenberger et al., 2001). Robinson's (1996) analysis shows that maintaining the psychological contracts between employers and employers includes the manager's belief in the employer's commitment to the employer. These commitments include salary, promotion, sufficient power, and long-term employment. Protection, training, professional development, etc. are closely related to the interests of professional managers. Whether this contract can continue to be maintained depends mainly on managers' evaluation of employers. If the employer ignores the work and life of the employee, the latter's lower evaluation of the employer can easily lead to the collapse of the contract and ultimately lead to the turnover of the manager (Robinson, 1996). A large number of social exchange theory studies provide sufficient empirical support. It is generally believed that the lack of social transaction relations will lead to higher turnover intentions, poorer job performance, less conducive organizational civic behavior to organization（OCBO）, and less conducive organizational civic behavior to superior (OCBS) (Takeuchi et al., 2015).

Bosses can take many forms to pay attention to subordinates. Suzanne and Luthans (2006) found that non-financial incentives such as recognition and performance feedback are good for employee retention. Social recognition and recognition refer to informal recognition, attention, praise, and affirmation of the performance from individuals or organizations (Kirchler and Palan, 2017; Li et al., 2016). According to Nelson (2001), 90% of managers believe that informal job admiration helps to motivate employees better, and 84% of managers believe that giving non-financial recognition to employees when they perform better can help improve their performance. Non-financial incentives are often viewed by employees as an effort to increase positive ambience, so employees will give corresponding returns to organizations by positive citizenship behaviors (Zagenczyk et al., 2015) and job involvement (Harter et al., 2002). Suzanne and Luthans (2006) believe that equity theory can provide a possible explanation for this. Employees who are sufficiently non-financially motivated will not easily leave the job.

The main reason why the employer factor is more important to Chinese corporate managers is that "in a relationship-oriented society, employers are more important than non-personalized organizations in affecting employee behavior and attitude" (Chen et al., 2002, p353). In Chinese private enterprises, especially small and medium-sized private enterprises, rules from people, rather than rules from the law, regulate the internal behavior of most organizations. Bosses dominate everything in the organization, and company leaders are often seen as a sign and symbol of the organization. Organizational individuals believe that employers' appreciation can help them obtain more resources and promotion opportunities (Selmer, 2001). They will naturally associate the degree of attention of their employers with their own indicators of the fate in the company. So, we can make the following hypothesis:

H14: *Employers' attention will affect the turnover intention of professional managers, the more satisfied the professional manager's perception of the employer's attention is, the lower the turnover intention.*

Employer leadership and achievement motivation

Employer leadership reflects the extent to which employers can lead the entire team to achieve business success. Employer's achievement motivation reflects employers' intention to make efforts to achieve business success. Since corporate success is crucial to the personal success of employees, employer leadership and achievement motivation naturally have important implications for employees' work attitude and turnover intention. Chen et al. (2002) believe that the employer's ability, quality, honesty, etc. will affect the employee's loyalty to the employer.

Leadership refers to 'the ability of individuals to influence, mobilize, and motivate others to contribute to the efficiency and success of their organization' (House and Javidan, 2004, p15). The leadership theory from the literature has long sought features that are relevant to effective leadership. Agreeableness, emotional stability, extraversion, and conscientiousness have been summarized as the main qualities of several kinds of leaders (Mark and Canger, 2004). Studies have found that these personality traits of leaders are highly correlated with their successful leadership behavior (Judge et al., 2002). Obviously, these dimensions of employer leadership also affect employees' turnover intention (Harris and Brannick, 1999), so hypotheses are made as follows:

H15: *Employer leadership influences the turnover intention of professional managers, the more satisfied professional managers feel about employer leadership, the lower the turnover intention.*

H16: *Employers' achievement of a motivating opportunity affects the turnover intention of a professional manager, the more satisfied a professional manager's perception of the employer's achievement motivation, the lower the turnover intention.*

Employer honesty

Employer honesty is one of the most crucial factors affecting professional managers entering and exiting private enterprises (Zhang and Huang, 2003; Zhang and Wang, 2003; Ji, 2008). The lack of integrity of private entrepreneurs not only hinders the entry of outstanding professional managers, but also leads directly to the betrayal of managers (Zhang, 2002; Robinson, 1996). Many literatures indicate that work-related attitudes and behaviors such as trust and commitment, job satisfaction, organizational citizenship behavior, and job performance are significantly positively correlated (De Jong et al., 2016). There are also many studies that directly lead to a negative relationship between trust and turnover intention (Schnake and Dumler, 2000). The meta-analysis by Bijlsma and Koopman's (2003) also confirmed that the trust relationship between employees and organizations helps to increase the loyalty of the former, which in turn reduces their turnover intention. Based on this, Mohamad and Nasurdin (2006) also found that increasing employees' trust in organizations or organizational agents does help reduce their turnover intentions.

Robinson's (1996) analysis shows that maintaining the psychological contracts between employers and employers includes the manager's belief in the employer's commitment to the employer. These commitments include salary, promotion, sufficient power, and long-term employment. Guarantees, training, professional development, etc. are closely related to the interests of professional managers. Whether this contract can continue to be maintained depends largely on managers' evaluation of the integrity of employers. Employers' lack of integrity can easily result in such contracts. The rupture of the system eventually led to the turnover of managers (Robinson, 1996, pp585-587). Susanna and Aryee (2003) used a sample of Chinese employees (N=152) from Hong Kong to conduct an empirical study on the relationship between psychological contract rupture, turnover intention and psychological turnover behavior. The results confirm the significant correlation between them, which is consistent with the conclusions of Alcover et al. (2017) and Turnley and Feldman (2000).

Susanna and Aryee (2003) pointed out that the two primary factors leading to the collapse of psychological contract are reneging and incongruence. The former refers to the employer's intention not to comply with the employee's commitment, and the latter refers to different understanding of a promise for employee and employer. In general, the integrity of employers is insufficient.

From the perspective of information economics, the lack of honesty of employers is essentially a question of the moral hazard of the client. It is an opportunistic act taken by employers after various trade-offs in the context of asymmetric information. Therefore, the existence of incomplete information or uncertainty is an important reason why managers value the honesty of their employers. If employers lack credibility, the probability that managers expect them to take opportunistic behavior will be high, and this reduces the manager's expected return. Kollock (1994) pointed out that uncertainties such as the acquisition of organizational resources, the determination of work objectives, decision-making information control, etc. require managers to have enough confidence in employers. The lack of integrity of employers will lead to occupations. Managers do not have the motivation to take this type of uncertainty. Zhang and Huang (2003) further pointed out that fraud in financial information would directly affect the manager's money income (such as equity income), and requiring managers to increase their own psychological costs and affect their own reputation. Moreover, the lack of honesty of employers will affect the long-term development of the company. The fate is that professional managers of enterprises are naturally reluctant to bury their own future in the hands of such employers.

In addition, the integrity of employers and of professional managers can influence each other. On one hand, as the trust mechanism is maintained by relying on informal rules agreed upon among the members of the society by default, the untrustworthy behavior of the employer will undermine the benign operation of the rule, reduce the psychological costs of the professional managers who also lose faith. "Betrayal has become something that some managers feel comfortable with" (Zhang, 2002, p107), managers would leave the organization without any apology. Chen et al. (2002) also pointed out that in the context of China, employees' trust in employers and the integrity of their employers will affect whether employees remain loyal to their employers. Wong et al. (2002) also reached a similar conclusion. On the other hand, when a manager enters a private enterprise and discovers that the employer is not good enough, to protect his interests from the employer's possible dishonesty, the turnover may be his best strategy. For skilled professional managers who are ready to enter private enterprises, employers who do not have integrity do not get him 'effective' (Zhang, 2003). Schwepker (2001) pointed out that ethical principles such as fair trade, trust, responsibility, and commitment are very important for the development of relational market transactions. Therefore, the level of integrity of employers will affect the professional manager's work attitude and turnover intention. The empirical studies of Zhang and Huang (2003) provide some support for this.

Because of the asymmetric information, managers cannot know the true level of honesty of the employer. The basis for his decision can only be based on his observation and experience, and his subjectively perceived employer integrity. This book uses four dimensions to construct employer honesty variables based on Huang (2007) and Ji (2008), and puts forward the following hypothesis:

H17: *The integrity of employers affects the turnover intention of professional managers, the more satisfied professional managers are with employers, the lower the turnover intention.*

Leadership fairness

Leadership fairness is an important dimension of organizational justice. In order to reflect the employer-influenced factors highlighted in this book, we deliberately separate it out to construct a variable. This approach can help us understand whether the path of fairness for managers to generate turnover intentions is different from other organizational variables, so as to build a professional manager turnover process model that is more in line with the actual situation of small and medium-sized private enterprises in China.

The principle of fairness in leadership is mainly concerned with whether the leaders of the company treat the subordinates equally and whether they give sufficient respect to the rights of subordinates. It comes from employees' perceptions of their boss's or employer's individual behavior and character, which directly affects the subordinate's perception of the superior and thus affects the relationship between the two sides (Cropanzano et al., 2003; Schwepker, 2001; Konovsky and Pugh (1994), and in turn has an impact on the loyalty of the former (Chen et al., 2002; Wong et al., 2002).

Erdogan et al. (2006) empirical evidence from 516 sample teachers in Turkey shows that one dimension of organizational culture, respecting employees, strengths the relationship between interactional justice and LMX. Interaction fairness refers to the degree of fairness in interpersonal communication and exchange. It is strongly correlated with LMX (Cohen-Charash and Spector, 2001). Takeuchi et al. (2015) found that employees' perceptions of procedural fairness and interaction fairness were similar. In this book, we directly include the dimension of respecting employees into the operational definition of fair leadership to reflect its impact on turnover intentions, so the following hypothesis is made:

H18: *Leadership fairness affects the turnover intention of professional managers, the more satisfied professional managers are with respect to leadership, the lower the turnover intention.*

Employer trust

Employer trust refers to the extent to which employers are willing to believe that employees will consciously safeguard the interests of employers and organizations. Employers' high level of trust means employers are willing to give more job support (Eisenberger et al., 2002; Farmer and Aguinis, 2005), higher positions (Selmer, 2000, 2001) and more authorization (Schriesheim et al., 1998; Chen and Aryee, 2007). Empirical studies for Chinese organizations in Taiwan and Singapore found that when Chinese companies hire employees, the main consideration is private trust, especially for senior positions (Kao, 1990; Tong, 1990). 'Only those who have a good relationship or are loyal to the boss will be promoted to higher positions' (Chen and Francesco, 2000). Therefore, the degree of employer's trust in managers plays an important role in the turnover decision-making process of professional managers.

An empirical study carried out by Susanna and Aryee (2003) shows that the rupture of the psychological contract between employees and organizations can lead to the turnover of the employees. Psychological contract refers to a belief of employees that involves the responsibilities, terms and conditions of reciprocal transactions between employees and their organizations. If employers show mistrust of employees, then this contract is easily broken (Schwepker, 2001). Many other studies have also found the relationship between psychological contract rupture and job satisfaction, organizational commitment, and turnover intention (Alcover et al., 2017; Robinson, 1996; Gupta et al., 2016; Turnley and Feldman, 2000).

Employer trust influences employee work attitudes and turnover intentions can also be explained within the lead-member exchange (LMX) framework. According to the theory of LMX, the high-quality social exchange relationships established by leaders are based on trust and mutual love with the members of the organization (Erdogan et al., 2006). On the contrary, low-quality social exchange is an economic exchange relationship, and its establishment will not exceed the scope of employment contracts (Zhang et al., 2015). Based on reciprocity norms, a sense of obligation for rewarding benefits enhances interpersonal relationships (Eisenberger et al., 2001). The mutuality of the trust relationship leads to the employer's trust in the manager and in turn affects the manager's trust in the employer. Therefore, the following hypothesis is made:

H19: *Employer trust affects the turnover intention of professional managers, the more satisfied professional managers feel about employer trust, the lower the turnover intention.*

5. Other factors

Work embeddedness

Research shows that the introduction of relationship constructs helps to improve the explanatory power of the turnover model. For example, Cohen (1999) found that certain non-working variables affect the actual employee turnover decision (Kevin et al., 2004). Kinship responsibilities will reduce the ease of turnover, thereby prompt them to exercise caution when leaving a job (Waldman et al., 2015). Related to this, the attitude model of Ajzen and Fishbein (1977) shows that individual behavior is influenced by the expectations of other people about how they should act, and other people who maintain a special relationship with them play a key role. For important decisions such as turnover, the expectations from other people cannot be ignored.

Mitchell et al. (2001) used the concept of 'embeddedness' (Granovetter, 1985) from socioeconomics to construct the concept of job embeddedness. They believe that this construct includes three dimensions: 1. The extent to which employees maintain links with other people and activities; 2. The extent of employee work and communication with other aspects of 'life space'; 3. The ease with which links are broken. That is the sacrifice if they leave the present company. Mitchell et al.'s empirical results show that work embeddedness has the ability to interpret both turnover intention and turnover behavior. In addition to job satisfaction, organizational commitment, other job opportunities, and job search, work embeddedness significantly increases model's interpretation of the turnover variance.

Further, on this basis, Lee et al. (2004) divide the work embedding degree specifically into two dimensions to measure: ie, on-the-job and off-the-job embedding. Relevant empirical results show that off-the job embeddedness is significantly related to voluntary turnover and automatic absence, while on-the-job embeddedness has no corresponding explanatory power on this; the on-the-job embeddedness is significantly related to organizational citizenship behavior and work performance, and off-the job work embeddedness has no corresponding explanatory power on this. In addition, work embeddedness also moderates the effects of absenteeism, organizational citizenship behavior, and work performance on turnover. These two studies fully demonstrated the necessity of introducing work-embeddedness constructs in the turnover influencing factor model. Since then there have been many other studies focusing on the explanatory power of relational constructs for employee turnover (eg Maertz and Campion, 2004; Mossholder et al., 2005; Hom and Xiao, 2006, etc.).

For Chinese economic organizations, the work embeddedness also contains a very special dimension: the private relationship with the employer. Scholars generally believe that there are influences of relationship of each country and society, but the special thing about China is that the relationships are ubiquitous and play a key role in daily life. The basis of relations in Chinese society can be divided into a blood foundation and a social foundation, both contain an important dimension, that is, the degree of closeness of the relationship. It depends on emotion ('ganqing', affection). Tsang and Eric (1998) pointed out that the characteristics of the relationship are value, scarcity and imitation. Xin and Pearce (1996) used interview data from China to test the importance of relations in Chinese society. They believe that personal relations are particularly important in countries that lack a stable legal and regulatory environment, and China's present stage also reflects such features.

In private enterprises in China, the special personal relationship between employees and employers does play an important role in the employment relationship (Xin and Pearce, 1996; Farh et al., 1998; Tsang, 1998). A study conducted by Farh et al. (1998) on mainland China and Taiwan indicated that outcome variables such as trust, mutual love, consensus assessment, frequency of communication, and consensual actions are all directly affected by 'relationships.' Another study from different samples also found that the quality of LMX, the subordinate's commitment, and the superior's evaluation of subordinates' work performance are all significantly related to 'relationships' (Chen and Francesco, 2000). Research conducted on Chinese organizations in Taiwan and Singapore also found that when companies employ employees, private trust is a major consideration, especially for senior positions (Kao, 1990; Tong, 1990). Therefore, only those who have a good relationship or are loyal to the boss will be promoted to higher positions. In turn, it can be assumed that employees who occupy high positions will have a better relationship with their employers. A good relationship means that employees should be loyal to his boss and be loyal to the organization because the boss has been treated as a representative and sign of the company. Therefore, an employee with a higher position should be more loyal to the boss or have a higher degree of commitment to the boss's personal representative organization (Chen and Francesco, 2000).

In Chinese society, employment decisions are often based on the consideration that a newly hired employee is a friend or relative of someone who has a relationship with the boss. This is the main reason why relations play such a key role in employment relations in China. The distribution of employees' social-emotional rewards (such as managerial friendliness) likes to use different rules according to various levels of closeness. Therefore, his perception of how close he is to the boss will affect the perception of interactional fairness (Wong et al., 2002). This perception in turn affects their turnover intention. So we can make the following hypothesis:

H20: *The degree of work embeddedness affects the turnover intention of professional managers, the higher job embeddedness sensed by professional managers, the lower the turnover intention.*

Suitability

The suitability implies that a certain type of organization has a culture that is attractive to a certain type of individual (O'Reilly et al., 1991). DelCampo (2006) pointed out that examining the negative correlation between individual-organization suitability and employee withdrawal behavior will be the focus of the turnover literature.

In the early literature, Chatman (1989) and Kristof (1996) focused on the concept of personal-organization matching. Recently, Swider et al. (2015) and Jiang (2016) have also studied on this. To sum up, the relevant term given in these documents refer to the degree of compatibility, that is, the degree of coherence of individual characteristics, beliefs, and personal values with organizational culture, strategic needs, norms, and organizational values. Another concept is organizational identity (van Dick et al., 2004). At the individual level, organizational identities are derived from the social identity literature, referring to the 'oneness' of individuals and organizations, and their perception of organizational success and failure as their own successes and failures. (Mitchell et al., 2001, p1107). According to this theory, the match between individuals and organizations means the feelings of the overlapping parts of self and group, as well as the internalization of organizational core values and identity features. It is a self-defined concept (van Dick et al., 2004).

Of course, many existing studies have found that suitability is negatively related to turnover intention. Some researchers have provided evidence that compatibility is a key process that affects job selection (Zimmerman et al., 2016). That is, when individuals evaluate the surrounding work environment, they will consider whether they are compatible with their own. The unfolding model of Lee and Mitchell (1994) also confirms the role of the matching process in multiple employee turnover paths. Individuals who think they are not fit with the organization usually do not stay too long in the company. Vandenberghe (1999) also found that in the healthcare industry, the congruence of organizational and personal values affects the employee's turnover intention. Kammeyer-Mueller et al. (2005) found that the suitability between newly recruited employee and the environment will affect his/her turnover intention.

In addition, O'Reilly et al. (1991) studied the relationship between suitability and organizational commitment, satisfaction, and performance. A recent study by Sun et al. (2007) pointed out that the perspective of the relationship of employment relationships emphasizes the process of hiring. In this process, the organization develops a high-quality, open-ended relationship with its employees. This relationship has characteristics of mutuality and mutual benefit. Interdependence means that employers and employees hold the same expectations for their relevant goals (Dabos and Rousseau, 2004).

The main theories used to explain the negative correlation between suitability and turnover intention include resource-based view and social identity theory (Farmer and Aguinis, 2005). The main points of the theory of resource dependence is that maintaining the identity of employees helps them to obtain sufficient resources to achieve their career goals. Therefore, the suitability of professional goals and organizational resources will influence their intention to retain this identity (Farmer and Aguinis, 2005). Social identity theory is sometimes referred to as identity theory, self-verification theory, or role identity theory (Burke, 1991; Brown, 2015), these theories point out that self is mainly defined by various social roles played by individuals (Brown, 2015). The theory of self-identification believes that the needs of subordinates should be met to establish, confirm, and maintain their identity. For individuals, the importance of a given identity is determined by the social and personal costs of not maintaining this role or abandoning the role expectations (Bench et al., 2015; Brown, 2015). The cost of an individual's calculation of meaning in the process of quitting or abandoning a character's expectations is called self-verification (Xu et al., 2015).

Van Dick et al. (2004) applied social identity theoretical framework to study individual behavior. They found that individuals would think and act in the direction of the interests of their respective groups, because the identity of this group member increases his social identity, and this will partly determine his self-esteem. Within the organization, stronger organizational identities are associated with lower turnover intentions. Van Dick et al. pointed out that since identity is a more general perception of the common destiny of employees and organizations, the relationship between identification and separation will be indirect, with more specific job satisfaction in between playing an intermediary role. The four samples of this article all support this hypothesis. This book will also examine the role of intermediary variables such as job satisfaction and organizational commitment in empirical research. The following hypothesis is made:

H21: *Suitability can affect the turnover intention of professional managers, the higher suitability of professional manager's perception between themselves and their organizations or employers, the lower the turnover intention.*

Other job opportunities

Many studies have confirmed the important influences of the ease of turnover intention and the turnover behavior. March and Simon (1958) once interpreted the ease of turnover as a function of the number of other job opportunities perceived by employees, which in turn was a function of the level of business activity, the number of external organizations, and the personal characteristics of employees. Later, this construct was again defined 'the availability of other opportunities' (Chen et al., 2016), 'cognitive opportunities' (Waldman et al., 2015), general job availability (Trevor, 2001), movement capital (Trevor, 2001), and the ease of mobility (Sun and Wang, 2011) etc.

Other job opportunities are the most important dimensions of the ease of turnover variable, and this book attempts to introduce it into the model for empirical testing. This variable often appears in the literature in such forms as: turnover costs (Kammeyer-Mueller et al., 2005), job opportunities (Judge et al., 2010), job search costs, informal organizations and unemployment rate (Maertz and Campion, 2004) and so on.

One of the most inspiring constructs is the Growth Opportunity Index (EOI) developed by Griffeth et al. (2005). After constructing the factor analysis, the EOI metric including five dimensions is finally obtained through factor analysis. They are, the ease of movement, the desirability of movement, the networking, the crystallization of alternatives and the mobility. A series of exploratory factor analysis and confirmatory factor analysis results show that the five-dimensional construct has satisfactory psychometric properties and construct validity and standard-related validity. The other job opportunity variables that we introduce in the model are designed with reference to this construct. Their reliability and validity in the context of China will be tested here through our samples.

Previous studies have shown that the perception of other job opportunities has a significant impact on employee turnover intentions (Griffeth et al., 2005). This effect may be direct or indirectly through job satisfaction (Price, 2001). A meta-analysis reported a correlation coefficient of 0.11 for these two variables (Griffeth et al., 2000). Lance (1991) pointed out that from the theoretical perspective of the transaction relationship, perceptions about the attractiveness of other job opportunities have a direct impact on organizational commitment (Rusbult and Farrell, 1983). The dynamic model proposed by Kammeyer-Mueller et al. (2005) strongly suggests that the turnover is significantly affected by the perceived cost of employee turnover. This research system confirms the key role of other job opportunity variables in the turnover model.

Other constructs related to other job opportunities have also been found to have complex effects on turnover intentions, such as unemployment rates (Sun et al., 2007). Earlier we mentioned the discussion in the literature about the relationship between job performance and turnover. One of the arguments is that high performance leads to high turnover (Salamin and Hom, 2005). There is an important hypothesis in this view that potential employers can observe that the employee is indeed with high-performance (Allen and Griffeth, 2001). Therefore, its transmission mechanism is that high performance leads to employees' perception of other job opportunities, while the latter increases the turnover intention. Jackofsky (1984) pointed out that performance directly affects the employee's own perception of other job opportunities. High-performing employees have a higher level of perception, which makes them more likely to leave. Lance (1988) believes that Jackofsky's (1984) opinion suggests that there is a positive correlation between job performance and voluntary turnover. However, if high performance increases employee satisfaction with other job opportunities while improving satisfaction, then the overall effect of performance on turnover is uncertain. Therefore, it is doubtful if high performance leads to the conclusion of a high turnover if the direct or modulating effects of other job opportunity variables are considered in the model.

It is obvious that the mechanism of other job opportunities affecting the turnover intention. According to Mobley's (1977) model of agency contact, employees had job search and job evaluation activities before they officially left the company. Through this process, employees will comprehensively evaluate the difficulty of searching for other job opportunities, the future value of other job opportunities and their advantages compared with the current work, and then make the final decision. Studies related to psychology and organizational behavior have shown that if there is not that much temptation, employees will not leave their job easily. However, if there are many other job opportunities, employees will not have incentives to overestimate the current job, and this will directly lead to turnover intentions (Kevin et al., 2004). So, we can make the following hypothesis:

H22: *The perception of other job opportunities affects the turnover intention of professional managers, the more job opportunities the professional manager perceives, the higher the turnover intention.*

Mediating and Moderating Variables

1. Mediating variables

In the classical model given by March and Simon (1958), the relevant antecedent dependent variable had a direct impact on the turnover. Based on this, Mobley (1977) proposes an intermediary contact model that considers more intermediate stages. The model deeply studies the specific process and mechanism of the relationship between job satisfaction and employee voluntary turnover. This process includes: status assessment, satisfaction perception, consider exit, evaluating the expected utility and cost of search behavior, search intention, search acts, other job evaluations, comparisons with the status quo, turnover intentions, actual turnover. Afterwards, many studies attempted to empirically find support for the intermediary role of these intermediate variables.

Griffeth et al. (2000) made meta-analysis and found that the direct antecedent variables of turnover, such as job satisfaction, organizational commitment, job search, other job opportunities, withdraw perception, and turnover intention, have a good explanation for the turnover behavior. These variables, in turn, are influenced by other variables like environmental variables, personal variables, and structural variables (Price, 2001). Price (2001) identified four media variables that cannot be ignored: job satisfaction, organizational commitment, job search behavior, and intention to stay. Hulin (1991) highlights employees' feelings of general withdrawal behaviors (departures, absenteeism, job conversions, etc.) and their influence on a series of withdrawal behaviors (Dickter et al., 1996). Wendy et al., (2005) applied a sample from managers to examine the recurrence relationship between job satisfaction and turnover by studying the interaction between job conversion and job satisfaction, and the dynamic mechanisms and processes of the interaction. Wendy et al. pointed out that low job satisfaction can lead to job conversions, which in turn can temporarily increase job satisfaction (honeymoon effect), and afterwards, job satisfaction is reduced again (hysteresis). Therefore, from the perspective of an employee's entire career, there is an interplay of endogenous relationships between turnover and job satisfaction.

Lance (1991) gives a comprehensive model including the overall job satisfaction, organizational commitments, and other direct antecedent variables of turnover. This article assumes a feedback relationship between job satisfaction and organizational commitment. Empirical results show that job satisfaction and organizational commitment, as direct antecedent variables, are affected by multiple sets of perceptions of the working environment. Work-scope awareness and fairness of reward systems have a direct effect on job satisfaction, while job involvement, organizational dependencies, and perceived other job opportunities have an indirect effect on job satisfaction through organizational commitment. In addition, there are three variables that have a direct impact on job satisfaction and organizational commitment, namely: leadership behavior, relationship with colleagues, and role pressure. Lance's research has brought a lot of enlightenment to scholars.

Job Satisfaction

Since the 1930s, there have been many documents devoted to this core intermediary variable in the turnover model. Hoppock (1935), based on surveys and interviews with workers in a community, found that certain elements of the work environment (such as bosses), family expectations, and 'emotional maladjustment' all affect job satisfaction (Brief and Weiss, 2002). Brief and Weiss (2002) concluded that, at least conceptually, endogenous variables in workplaces that affect employee emotions and emotions can be divided into such categories: stress events (or counter-stimulation), superiors (George, 2000), work team characteristics, physical settings (such as work complexity, work environment, etc.), organizational returns and penalties (Weiss et al., 1999). The effect of these variables on job satisfaction can be mediated by organizational and social support (Rhoades et al., 2001).

Job satisfaction is the most studied variable in the factors affecting turnover (Hom and Kinicki, 2001; van Dick et al., 2004). Since March and Simon (1958) identified the two main causes of employee voluntary turnover, the desirability of leaving and the ease of turnover, the conceptualization of job satisfaction has been the focus of the turnover study. According to a search of the PsycINFO database, the database includes as many as 7855 studies on topics related to job satisfaction from 1976 to 2000 (Harter et al., 2002). Although the search does not specifically address the study on turnover, however, the sheer number of people is enough to show that the academic community attaches importance to the job satisfaction variable.

The early construct of work satisfaction mainly examined its affective status. In 1976, Locke (1976, p.130) gave a definition of job satisfaction, which was later quite influential, namely: "a pleasant or positive emotional state brought about by the employee's evaluation of his/her work or work experience". At this time, job satisfaction is seen as an emotional response of employees to the work itself. About 10 years later, Organ and Near (1985) realized that job satisfaction has both emotional dimensions and cognitive dimensions. Based on this, Motowidlo (1996) defines self-reported job satisfaction as "judgment about workability's favorability" (p176). Weiss (2002) is consistent with this and understands it more succinctly as a mental attitude. He defines job satisfaction as "a positive (or negative) evaluative judgment that employees use for their work or work situation" (p6). Brief (1998) adopts a job satisfaction construct that is closest to a psychological attitude, namely: "Employees' emotional and/or cognitive evaluation of work experience with a certain degree of desirability, and the internal conditions expressed through this evaluation are called job satisfaction" (p.86).

The factors found in the literature that have a significant impact on employee job satisfaction are numerous. Brief and Weiss (2002) believe that, at least conceptually, endogenous variables in workplaces that affect employee emotions can be divided into several categories that are not necessarily independent of each other: stress events (or counter-stimulation), work team characteristics, work settings (such as work complexity, work environment, etc.), organizational returns and penalties. Other studies have pointed out that subordinates' emotions are also influenced by leaders (George, 2000). Weiss et al. (1999) found that the results of organizational rewards also affect employee well-being, while procedural fairness is only playing a minor role, but it still has an impact on satisfaction. Lance (1991) pointed out that job satisfaction is affected by multiple sets of perceptions of the working environment. He found that five variables, such as work scope awareness, fairness of reward system, leadership behavior, relationship with colleagues, and role pressure, have a direct effect on job satisfaction. Gaertner (1999) applied the meta-analysis structural equation model method to test the antecedent structural variables of job satisfaction and organizational commitment in the turnover model. It was found that most of the structural variables are directly related to job satisfaction. The notable exception is that the effect of the salary is not that much significant.

As a large number of studies have shown that employees' attitudes toward work and organization directly affect their turnover intentions (Steel, 2002; Kammeyer-Mueller et al., 2005), thus job satisfaction plays a major role in all turnover theories. In most turnover studies, it is treated as a key psychological predictor variable (Dickter et al., 1996). A five-dimensional average correlation coefficient of job satisfaction constructs and turnover intentions was found to reach 0.31 (Kinicki et al., 2002). Several meta-analyses report the correlation between job satisfaction and turnover, respectively: -0.24 (Tett and Meyer, 1993), -0.28 (Steel and Ovalle, 1984), and -0.19 (Griffeth et al., 2000; Hom and Griffeth, 1995).

Harter et al. (2002) based on a sample of 36 companies with 7,939 business units, applied meta-analysis methods to examine employee satisfaction at the business unit level -- the relationship between engagement and outcome variables, productivity, and so on. It was found that employee satisfaction and engagement are related to turnover at the business unit level. These correlations are common to all companies and are therefore of great significance to most organizations. Du et al. (2006) applied a sample from Hubei, China to study a turnover model for professional managers in the Chinese construction industry. The results show that seven job satisfaction (JS) and organizational commitment (OC) variables affect the turnover intention of construction industry managers.

Further, many theoretical models and empirical studies have pointed out that job satisfaction acts as an intermediary (or part of an intermediary) on the relationship between related work and organizational characteristics (such as compensation, nature of work, promotion opportunities, work group relations) and turnover (Wendy et al., 2005). Trevor (2001) believes that the impact of job satisfaction on voluntary turnover will be mediated by training in education, cognitive ability, and occupation-specific training. At the same time, there are two interaction effects of job satisfaction and other variables in the departure model, namely: the interaction effect of job satisfaction and general job availability on turnover; the interaction effect of job satisfaction and working capital. The article points out that the role of general work availability in regulating the relationship between job satisfaction and turnover has been discussed in several conceptual models (Pindek et al., 2017). The main point is that when there are not many other job opportunities, the relationship between satisfaction and turnover will be weakened because employees will hesitate about uncertain prospects before making actual turnover decisions. When the employees' personal ability is strong enough and the working capital is relatively abundant, when there are many job opportunities to choose from, the relationship between job satisfaction and turnover is closer. This is easy to understand. If an individual has no confidence in the ability signals he sends to the labor market, he will not easily leave because of dissatisfaction with his job. Jackofsky (1984) pointed out that high-performing employees are more likely to find other job opportunities, so their level of satisfaction is stronger than those of low-performing employees. That is, the relationship between job satisfaction of high-performing employees and turnover tis even closer.

Based on the above-mentioned literature, this book examines the predictive effect of job satisfaction on turnover intentions and its intermediary role in the relationship between relevant prior-independent variables and turnover intentions. Therefore, we propose the following hypothesis:

H23: *Job satisfaction affects the turnover intention of professional managers, the higher job satisfaction perceived by professional managers, the lower the turnover intention. In addition,* *job satisfaction plays an intermediary role between the related former variable and turnover intention.*

Organization commitment

Research shows that employees' organizational commitment (OC) is negatively related to their turnover intention (Schwepker, 2001). In the turnover literature, organizational commitment and job satisfaction together form the most important attitude variable that influences turnover intention, and its predictive power for turnover is gradually accepted by scholars.

Early scholars used a relatively broad commitment variable in the human resources management literature, which was mainly used to explain the influence of commitment on relevant outcome variables. The work of Morrow (1983, 1993) identified five several types of commitments: commitment to the job itself, career, job role, organization, and alliance (Lee et al., 2000). Because the meaning of commitment outside of organizational commitments can be captured by other constructs, organizational research has gradually focused on employee commitment to the organization's specific object: organizational commitment. A well-accepted organizational commitment classification is based on the difference between individual attitudes and behaviors, i.e., organizational commitments are divided into attitudinal commitments and behavioral commitments (Zimmerman et al., 2016; Reichers, 1985).

In a broader sense, organizational commitment refers to personal loyalty and connection with his organization (Bozeman and Perrewe, 2001). OC is defined and conceptualized by researchers from various aspects and perspectives. They define it as "personal identification" and "involvement" of a specific organization (Bozeman and Perrewe, 2001, p604). This concept consists of three dimensions: the strong belief in the goals and values of the organization and the intention to accept it, willing to work for the benefit of the organization, and retain the membership of the organization (Zimmerman et al., 2016). Since then, a variety of OC metrics have appeared in the literature, single-item, multi-item, etc.

The most cited literature in organizational commitment research is the highly creative work of Meyer and Allen (1991). Meyer and Allen go beyond the classification of attitude commitments and behavioral commitments of existing research, and considers organizational commitments as a mental state that includes at least three separate components: desire (emotional commitment), need (continuous commitment), and obligation (normative promise). They believe that the three preceding sections are determined by different antecedent variables, which have different meanings for work-related behaviors. Meyer and Allen pointed out that the attachments previously mentioned in the literature regard commitment as a personal trend toward an organization. This construct corresponds to the book's emotional commitment dimension, that is, it wants to do so. The perceived cost mentioned in the existing research comes from the perception that individuals have a cost to leave the organization, which corresponds to the book's continuous commitment, that is: need to do so. A few scholars regard commitment as an obligation that should remain in the organization, which corresponds to the normative commitment of the book, that is: ought to do so.

Based on the newly constructed three-dimensional organizational commitment constructs, Meyer and Allen (1991) examined the influencing factors of each dimension of organizational commitment. First, Meyer and Allen pointed out that the affecting factors of (emotional) commitments could be grouped into four categories: personal characteristics, structural characteristics, work-related characteristics, and work experience. Second, continuous commitments reflect employee perceptions of the cost of turnover. Anything that may increase this perceived cost can be viewed as an antecedent variable. The most commonly mentioned are side bets or investments and the availability of alternatives. Therefore, variables such as age and length of service that may reflect bets and human capital investment are related to continuous commitments. Finally, Meyer and Allen believe that the theoretical development of most normative commitments so far is theoretical rather than empirical. Wiener (1982) pointed out that the sense of obligation retained in an organization comes from the internalization of normative pressure exerted on the individual. It is either produced before the individual enters the organization (family or cultural socialization) or is accompanied by organizational socialization, so the influencing factors of the normative commitment are with more social nature.

An empirical study by Rhoades et al. (2001) found that organizational support (POS) affects affective commitment (AC), and that the negative relationship between POS and employee voluntary turnover is played by AC in the medium. These results show that good working conditions can help improve feelings of commitment through organizational support perceptions, thereby reducing employee withdraw behavior. Lance (1991) pointed out that from the theoretical perspective of transaction relations, the perception of the attractiveness of other job opportunities also has a direct impact on organizational commitment (Rusbult and Farrell, 1983). Work involvement, organizational dependencies, and perceived other job opportunities have an indirect effect on job satisfaction through organizational commitment. Payne and Ann (2005) through a survey of more than 1,000 officers over a two-year period found that mentoring could greatly improve the commitment of new officers (composed of an affective commitment and continuance commitment). Relevant, this relationship is influenced by supervisory versus nonsupervisory and is not related to the type of career-related versus psychosocial.

Although scholars pay attention to organizational commitment structure because of its strong explanatory power to many organizational effectiveness variables, in fact, the most involved in organizational commitment research is employee voluntary turnover. A meta-analysis of 178 independent samples reported by Tett and Meyer (1993) also reached a similar conclusion (Schwepker, 2001), which found that the correlation coefficient between organizational commitment and turnover reached -0.33 (Kammeyer-Mueller et al.,

2005). Snape and Redman (2003) found that there is a negative relationship between normative commitment and turnover intention. A large number of other studies have confirmed the negative relationship between commitment and turnover (Sheridan and Abelson, 1983; Mercurio, 2015; Simons and Roberson, 2003).

In order to study the different influences of the three dimensions of organizational commitment, Somers (1995) examines the effects of these three dimensions on work withdrawal intentions, turnover, and absenteeism. It was found that emotional commitment was the most consistent predictor of these outcome variables, and was the only variable that was both related to and related to absence. In contrast, normative commitments are only related to withdrawal intentions, while the direct effects of successive commitments have not been observed. However, the interaction between consecutive commitments and emotional commitments can predict work withdrawal intentions and absenteeism. The interaction takes the form of a higher sunk cost that eases the relationship between emotional commitment and related outcome variables. The study pointed out that the continuous commitment and normative commitment dimension have only a small ability to explain the variance of the turnover and absence behavior. The employee's emotional connection to the organization (ie, emotional commitment) is often considered to be an important determinant of employee contributions and loyalty to the company (Rhoades et al., 2001). Employees with a high degree of emotional commitment are having a sense of belonging and identity with the company. This will increase their involvement in organizational activities and their intention to pursue organizational goals, and their desire to stay in the organization will become stronger. (Meyer and Allen, 1991; Zimmerman et al., 2016).

Yao and Wang (2006) used 242 samples from China to examine the impact of regulatory commitments on employee turnover. The authors point out that traditional research based on the three-dimensional organizational commitment of Meyer and Allen (1991) believes that emotional commitment has the best ability to explain employee attitudes, turnover intentions and behaviors (Wong et al., 2002). However, as intercultural studies become more common, the role of normative commitment has also received more attention (Wasti, 2003). Wasti (2003) pointed out that in a collectivistically oriented Turkish society, normative commitments are very important in predicting turnover intentions. In China, a society with a strong tendency towards collectivism, many empirical studies also support the importance of normative commitments (Chen and Francesco, 2003). According to the empirical study of Yao and Wang (2006), emotional commitment is an important predictor f organizational satisfaction, but normative commitment has the greatest impact on employee turnover behavior. Idiocentrism and allocentrism have a moderating effect on this relationship. Therefore, different dimensions of organizational commitment have different effects. This finding implies the importance of normative commitment in predicting organizational behavior, especially in the context of the prevailing collectivist concept.

Based on the above analysis, we can see that organizational commitment may play an intermediary role in the relationship between the relevant previous variable and turnover intention. Cropanzano et al. (2003) gave some empirical support for this in the same model. The authors found that the relationship between emotional exhaustion and effective work behavior (eg, the intention to stay) is mediated by organizational commitment. Rusbult and Farrell (1983) also found that organizational commitment mediates the relationship between job involvement and turnover (Mitchell et al., 2001). Our research will also introduce organizational commitment variables in the structural equation model with the role of mediating variables.

As mentioned above, organizational commitment and job satisfaction are the most important attitude variables affecting employee turnover. Therefore, many studies in the literature attempt to examine the causal relationship between these two variables. Regardless of the direction, as long as there is a progressive relationship between the two, or the related prevariable variables have similar influence effects on these two attitude variables, one of the variables can be abandoned in the study, and focusing on another variable with most explanatory power. But so far, the researchers' attempts have not been successful, and the relevant literature gives quite confusing results.

The main assumptions and opinions in the literature are that satisfaction affects organizational commitment, and it is supported by many theoretical and empirical studies. According to Currivan (1999), at least two studies have found that organizational commitment precedes satisfaction (e.g., Vandenberg and Lance, 1992). These studies indicate that employees will adjust their level of satisfaction to match the current level of commitment. Of course, there are studies that believe that the two are feedback relationships or have no significant relationship. Scholars who hold the latter view point out that the correlation between the two may come from the "pseudo-relationship" caused by common determinants. In response to this confusion, Currivan (1999) examines the four possible relationships between job satisfaction and organizational commitment. The analysis of the structural equations given by the authors found that the four models have basically the same fitting indicators. This means that the correlation between satisfaction and organizational commitment may indeed come from the problem of common antecedent variables, and there is no real causal relationship between them.

However, there are many different conclusions about this common antecedent variable problem in the literature. Some studies have found that all structural variables are related to satisfaction and organizational commitment (George, 2015); others find that all structured variables are only related to job satisfaction (Price and Mueller, 1986). Another view is that different structural variables have different effects on job satisfaction and organizational commitment (Hom and Griffeth, 1995). Some studies report that job satisfaction is a direct predictor for withdrawing perception (Hom et al., 2017; Hom and Griffeth, 1991; Tett and Meyer, 1993). Other studies point out that the relationship between job satisfaction and withdraw perception is mediated by organizational commitment (Zimmerman et al., 2016). DeConinck and Stilwell (2004) gave an example of organizational commitment, turnover intention and actual turnover behavior.

Gaertner (1999) applied the meta-analysis structural equation model method to test the antecedent structural variables of job satisfaction and organizational commitment in the turnover model. As a result, it was found that only three structured variables (distributive equity, development opportunities, and superior support) had a direct impact on organizational commitment beyond job satisfaction. However, these direct relationships are less effective because they are not detectable in small samples. On the other hand, Gaertner also found that most structural variables are directly related to job satisfaction.

Based on the above analysis, we propose the following hypothesis:

H24: *The degree of organizational commitment will affect the turnover intention of professional managers, the higher the professional manager's organizational commitment, the lower the turnover intention. In addition, the organization commitment mediates the relationship between the relevant dependent variable and the turnover intention.*

Work initiative and work status

Managers have noticed that employees' performance is predictive of their future turnover (Mobley, 1982). First, employees with better job performance may be more likely to leave because they are more likely to get other job opportunities in the labor market. Of course, this requires their working ability to be known to other employers (Schwab, 1991; Salamin and Hom, 2005). Second, contrary to the foregoing, the more employees with better job performance feel that they have found a suitable position in the company, the lower the turnover intention may be (Lance, 1988; Hom and Griffeth, 1995). Again, some studies have pointed out the nonlinear relationship between them (Jackofsky et al., 1986). Finally, the idea of employee turnover may in turn affect their work performance, especially outside work performance such as organizational citizenship behavior, organizational altruism, and so on. Empirical studies have given partial support to these conclusions, but so far have not come up with a unified conclusion (Allen and Griffeth, 2001). In view of this, the book will focus on the aforementioned fourth viewpoint, turning the performance within the job into a working state variable, turning the out-of-job performance operation into a work initiative variable, and trying to test the relationship between them and the turnover intention.

Many meta-analysis results show a negative correlation between job performance and turnover (Hom and Griffeth, 1995; Williams and Livingstone, 1994), which means employees of poor performance are more likely to leave the company. Despite these consistent findings, some scholars believe that these conclusions are too simplistic (Trevor et al., 1997). Applying a more sophisticated approach, Trevor et al. (1997) provide strong evidence that there is a curve connection between performance and turnover. Allen and Griffeth (2001) also pointed out that the nonlinear relationship is more common than previously people believed.

It is generally believed that the performance of employees can be divided into two types: on-the-job performance and out-the-job performance. The former is often referred to as in-role performance or job performance (Lee et al., 2004). The latter is often referred to as extra-role performance (Eisenberger et al., 2001), organizational citizenship (Lee et al., 2004), contextual performance (Harrison et al., 2006), organizational spontaneity (Eisenberger et al., 2001), and help behavior (Sparrowe et al., 2006). On-the-job performance is easy to understand and will not be discussed below. The following analysis revolves around out-the-job performance.

In the organization, we will observe that some employees will go beyond simple role requirements and actively carry out innovation and spontaneous activities. This kind of activity has not been stipulated by the formal rules of the organization, and it is not the employee's responsibilities. Therefore, the motive of his behavior mainly comes from the employee's loyalty to the organization. Smith et al. (1983)

called this activity Organizational Citizenship Behavior (OCB). Formally, organizational citizenship behavior is an employee behavior that is not required by the role. It is voluntarily taken by employees. The actor is usually unable to obtain the return from the organization's formal remuneration system. Although there is no formal incentive, such behavior is necessary for organizational efficiency (Konovsky and Pugh, 1994). According to the definition of George and Brief (1992), extra-role activities include helping colleagues, taking actions to protect the organization from risks, providing constructive advice, gaining knowledge and skills that benefit the organization, etc. (Eisenberger et al., 2001). Bettencourt et al. (2001) developed a three-dimensional service-oriented organizational citizenship behavior framework: loyalty, participation, and service (Sun et al., 2007). Sparrowe et al. (2006) pointed out that helping behavior is a kind of self-conscious behavior taken by group members for the benefit of other group members or the whole group. It is closely related to the altruism dimension of OCB. Taken together, out-the-job performance typically includes helping working partners, boosting morale, recognizing, supporting, and defending organizational goals (Harrison et al., 2006). The book turns this construct into a work-initiative variable. Correspondingly, we used the work status constructs to indirectly measure the performance of the managers' work.

Since the work initiative comes from employee loyalty and identification with the organization, the lack of job initiative can be considered as one of the manifestations of low loyalty and recognition of the organization, and its ability to predict employee turnover intentions cannot be ignored. The reduction of employees' organizational citizenship behavior means that employees will reduce their work efforts and their work participation (Chen et al., 1998). If the performance of non-workers including morale establishment, relationship promotion, etc. (Aryee et al., 2017) is the employee's advance payment of the employer's ultimate good return, then the decrease in performance in this aspect is a signal of turnover. Similarly, in the job embeddedness model of Mitchell et al. (2001), one of the main factors that prevent employees from leaving their jobs is the interpersonal relationship developed through non-work and mutual help behaviors. Mossholder et al. (2005) also provide evidence that employees who have fewer interpersonal connections in the company are more likely to leave. Most of the favorable interpersonal relationships are due to spontaneous citizenship behavior. If employees reduce the investment in such behavior, their turnover intention becomes obvious.

Based on these analyses, we make the following hypotheses:

H25: *The work initiative has the ability to predict the turnover intention of professional managers, the higher the initiative of professional managers, the lower the turnover intention. In addition, the work initiative plays an intermediary role between the related previous variable and the turnover intention.*

H26: *The job status has the ability to predict the turnover intention of professional managers, the better the job status of professional managers, the lower the turnover intention. In addition, the working state plays an intermediary role between the related pre-variable variables and the turnover intention.*

Job search intention

The mediation model indicates that job search plays a very important role in the employee's departure decision process (Mobley, 1977). An employee who has no other real job opportunities will not easily decide to leave the organization. Before it officially declares that it has left the organization, it usually conducts certain job search activities to minimize the risks that it may face during its work transition.

Some studies have found that when other job opportunities are limited, the relationship between job satisfaction and turnover will be weakened (Pindek et al., 2016). Before making the final turnover decision, the employee will hesitate about uncertain prospects. In addition, many studies have pointed out that when employees have strong personal abilities and fluid capital, and there are many job opportunities to choose from, the relationship between job satisfaction and turnover is closer, and on the contrary, it is relatively weak (Trevor, 2001). This is easy to understand. If an individual has no confidence in the ability signals he sends to the labor market, he will not easily leave because of unsatisfactory work. Therefore, when the employee's job satisfaction, work initiative, organizational commitment, and employer commitment are reduced, he/she will do job search as much as possible before making actual turnover decisions (Liu et al., 2015; Cropanzano et al., 2003). Once there are better other job opportunities, the turnover intention becomes higher.

However, strangely enough, few studies in the existing literature have found a meaningful relationship between job search behavior and turnover. Kammeyer-Mueller et al. (2005) pointed out that this might be because most studies use static data for testing. We believe that, no matter what, the intention to find work will certainly play a key role in the employee's decision-making process. Now we make the following hypothesis:

H27: *The job search intention has the ability to predict the turnover intention of professional managers, the higher the professional manager's job search intention, the higher the turnover intention. In addition, job search intention plays an intermediary role in the relationship between the relevant attitude variables (such as job satisfaction, employer leadership, etc.) and turnover intention.*

2. Moderating variables

This book examines six moderator effects. The moderating of the first three types of job involvement, commitments, and entrepreneurial motives has been hypothesized in the previous related sections. The following three moderations are discussed below.

Concept consciousness

Many scholars who have studied the issue of human resource management in the context of China have noticed that the conclusions drawn from Western organizational theory may not be entirely suitable for China. Correspondingly, the HR management measures that pass through the western world are often unsatisfactory (e.g., Tsui, 2004; Hom and Xiao, 2006; Farh et al., 2007, etc.). This book examines the manager turnover of private enterprises in China. It also cannot ignore the influence differences in the concept of consciousness caused by cultural differences between the East and the West.

In the literature, the differences in the sense of concept between East and West employees are often attributed to differences in two values, ie, self-centered tendencies and group-centered tendencies, which in turn are closely related to broader social norms of individualism and collectivism (Schaubroeck et al., 2000). Hofstede (1991) and other researchers point out that individualism and collectivism are the key features of diverse cultural orientations. At the same time, self-centered and group-centered concepts reflect the characteristics of cultural values at the individual level (Wagner, 1995). Wagner's (1995) empirical study of samples from 492 undergraduate students found that group size, individual identifiability, shared responsibility, and individualism/collectivism can affect the horizontal cooperation of class groups. The level of individualism or collectivism plays a moderating role in the relationship between group size, identifiability, and cooperation.

Individualism-collectivism is an analytical dimension that gives relative weights on which individuals pursue personal and common interests (Wagner, 1995). Individualists are more concerned with their own interests and tend to ignore collective interests, especially if they are in conflict. On the contrary, the collectivists pay more attention to the interests of the groups to which they belong, and even require the rejection of personal interests (Wang et al., 2013). Individualism values individuals' rights and freedoms, while collectivism values the good relationships between groups and group members (Thomas et al., 2016). Chinese traditional Confucian culture has a strong collectivism. This traditional culture pays special attention to harmony, reciprocity and loyalty (Earley, 1989; Liang, 2005). This has become the main principle that guides people in dealing with interpersonal relationships and is accepted by all strata of society (Selmer, 2000; Wong et al., 2002).

Markus and Kitayama (1991) also observed that Westerners have an independent view of self-reporting, emphasizing independence, idiosyncrasies, and the intrinsic characteristics of individuals, while Asians hold an interdependent view of self, emphasizing connections, social factors, and relationships etc. (Huang, 2005). In a comparative study of university students in China and the United States, Brockner and Chen (1996) also came to the same general conclusion. Brockner and Chen's work is unique in the cross-cultural study of organizational behavior. It provides a complete theoretical framework for analyzing the differences between the two cultures. Earley (1989) compared the influence of cultural values on social loafing between American and Chinese managers. It was found that American managers performed better when working independently, while Chinese managers worked better in teams. These studies show that in an individualistic society, self refers to the individual. In a collectivistic society, the self is generalized to include a network of individuals (Markus and Kitayama, 1991; Fei, 2005).

The above-mentioned difference in concept consciousness has been found to influence the relevant outcome variables. Of course, most of the influences are exerted on the specific relationship in the model through the regulation effect. Schaubroeck et al. (2000) examines the moderating effects of cultural factors and different efficiency perceptions when studying job control treat job demands. The results show that in the United States, for those employees who reported higher levels of self-efficacy, higher levels of perceived control can ease the impact of job demand on mental health and turnover intentions; but for those American employees reporting lower levels of self-efficacy, the level of control will increase the effect of job demand. However, for a matching Hong Kong sample, the collective efficacy interacts with the level of control in the same way to influence the impact of work requirements. This difference was attributed to the difference in the concept of consciousness between the East and the West.

In recent years, some studies have often referred to traditional concepts as examining traditional concepts (Farh et al., 1997, 2007; Chen and Aryee, 2007, etc.). The main reason for this is that, as China becomes more and more open, more and more employees are influenced by modern education and modern cultural trends, and young people who hold the concept of typical Eastern culture are becoming less and less frequent in the eyes of modern people. The individuals who hold the consciousness of Confucian culture, collectivism, and group orientation are more 'traditional'. Therefore, it is reasonable to describe the difference of concept consciousness with the degree of maintaining traditional concepts.

In the 1980s, the concept of Chinese individual traditionality was proposed, and defined as: "The typical model of most Chinese people in traditional Chinese society is related to the characteristics of motivation, value, attitude, and temperament. This model can still be observed in contemporary Chinese communities like Taiwan, Hong Kong, and Chinese mainland" (Farh et al., 2007, p717). Schwartz (1992) defines the traditional concept as the respect and acceptance of the customs and norms of traditional society. In Chinese society, the decisive characteristics of traditional culture include: respect for authority, filial piety, ancestor worship, fatalism, and universal awareness of powerlessness. Since respect for authority is a key dimension of traditional concepts (Farh et al., 1997). Researchers believe that employees with higher traditional beliefs should have characteristics like those who hold higher recognition of power distance (Ma et al., 2016).

High-traditional employees are more willing to obey the guidelines of leaders, less inclined to play the role of leaders, and therefore, even when they are empowered, they may even feel uneasy. The reluctance of a high-class employee to accept job responsibilities arises from their sense of powerlessness or low sense of agency. Therefore, empowerment will not improve the self-concept of high-traditional employees. Kirkman and Shapiro (1997) pointed out that employees with high power distance do not like the work with strong autonomy and heavy responsibility. The latter is precisely the main feature of high self-management (Chen and Aryee, 2007).

Farh et al. (1997) found that for employees with less traditional ideas and higher modern values, organizational justice (distributive fairness and procedural fairness) is most strongly related to their organizational citizenship behavior (OCB), that is, employees with traditional concept will moderate the relationship between organizational fairness and OCB. Yao and Wang (2006) used 242 samples from China to study the impact of normative commitments on employee turnover behavior. The results show that emotional commitment is an important predictor of organizational satisfaction, but normative commitment has the greatest impact on employee turnover. Traditional ideology (ie, individualistic tendencies/collectivist tendencies) has a moderating effect on this relationship. The different dimensions of organizational commitment have different effects on resignation under the perception of different employees. This finding implies the importance of normative commitment in predicting organizational behavior, especially in the context of the prevalence of traditional concepts (ie, collectivist tendencies). Bontempo and Rivero (1992) have similar findings. They point out that the more social orientation the individual tends to be, the better predictive the attitude can be for individual behavior than the norm. On the contrary, the more the society tends to collectivism, the better predictability the norms have. Wasti (2003) also used a sample from Turkey to examine the effect of social orientation on the relationship between organizational commitment and turnover intention. The relevant hypotheses were empirically supported.

Farh et al. (2007), under the guidance of the aforementioned research, conducted empirical research on samples taken from 163 pairs of superiors and subordinates in mainland China. It was found that power distance and traditional concepts changed the relationship between organizational support and work results. When the power distance is low or the traditional concept is weak, the relationship between the two is stronger, and on the contrary, it is weaker. The article also found that power distance is a stronger and more consistent moderating variable than traditional concepts. However, the latter is often included in the previous construction in the literature (Ma et al., 2016). In addition, Farh et al. also found that traditional concepts can moderate the relationship between fairness perception and employee performance (including emotional commitment, job performance, and multiple dimensions of OCB). Farh et al. explained that due to obedience and respect for authority, employees who have high recognition of power distances rarely consider their own contributions to the company based on reciprocity norms. Conversely, employees who have low recognition of power distance are more likely to use reciprocity norms as the main principle of their human capital transactions with the company.

In addition, Chen and Aryee (2007) found that in the Eastern context, the relationship between empowerment and emotional commitment is based on the organization-based self-esteem and perceived insider status. The mediating role plays a part in mediating the relationship between empowerment and job satisfaction, while the traditional concept moderates the relationship between empowerment and these intermediary variables, the weaker the traditional concept, the stronger the relationship between authorization and mediator variables, and vice versa.

Therefore, we expect that for professional managers of small and medium-sized private enterprises, their personal values will also moderate the relationship between the perceptions of relevant variables and turnover intentions. Now we put forward the following hypothesis:

H28: *The sense of ideology held by professional managers plays a moderating role in the relationship between relevant antecedent variables and turnover intention, the stronger the traditional sense of concept, the weaker the correlation.*

Risk aversion

The pioneering study of March and Simon (1958) pointed out that the ease of turnover would directly affect the employee's turnover intention. Studies by Kevin et al. (2004), Griffeth et al. (2000) and Ravichandan, (2015) confirmed this view. Although not explicitly pointed out, the ease of turnover itself contains risk factors. Therefore, for employees, under the same other conditions, the smaller the risk of work conversion of the employee, the higher the ease of turnover. However, because people have various levels of risk appetite, other job opportunities that include the same risk have different attractiveness for employees with different risk aversion. Therefore, it is necessary to formally introduce the influence of risk aversion in the turnover model. Unfortunately, we have not found too much research in the literature that considers the effects of risk-aversion moderation. One exception is an empirical analysis done by Allen et al. (2005) in recent years.

The main purpose of Allen et al. (2005) is to test the moderating effect of individual differences on the relationship between turnover intention and actual turnover behavior. The results show that risk aversion plays a regulatory role in the relationship between intention and behavior. Specifically, for employees with lower risk aversion, turnover intentions have a better predictive effect on turnover behavior. Employees who report a higher turnover tendency will most likely convert their wish into actual behavior. Allen et al. believe that the reason for this regulatory effect of risk aversion can be attributed to two aspects: 1. the turnover behavior includes costs, risks and potential obstacles, but the intention express does not include costs; 2. some people will show a more systematic consistency of attitudes, beliefs, and behaviors, which leads to a closer relationship between their intention and behavior.

Since we cannot obtain longitudinal data on the factors that influence the actual turnover behavior, it is difficult to verify whether the findings of Allen et al. (2005) are applicable to this book. Here, we try to introduce the role of risk aversion in the relationship between the direct antecedent variable and turnover intention, and examine whether the regulatory effect of risk aversion at this stage is significant. Present relevant hypothesis is as follows:

H29: *The degree of risk aversion of professional managers plays a role in regulating the relationship between the related antecedent variables and turnover intention. the greater the degree of risk aversion, the weaker the correlation.*

Employer factors

Employer-related factors will affect managers' turnover intention. But equally important is that the employer factor also plays a role in regulating the impact of other relevant variables (such as organizational factors, work factors) on turnover intention.

As mentioned above, under the influence of traditional Confucian culture, employers have a prominent position in the eyes of Chinese employees (Farh and Cheng, 2000). There is a 'five-status' theory in the Confucian ethical order. In the 'five-status' relationship, individuals with lower status have the obligation to obey and be loyal to their respected superior figures (Wong et al., 2002), while high-ranking figures think that it should show charity and love for subordinates. Employees are sometimes more loyal to individuals than to organizations and systems (Redding, 1990). In this case, even if the manager's job satisfaction and organizational commitment are reduced, he will not easily leave the organization because it will cause him to 'betray against' his employer. Conversely, when the manager's commitment to individual employers is reduced, the attitude variables such as job satisfaction and organizational commitment have a stronger impact on turnover intentions because the organization is no longer worthy of nostalgia.

It is also worth noting that even though China's legal system has achieved some progress in the modern era, in general, Chinese society still retains the rule of man rather than rule of law in many aspects (Chen and Francesco, 2000;). In this context, individuals prefer to link their future to the employer's individual rather than the organization itself. This has been partially verified by our previous field surveys.

For professional managers, loyalty to the boss can help them obtain direct benefits from the organization or get better promotion opportunities (Selmer, 2001; Wong et al., 2002). "In a relationship-oriented society, employers are more important than non-personalized organizations in influencing employees' behaviors and attitudes" (Chen et al., 2002, p353). Therefore, employers who have a considerable influence on managers' future and destiny are more valued than professional managers of the organization itself. Managers will not easily make a turnover decision when they are dissatisfied with the organization, they must consider whether they should continue to follow the boss. So, we can make the following hypothesis:

***H30:** Employer-related factors moderates the relationship between organizational factors and turnover intention, the higher the employer's perception of employer satisfaction, the weaker the correlation.*

Dependent Variables and Control Variables

1. Turnover intention and turnover behavior

Turnover intentions are highly correlated with actual turnover behavior (Schwepker, 2001; Murray and Zimmerman, 2005), but just as individual attitudes do not necessarily translate into individual actions, turnover intentions do not necessarily imply actual turnover behavior. If the employee's turnover intention does not usually translate into behavior, then turnover intention is not a fundamental problem for the company. However, if the high turnover intention means a high probability of turnover rate, then before the actual turnover behavior, the company will have a certain 'buffer time' to change the attitude of its employees and thus retain the employees at the last minute. Therefore, it is an important task for the turnover literature to examine the essential meanings and mutual relations of the two concepts of turnover intention and turnover behavior.

There are 23 turnover studies reporting a significant positive correlation between turnover intention and actual turnover behavior (Schwepker, 2001). Many studies such as O'Keefe and Delia (2016) also pointed out that intention is the best predictor of behavior. Among them, Mitchel (1981) has verified this by applying a sample from managers. Murray and Zimmerman (2005) concluded that, in general, turnover intention is one of the best predictors of actual turnover behavior, because the intention to take a certain behavior is often found to be the best predictor of its corresponding behavior (Ajzen and Fishbein, 1977).

Other studies examine the differences and interrelationships of turnover intention and turnover behavior from the perspective of the impact of the relevant antecedent variables on them respectively. A meta-analysis found that the correlation between emotional exhaustion and turnover intention reached 0.44 (Cropanzano et al., 2003). Other studies confirmed the high correlation between emotional exhaustion and actual turnover behavior (Liu et al., 2015). This means that the same antecedent variables can affect employee turnover intention and turnover behavior, and the turnover intention and turnover behavior are likely to have a high degree of connection.

Of course, many studies have pointed out that most of the employees who expressed their turnover intention do not end up with turnover behavior, and their attitude variables can only explain the 5% deviation in the turnover behavior (Allen et al., 2005). At the same time, the explanatory power of turnover intentions rarely exceeds 10%-15% (Griffeth et al., 2000; Hom and Griffeth, 1995). This result can be explained by the theory of planned behavior, which states that the relationship between intention and behavior can be influenced by some other factors (Ajzen, 2002). Since the intention is hypothetical, they tend to overestimate the good side of consensual behavior, especially when actual behavior has costs and risks. Therefore, when there are other factors in the process of transforming intentions into behaviors, relevant behaviors may not appear.

Allen et al. (2005), based on this theory, examines the moderating effect of individual differences on the relationship between turnover intention and actual turnover behavior. The results show that self-monitoring and risk aversion can moderate the relationship between the intention and the behavior. Specifically, the relationship between turnover intention and turnover behavior is stronger for people with lower self-monitoring ability and less risk aversion. The author explains that the two reasons why personality factors play a role in this moderation are as follows: 1. The turnover behavior includes costs, risks and potential obstacles, but the intention expression does not include costs; 2. Some people will show a more systematic consistency of attitudes, beliefs, and behaviors, which leads to a closer relationship between their intention and behavior. In addition, Somers (1995) also found that the relationship between job-related variables and turnover intention seems to be more closely related to the actual turnover behavior, which is also influenced by many other factors.

Therefore, if the turnover intention can be a good predictor of turnover behavior is largely influenced by personal, organizational, work, and other factors. Due to the formal inspection of the relationship between the two requires vertical data, given the limited conditions, we cannot obtain such data temporarily, so this book does not intend to conduct a rigorous empirical analysis. But considering the importance of this issue, we have conceived a sub-optimal alternative approach. Through the retired data of the retiring experience manager's evaluation of the former job company, combined with the sample of the current job company, through variance analysis, Logit discrete variable model and other measurement methods, try to examine the forecasting effect of turnover intention on the turnover behavior. As this practice has not appeared in the existing literature, its reliability has not yet been verified. At the same time, retrospective data may face the so-called recall biases pointed out by Kammeyer-Mueller et al. (2005), so the relevant results are only of reference significance. The relevant hypothesis is put forward as follows:

H31: *Turnover intention is related to actual turnover behavior, the higher the professional manager's turnover intention, and the higher the probability of actual turnover behavior.*

2. The main control variables

The control variables introduced in the empirical tests of relevant process models and factor models in the turnover literature mainly include: age (Mitchell et al., 2001; Chen and Francesco, 2000), gender (Krishnan et al., 2006; Mitchell et al., 2001), marital status (Mitchell et al., 2001), education level (Hom et al., 2017; Chen and Francesco, 2000; Trevor, 2001), length of service in the company (Mossholder et al., 2005; Griffeth et al., 2000; Sommer et al., 1996; Jovanovic, 1979; Kammeyer-Mueller and Wanberg, 2003), average length of service in other companies before entry (Murray and Zimmerman, 2005; Fleishman, 2010; Hom et al., 2017), the length of service in the previous company (Cascio, 1976), total length of service (Mitchell et al., 2001; Chen and Francesco, 2000), job position and work level (Mitchell et al., 2001), company size and years of business (Sun et al., 2007), work experience or career stage (Lucas et al., 1987; Russ and Mcneilly, 1995), difference between individual population background and group population background (Charles et al., 1989; Dulebohn et al., 2016) and other individual psychological and demographic characteristics (Krishnan et al., 2006).

Based on this, the book considers the introduction of gender, marital status, age, position, length of work, the company's length of service, level of education, previous work experience, and other control variables in the factor model. We will classify the samples according to their needs according to some meaningful control variables. Through grouping inspections, we will further understand the main turnover influencing factors of several types of professional managers, and provide basis for the targeted turnover governance mechanism in this book.

Empirical Test Procedures

1. Scale validity and reliability test

We initially find out the variables to be investigated and related measurement items based on literature, and then extend and cut down on the basis of in-depth interviews and qualitative research of the previous period, so as to form a preliminary survey scale. The initial survey and revised scale are followed by a formal large-scale survey. After the data is acquired, the exploratory factor analysis of the original data is first performed using the data compression function of the SPSS software. The measurement items with the load below 0.5 are deleted, and the variables and the corresponding measurement items are redefined according to the attribution of the factor load. Afterwards, LISREL software was used to perform a confirmatory factor analysis (CFA) on the regenerated model, and the items with a latent variable load below 0.5 were deleted (Zhang, 2006) to ensure the validity of the convergence of the formal analysis items. Finally, the reliability test of SPSS software was used to test the reliability of the variables tested by validity. The variable whose Cronbach' α coefficient was lower than 0.7 retained only one measurement whose meaning was closest to the definition of the construct. The variables and measures and the corresponding sample data after this series of testing procedures are used for formal empirical analysis.

2. Structural Equation Model analysis (SEM)

This book adopts the LISREL8.72 software that is more popular in the world to analyze the structural equation model. The preliminarily set path is:

1) The perceived variables X1 ... X19 influence the attitude variables Y1... Y3.

2) The perceived variables X20... X23 and the attitude variables Y1... Y3 together affect the attitude variables Z1 and Z2.

3) The attitude variables Z1 and Z2 influence the turnover intention T1.

The process model composed of this series of stages will be applied to relevant test methods for analysis. Through the theoretical research and the comparison of the index, the revised index fed back from the initial model will continuously moderate the path among the relevant variables, finally find the process model that has the highest degree of fit to the actual survey data, and lay the foundation for the next study.

3. Robustness and moderating effects test

Based on the SEM analysis, Eviews software was used to further examine the influencing factors of professional manager turnover through OLS or Logit discrete variable models. In order to test the robustness of the relevant significant influence factors, we designed two indicators of measures of turnover intention in advance, and placed them in different parts of the questionnaire to ensure its reliability. One is that: 'I hope to work in the company until retirement' (the reverse question). This indicator adopts Likert 7-point system. The other is: 'I am going to spend my entire career in the company' (the reverse question). This indicator uses two choices and the questioner answers 'yes' or 'no'. We will use these two explanatory variables to construct a model, and compare the estimated parameters of the two models to determine the robustness of the factors affecting the turnover of professional managers.

On this basis, we further examined the six groups of moderating effects proposed in the previous section, and introduced the corresponding cross terms into models to examine the regulatory effects of these variables. In addition, we will selectively group the samples according to some meaningful control variables, and examine the relevant models separately to reveal more information and provide further support for the proposed targeted management turnover of professional managers.

4. Consistency analysis of the effects of turnover intention and turnover behavior

Through the Logit discrete variable turnover model and analysis of variance, it will examine whether the turnover behavior is consistent with the prediction of the attitude towards turnover intention. Of course, since the methods applied here have not appeared in the literature, the conclusions are only instructive.

Chapter 5

Empirical Test of Turnover Process Model

Our survey was conducted by professional managers. We first determined the antecedents, mediators, and regulators that introduced the book model for empirical testing through literature screening. And according to the scale provided by the relevant literature, the measurement index is designed. Then, according to the company's field survey and in-depth interview data, the preliminary scale is further revised and expanded. Subsequently, through several rounds of internal and external conference discussions, according to the English original and Chinese language habits, the relevant variables, items and their descriptions have been modified and expanded, so that they are consistent with Chinese expression conventions and are easy to understand. Finally, the scale formed by this requires 5 on-the-job professional managers with various levels of education and 5 non-major students in the school to fill in the test. They give the feelings and suggestions based on the test, based on which then through an internal conference discussion, the final scale for formal investigation (see Appendix 2) is determined.

Samples and Measurements

1. Samples

Sample data were taken from small and medium-sized private enterprises in Guangdong Province. The questionnaire is issued through on-site filling, mailing, and email. 1500 copies were issued and 568 were recovered. The recovery rate reached 38%. After removing the questionnaire containing too many missing items or obviously filled in, there were 550 valid questionnaires. The survey included 332 males, 201 females, and 17 individuals who did not mention the gender; 217 were married, 316 were unmarried, and 17 were unfilled. According to the simple description statistics provided by the effective questionnaire (see Table 5-1), the samples used for empirical analysis can fully represent the sampling population.

Mean Maximum Median Minimum Standard Deviation Number of Samples

Table 5-1 Sample information

Variables	Average value	Maximum	Median	Minimum	Standard Deviation	Number of Samples
Age	28.45	60	27	18	5.79	528
Occupation	1.61	3	2	1	0.64	524
Total length of service (years)	6.92	37	5	0.5	5.80	509
Current company's length of service (months)	33.42	214	24	1	29.50	517
Education	2.16	4	2	1	0.88	528
Company size	1.80	3	2	1	0.58	522
Years since the company was founded	10.22	100	9	1	8.04	509
Work experience (times)	2.11	13	2	0	1.70	508

2. Variables and measures

Most of the indicators used the Likert 7-point system. 1 point indicated that they completely disagree with the corresponding description, and 7 points indicated that they fully agree. The following is a brief introduction of the relevant circumstances.

Job Satisfaction (Q1). Four items, the relevant indicators originally come from the four dimensions of Currivan (1999). We modify the two measures of the reverse measures in the original scale to positive measures, to ensure that they conform to the Chinese people's understanding habits. A representative description is 'I can get satisfaction from my job'.

Organizational Commitment (Q2). Three items, originally from Eisenberger et al. (2001), it is described as 'I have a keen sense of belonging to the company'.

Job Initiative (Q3). Three items, from Eisenberger et al. (2001). It is partially revised with reference to other relevant documents. The representative description is 'I often help my co-workers to do tasks beyond my responsibilities'.

Career Commitment (Q4). Three items, originally from Chen et al. (2002). Based on the discussion results, the promised object is changed to "company". The representative description is 'I was honored for the company's achievements'.

Job Attitude (Q5). Two items, from Currivan (1999). It is representatively described as 'I sometimes feel sorry for working at the company'.

Organizational Attraction (Q6). Three items, from Huang (2007). The representative description is 'I would like to recommend a friend to work for the company'.

Job Searching Intention (Q7). Three items are referred to by modifying the relevant items of the "work-seeking behavior" variable of Price (2001). The representative description is 'I cannot find other work within the next three years'.

Organizational Return System (Q9). Three items, originally from Rhoade et al. (2001), is described as 'employees have the opportunity to obtain higher pay in the company'.

Salary (Q10). The three items of measurement are given based on the remuneration theory, and are partially revised according to the previous survey data. The representative description is 'I am satisfied with my overall salary'.

Organizational Conditions (Q11). The four measurement items are based on Zhang and Wang (2003), which were modified from the interview data. The representative description is 'there is a perfect company management system'.

Social Relationship (Q12). The three items are designed based on the preliminary investigation data. The representative description is

'There is a harmonious relationship between the superior and subordinates in the company'.

Fairness (Q13). Three items, the first two are taken from the two items with the highest load in the corresponding indicator of the 'procedural fairness' variable in Rhoades et al. (2001) (0.72 and 0.68, respectively). The latter one is taken from Simons and Roberson (2003). The representative description is 'the opinions of the relevant persons will be sought when making decisions at the top level'.

Career Growth Opportunity (Q14). The three items are referenced by Benson et al. (2004) and combined with Zhang (2006) and interview data. The representative description is 'I have the opportunity to learn new knowledge and new skills in the company'.

Job Autonomy (Q15). Three items, from Currivan (1999). The representative description is 'I can control my own work process'.

Job Pressure (Q16). Four items, originally from Price (2001). It uses the measure with the highest factor load value from the four dimensions of Zhang Jian (2006) related constructs. The representative description is 'My work load exceeds the tolerated range'.

Job Challenge (Q17). Three measures, from Cavanaugh (2000). It selects three indicators that have higher loads and are most relevant to the theme of the book. The representativeness is described as 'my job responsibilities are significant'.

Employer Appreciation (Q18). Three measures, originally from the three indicators of Eisenberger et al. (2001), that is 'Organization Support Level (POS)' structure, with a load greater than 0.70. We change the 'organization' in the original measurement item to 'leadership'. The represented description is 'leaders value my contribution to the organization'.

Leadership of Employer (Q19). Three items, under the guidance of Chen et al. (2002). It refers to the entrepreneurial leadership theory to design relevant indicators. The representative description is 'the boss has a strong entrepreneurial ability'.

Employer Honesty (Q20). The four items are derived from the four most relevant items of Huang (2007) and Ji (2008). The representative description is 'the boss usually fulfills his promise to employees'.

Leadership Fairness (Q21). Three items are designed based on the leadership fairness theory (Cropanzano et al., 2003). A representative description is 'the boss treats all employees equally'.

Employer Achievement Motivation (Q22). The three items are designed based on the theory of individual achievement motivation. The representative description is 'the boss regards work as the most important thing in life'.

Job Embeddedness (Q23). The three items are designed under the guidance of Mitchell et al. (2001) and combined with the preliminary survey data. The representative description is 'I was introduced to the company by acquaintance'.

Personal-company Match (Q24). Four measures, based on the three variables with the highest load of the corresponding variables in Mitchell et al. (2001), combined with the design of social identity theory. The representative description is 'I can give full play to my talents in the company'.

Other Job Opportunities (Q25). Four items are measured by the ease-of-conversion sense construct (EIO) from Griffeth et al. (2005), which has five dimensions and a total of 14 items originally. This book selects the highest load in each dimension, and combines the two indicators with similar meanings in Chinese translation. Finally, four items are remained, the representative description of 'If you leave the company, I will find a better job'.

Employer Trust (Q26). According to Huang (2007), combined with previous survey data design, the three representative items are described as 'the boss believes that the employees will consciously safeguard the interests of the company'.

Organization Change (Q27). One measurement item, based on Susanna and Aryee's (2003) research on the breakdown of psychological contract, combined with previous survey data. The question is designed as 'Is the company undergoing or will undergo a major organizational change or adjustment?', and the respondents need to answer 'yes' or 'no'.

Job Involvement (Q29). Three items, from Mirvis and Lawler (1977). The original construct consists of four items. This study selects three with a load greater than 0.7. The representative description is 'Work is my main pleasure'.

Risk Aversion (Q30). Three items, from Gomez-Mejia and Balkin (1989). Originally there are four items, one of which is not related to the theme of the book. The representative description is 'I prefer to work with stable income and low risk'.

Conceptual Awareness (Q31). The three items are from the 'Chinese traditional concept' or 'power distance' construct of Farh (2007). There are six items in the original text. The book uses three items that are most closely related to the turnover in terms of meaning. This construct was originally constructed by Dorfman and Howell (1988) for research in Taiwan. The representative description is 'In case of dispute, the ruling should be given to people with higher status'.

Commitment Propensity (Q32). Three items, from Price (2000) and Zhang (2006). The representative description is 'I am willing to work in a company for a long time'.

Entrepreneurial Motivation (Q33). The three measurement items are designed based on preliminary enterprise interviews and surveys. The representative description is 'If the conditions are ripe, I will consider self-employment'.

The explanatory variable is the 'turnover intention'. In order to enable respondents to report their true ideas as much as possible, we use neutral vocabulary names such as 'plan' and 'expectation', and use reverse quizzes to dispel their concerns. In the actual investigation, to carry out the robustness test during the formal analysis, we've designed two indicators to measure the turnover intention and placed it on various parts of the questionnaire to ensure the reliability of the information obtained. One is 'I hope to work in the company until retirement' (Q8), adopting Likert 7-point system; the other is 'I plan to spend my entire career in the company' (Q28), and the respondents need to answer 'yes' or 'no'.

In addition, to avoid the problem of common method variance (CMV), we placed explanatory variables and mediating variables in the front part of the questionnaire, so that the respondents would reflect their true tendencies in the initial stage of answering the questions.

3. Exploratory Factor Analysis (EFA)

To compress data and merge variables so as to avoid multiple collinearity problems, and to ensure the convergence of relevant variables, we first applied SPSS16.0 software to conduct exploratory factor analysis on the survey data. The KMO test statistic is 0.938 and the Bartlett's spherical test statistic is 3160 ($p<0.001$), indicating that our data is very suitable for factor analysis. After the factor structure is obtained, the variables and merging are redefined based on the meaning of the correlation factor load matrix and its corresponding measurement items for further analysis. Table 5-2 shows the factor load matrix obtained by rotating Varimax. The indicator with a load value below 0.5 has been deleted. The newly defined and named new construct and its corresponding measurement items are also given in the table. The following is a brief introduction of the new constructs.

Organization Condition and Opportunity (OSC). Based on the original scale and the results of the exploratory factor analysis in Table 5-2, the measurement attributed to this new constructive idea (load value greater than 0.5) was originally attributed to 5 constructs, namely: organizational returns, compensation, organizational conditions, fairness, and organizational attractiveness. This construct reflects mainly the most crucial factors in the organization, and the explanatory power of these factors for managers' turnover intention is condensed into a factor. Although we only extracted the four items with the largest load value for formal analysis, it should be noted that the results obtained reflect the influence of organizational factors such as organizational returns and salary on the turnover intention. Therefore, in interpreting the meaning of empirical results, we can start from the perspective of the original construct.

Leadership of Employer (BLH). The measurement items included in this construct were originally attributed to the three original variables: the employer's achievement motivation, employer leadership, and employer honesty. These factors are all related to the employer's ability and moral conduct, and reflect the impact from employers.

Employer Fairness and Trust (BFT). The measurement items contained in this construct were originally attributed to three original variables: fairness in leadership, employer integrity, and employer trust. The construct reflects the way the employer treats subordinates and reflects the LMX quality between the employer and employees. According to the assumptions presented earlier in this book, such factors have an important influence on the turnover intention of managers.

Employer Appreciation (BCI). The measurement items included in this construct were originally attributed to BCI and the challenges of the job. It reflects the extent to which employers care about train employees.

Job Satisfaction and Commitment (JSC). As mentioned earlier, job satisfaction and organizational commitment are different attitude variables. However, in this study we found that the two constructs are highly correlated. The PHI matrix estimated by LISREL shows a correlation coefficient of up to 0.57 ($t=12.59$, $p<0.001$). Therefore, it is not an unexpected result that EFA shows that both factors belong to the same factor. In fact, this construct is similar to the "Total Work Attitude" constructed by Harrison et al. (2006), which has been found to have a significant impact on employees' overall performance standards, including turnover intentions. When we are interpreting relevant empirical results, we no longer distinguish between the two items.

Job Initiative (JFC). The measurement items included in the construct were originally attributed to the variables of JC and PC. The original intention of designing these two constructs was to examine the JC respectively from the manager's attitude toward the work itself and the organization. However, EFA shows that both actually reflect the same thing, that is, job performance.

The variables that were deleted in the EFA due to under-loading include the career growth opportunities and matching degree, indicating that the validity of the two constructs in this book cannot meet the analysis requirements. In addition, all other constructs make empirical analysis process according to the original definition and measurement.

Table 5-2 EFA Factor Load Matrix

Measurement items	**OSC**	**BLH**	**JSC**	**BFT**	**BCI**
Q9_1	0.80				
Q10_1	0.78				
Q9_3	0.77				
Q10_2	0.75				
Q9_2	0.70				
Q11_2	0.68				
Q13_3	0.65				
Q10_3	0.65				
Q13_2	0.57				
Q11_1	0.55				
Q6_2	0.53				
Q6_1	0.53				
Q22_3		0.83			
Q22_1		0.79			
Q22_2		0.70			
Q19_3		0.68			
Q19_1		0.67			
Q20_1		0.65			
Q20_4		0.62			
Q20_3		0.55			
Q1_1			0.72		

Measurement items	OSC		BLH	JSC	BFT	BCI
Q1_3				0.70		
Q1_2				0.68		
Q1_4				0.67		
Q2_2				0.58		
Q2_1				0.58		
Q2_3				0.54		
Q21_3					0.63	
Q20_2					0.61	
Q21_1					0.59	
Q21_2					0.57	
Q26_2					0.57	
Q18_1						0.71
Q18_3						0.61
Q18_2						0.60
Q17_3						0.55
Q17_2						0.53
Q16_2	0.75					
Q16_4	0.74					
Q16_3	0.73					
Q16_1	0.71					
Q33_2		0.89				
Q33_1		0.87				
Q33_3		0.84				
Q3_3			0.65			
Q4_1			0.60			
Q3_2			0.60			
Q4_2			0.59			
Q4_3			0.55			
Q32_1				0.78		
Q32_2				0.70		
Q32_3				0.63		

Measurement items	**OSC**		**BLH**	**JSC**	**BFT**		**BCI**
Q7_2					-0.73		
Q7_1					-0.72		
Q7_3					-0.52		
Q15_2						0.68	
Q15_3						0.64	
Q15_1						0.57	
Q29_2							0.82
Q29_3							0.76
Q29_1							0.53
Q12_2	0.69						
Q12_3	0.63						
Q12_1	0.52						
Q25_2		0.79					
Q25_3		0.69					
Q31_2			0.74				
Q31_1			0.66				
Q31_3			0.55				
Q23_1				0.74			
Q23_2				0.71			
Q30_3					0.70		
Q30_2					0.61		
Q30_1					0.58		
Q5_1						-0.53	
Q5_2						-0.52	
Q27							0.68

Note: The factor load values of the items listed in the table are all higher than 0.5.

4. Confirmatory Factor Analysis (CFA) and reliability test

Based on the factor structure given by EFA, we select the four items with the largest load value included in each factor (those with less than four items are all selected). Then the LISREL 8.72 software is used for confirmatory factor analysis (see related procedures in Appendix 3). The verification of confirmatory factor analysis ($\lambda > 0.5$) is used for further reliability test. Specifically, the Cronbach's α coefficient given by the data reliability analysis function of SPSS is used for judgement, and the variable with coefficient $\alpha > 0.7$ passes the reliability test. The CFA load matrix is given in Table 5-3, and the latent variable descriptive statistics and the corresponding Cronbach's α reliability coefficients are shown in Table 5-4.

Empirical Test Method

Data from previous tests of validity and reliability were used for subsequent empirical analysis. The SEM is applied to the path analysis program of LISREL 8.72 software (see Appendix 4 for the original program). We first fit the initial model according to the assumed path given in the previous chapter, and then modify the model gradually according to the feedback correction index and relevant theories. Finally, a "good" model with the best fit and theory is obtained.

Table 5-3 CFA Latent Variable Load Matrix (LISREL Standard Estimated Value)

Constructs	No. of Measurement Items	1	2	3	4
Explanatory Variables					
JSC	4	0.83	0.81	0.78	0.7
JFC	4	0.5	**0.48**[a]	0.82	0.81
JA	2	0.86	0.74	——	——
JL	3	0.53	0.63	0.81	——
OSC	4	0.83	0.84	0.78	0.79
SR	3	0.82	0.78	0.79	——
JC	3	0.64	0.73	0.75	——
JP	4	0.65	0.7	0.7	0.8
BCI	4	**0.46**	0.74	0.82	0.8
BFT	4	0.75	0.9	0.87	0.86
BLH	4	0.84	0.79	0.92	0.69
JE	2	0.52	0.8	——	——
OJ	2	**0.48**	0.94	——	——
JI	3	0.7	0.88	0.81	——
PC	3	0.79	0.7	0.77	——
EM	3	0.87	0.91	0.72	——
CR	1	1[b]	——	——	——
Dependent Variable					
TOVL	1	1	——	——	——

Note: a. The load value of the measured items on the corresponding latent variable λ <0.5 is deleted when performing the next analysis. b. When only one measurement item is constructed in the LISREL program, it assumes that it has no measurement error and forces the corresponding λ =1.

Table 5-4 Descriptive Statistics of Latent Variables and Reliability Factor

CN	Latent Variables	N	Min	Max	Mean	Std. Deviation	Cronbach's α
1	JSC	541	1	7	5.53	1.04	0.860
2	JFC	539	3	7	6.15	0.79	0.710
3	JA	501	1	6.5	2.44	1.47	0.777
4	JL	540	1	7	3.60	1.51	0.725
5	TOVL	528	1	7	4.26	2.06	——[a]
6	OSC	536	1	7	4.53	1.40	0.883
7	BLH	532	1	7	6.18	1.01	0.865
8	BFT	534	1	7	5.23	1.37	0.907
9	BCI	536	1	7	4.52	1.40	0.865
10	JP	536	1	7	3.26	1.44	0.806
11	EM	529	1	7	4.98	1.49	0.869
12	PC	532	1	7	5.14	1.33	0.798
13	JC	536	1	7	5.41	1.11	0.749
14	JI	531	1	7	5.30	1.20	0.828
15	SR	536	1.67	7	5.50	1.05	0.839
16	OJ	534	1	7	2.52	1.78	——
17	JE	533	1	7	2.53	1.92	**0.573**[b]
18	CR	505	0	1	0.71	0.45	——
19	RA	531	1	7	4.26	1.25	**0.554**
20	VI	531	1	7	4.65	1.24	**0.656**
Valid N (listwise)				460			

Note: a. There is only one measurement item for this type of variable and no internal consistency check is required. b. The reliability coefficient of the corresponding variable is α <0.7, indicating that the reliability of the measurement using these three measures cannot be guaranteed. Therefore, in the next analysis, the measurement item closest to the definition of the construct is used to replace the corresponding constructs (Zhang, 2006).

Structural Equation Model Test Results

1. Latent variable pearson correlation coefficient matrix

From the simple correlation coefficient matrix in Table 5-5, it can be seen that the correlation between manager's turnover intention and each explanatory variable is significant, and is fully consistent with the hypothesis. Among them, the six variables with the strongest correlation ($r>0.3$) to turnover intention are: JSC (-), JL(+), OSC(-), BFT(-), BCI(-), and PC(-). It suggests that we need to focus on these explanatory variables in the subsequent empirical analysis.

Table 5-5 Latent Variable Pearson Correlation Coefficients Matrix

	JSC	JFC	JA	JL	CR	OSC	BLH	BFT	BCI
JSC	1.000								
JFC	0.460	1.000							
JA	-0.531	-0.330	1.000						
JL	-0.401	-0.117	0.221	1.000					
CR	0.062	0.061	-0.124	0.059	1.000				
OSC	0.353	0.069	-0.288	-0.368	-0.366	1.000			
BLH	0.394	0.430	-0.328	-0.278	-0.254	0.281	1.000		
BFT	0.422	0.188	-0.280	-0.439	-0.394	0.621	0.524	1.000	
BCI	0.438	0.202	-0.255	-0.385	-0.339	0.455	0.268	0.468	1.000
JP	-0.316	-0.166	0.408	0.165	0.176	-0.247	-0.191	-0.267	-0.240
EM	-0.002	-0.007	0.084	0.030	0.078	-0.031	0.122	-0.019	-0.009
PC	0.389	0.264	-0.222	-0.405	-0.519	0.302	0.370	0.409	0.298
JC	0.507	0.367	-0.409	-0.226	-0.299	0.401	0.414	0.420	0.492
JI	0.413	0.382	-0.309	-0.235	-0.276	0.310	0.384	0.391	0.228
SR	0.418	0.257	-0.311	-0.244	-0.243	0.467	0.461	0.530	0.444
OJ	-0.100	-0.226	0.184	0.125	0.192	-0.154	-0.309	-0.196	-0.179
JE	0.162	-0.113	-0.083	-0.294	-0.214	0.168	-0.053	0.170	0.347
TOVL	-0.368	-0.154	0.275	0.519	0.033	-0.366	-0.254	-0.394	-0.339

Table 5-5 Latent Variable Pearson Correlation Coefficients Matrix (Continued)

	JP	EM	PC	JC	JI	SR	OJ	JE	TOVL
JSC									
JFC									
JA									
JL									
CR									
OSC									
BLH									
BFT									
BCI									
JP	1.000								
EM	0.143	1.000							
PC	-0.178	-0.065	1.000						
JC	-0.300	0.024	0.319	1.000					
JI	-0.146	-0.018	0.357	0.345	1.000				
SR	-0.325	-0.004	0.343	0.433	0.263	1.000			
OJ	0.220	0.165	-0.082	-0.197	-0.170	-0.185	1.000		
JE	-0.044	-0.125	0.128	0.168	-0.004	0.054	-0.007	1.000	
TOVL	0.176	0.078	-0.519	-0.299	-0.276	-0.243	0.192	-0.214	1.000

2. The goodness-of-fit of professional manager turnover process model

The basic structure of the two models going to be selected is shown in Figures 5-1 and 5-2. The main fitting indices of the original model M1 and the revised model M2 are given in Table 5-6. According to Hou et al. (2004), for □□, RMSEA, and AIC information index, the smaller, the better, and for other indices, the larger, the better. Among them, the relative fitting index NFI, NNFI, and CFI above 0.9 are acceptable. The closer it is to 1, the better the degree of fit to the data. It is easy to see that revised model M2 has lower □□, RMSEA and AIC, and has higher NFI, CFI and GFI. Therefore, it can be determined that

M2 has a high degree of goodness-of-fit for the sample data in this study, and is a "good" model, which can be determined as the final process model of the turnover intention of professional managers.

3. Standardized path coefficient and its significance

Table 5-7 shows the normalized path coefficients and significance of the final selected model M2 (see Appendix 5 for specific factor load values and path coefficients). In terms of mediating variables, JL significantly affects managers' turnover intention ($p<0.001$); JA also has a significant effect at the level of 0.05. In addition, JSC significantly affects JFC and JA ($p<0.001$). There is no meaningful relationship between JFC and JA; the relationship between JSC and JA is also not significant, indicating that its impact on turnover intention is mainly transmitted indirectly through JA variables.

Table 5-6 Comparison of SEM Model Fitting Index

Models	χ^2	df	RMSEA	AIC	NFI	NNFI	CFI	GFI	AGFI
M1	2630.16	1069	0.057	3042.16	0.94	0.96	0.96	0.81	0.78
M2	2471.02	1058	0.054	2905.02	0.95	0.96	0.97	0.82	0.78

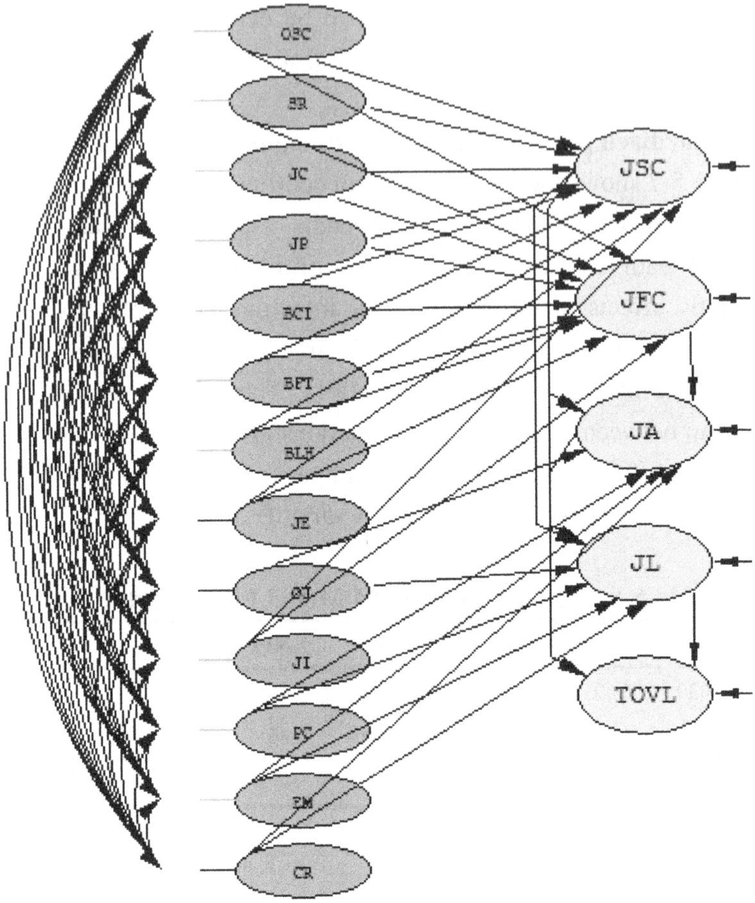

Figure 5-1 Original Model M1

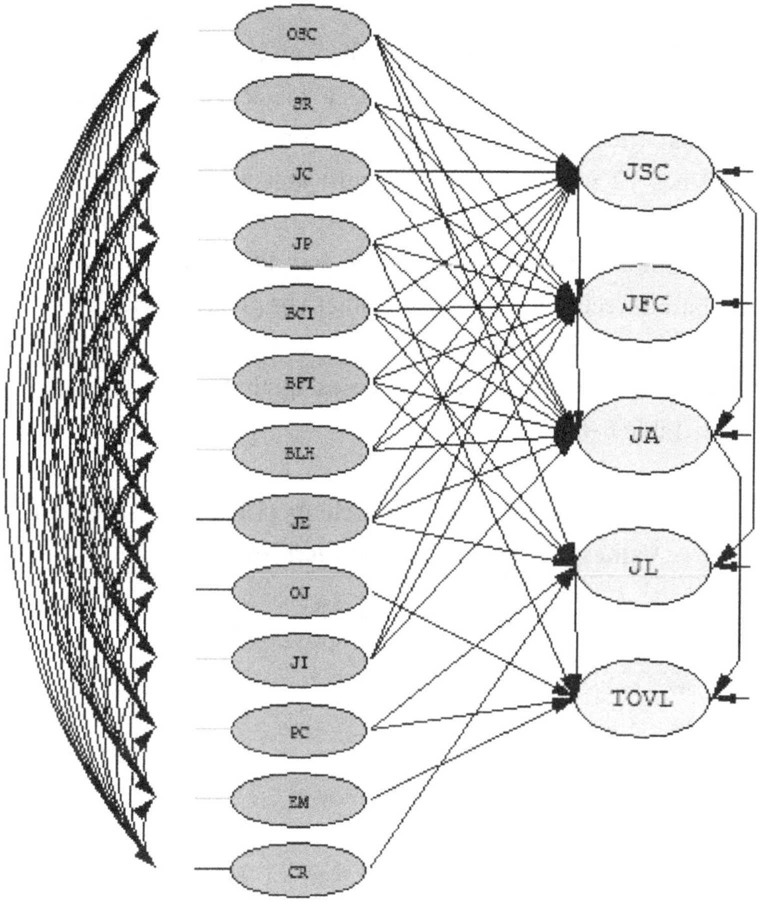

Figure 5-2 Revised Model M2

In terms of antecedent variables, BCI, JC, JI, and SR have a significant impact on manager's JSC; BLH, BFT, JC, JI and JE have a significant impact on JC; BCI, JP and JC significantly affect the manager's working status; variables that have a direct impact on the JL include the BCI, JC, JE, PC and CR etc. Finally, JP and OJ have a direct and significant effect on turnover intentions.

4. Influence effect decomposition of related variables on turnover intention

Table 5-8 shows the direct, indirect, and total effects of each variable on the interpreted variables. This is the core result of this book. As far as total effects are concerned, apart from JC, BLH, BCI, SR and EM, the other 12 variables have a significant effect on the turnover intention of managers. Among them, JA, JL and OJ all affect the turnover intention in a direct way; JP and PC affect the turnover intention both directly and indirectly; other significant variables affect the turnover intention through indirect ways. For ease of reading, we have summarized the relevant hypotheses in this and the following chapters in Table 6-12 of Chapter 6.

Table 5-7 Standardized Path Coefficients (LISREL Estimated Values) of Structural Equation Model M2

Variables		JSC	JFC	JA	JL	TOVL
Mediating Variables	JSC	——	0.39***	-0.43***	-0.09	——
	JFC	——	——	0.09	——	——
	JA	——	——	——	——	0.12**
	JL	——	——	——	——	0.54***
Antecedent Variables	OSC	-0.02	-0.10	-0.10	-0.18**	——
	BLH	0.09	0.37***	0.11	——	——
	BFT	0.02	-0.16*	0.07	-0.13	——
	BCI	0.14*	-0.02	0.2**	-0.12*	——
	JP	-0.08	-0.05	0.48***	——	-0.16***
	JC	0.17**	0.18**	-0.22***	——	——
	JI	0.26***	0.15**	-0.04	——	——
	SR	0.25***	-0.02	0.13	——	——
	JE	0.06	-0.13***	0.03	-0.16***	——
	EM	——	——	——	——	0.05
	PC	——	——	——	-0.31***	-0.23***
	OJ	——	——	——	——	0.09**
	CR	——	——	——	0.10**	——
R^2 (N=456)		0.53	0.55	0.56	0.53	0.52

Note: "*" indicates being significant at the level of 0.10, "**" indicates being significant at the level of 0.05, and "***" indicates being significant at the level of 0.01.

Table 5-8 Decomposition of Effects of Variables (LISREL Estimated Value)

Variables		Direct Effect	Indirect Effect	Total Effects
Mediating Variables	JSC	——	-0.10**	-0.10**
	JFC	——	0.01	0.01
	JA	0.12**	——	0.12**
	JL	0.54***	——	0.54***
Antecedent Variables	OSC	——	-0.11**	-0.11**
	BLH	——	-0.02	-0.02
	BFT	——	-0.07*	-0.07*
	BCI	——	-0.05	-0.05
	JP	-0.17***	0.07**	-0.10**
	JC	——	-0.04**	-0.04**
	JI	——	-0.03**	-0.03**
	SR	——	-0.01	-0.01
	JE	——	-0.09***	-0.09***
	EM	0.05	——	0.05
	PC	-0.23***	-0.17***	-0.40***
	OJ	0.09**	——	0.09**
	CR	——	0.06**	0.06**

Note: "*" indicates being significant at the level of 0.10, "**" indicates being significant at the level of 0.05, and "***" indicates being significant at the level of 0.01.

Discussion

1. Influence-effect of mediating variables

The intermediary connection model proposed by Mobley (1977) pioneered the concept of turnover as a "process". Later many related studies have shown that the turnover of employees is not a simple point-in-time decision. It involves complex stages and procedures such as subjective perception, reduced satisfaction, information search, and comparative evaluation. This book has obtained a process model through structural equation model test. This model shows that the turnover of professional managers of small and medium-sized private enterprises will undergo a complex process. Starting from the situation perception on the organizations, employers, and the job itself, the managers would experience a decline in satisfaction, a decline in enthusiasm for work, job search motives, and a low work level etc., finally leading to turnover intention.

As can be seen from Table 5-8, in terms of the total effect, three of the four mediating variables have a significant effect on the turnover intention of managers. First, JSC reduces the manager's turnover intention ($p<0.05$). This result supports our hypotheses H23 and H24. When the manager's job satisfaction and organizational commitment increase by 1 unit, the turnover intention tends to decrease by 0.1 unit. This result means that, whatever the cause, dissatisfaction with work and a reduction in loyalty to the organization will greatly increase the likelihood of manager turnover. From Table 5-7, we can further see that the effect of JSC is achieved indirectly through JFC and JA. The relevant standardized path coefficients are 0.39 and -0.43, and both are significant at the level of 0.01. The transmission mechanism here can be summarized as follows: Influenced by the perception of related factors such as organization and work, the managers' working attitude changes, this in turn reduces the work enthusiasm. And the work performance within the scope of duties falls, resulting in the occurrence of turnover intention. Whether the managers are full of work enthusiasm, whether they can get satisfaction from work, and whether they are emotionally loyal to the company have a considerable influence on their willingness to stay in the company. Although existing research shows that there are many reasons leading to such changes in mental attitudes (Price, 2001), managers' perceptions of relevant individuals, organizations, employers, jobs, and other opportunities are the core influence variables. These factors indirectly lead to managers' turnover intentions in this way.

Second, JA has strong explanatory power for turnover intention ($\eta = 0.12$, $p < 0.05$), and supports our hypothesis H26. In our final selected process model M2, the effect of JA on turnover intention is straightforward. Although the causal relationship between the two cannot be completely determined, it is at least certain that the poor working conditions are accompanied by higher turnover probabilities. If the organization observes that the manager is in a poor JA, this probably means that the manager will leave the company in the near future. JA reflects the extent to which managers are willing to work hard, in order to obtain organizational rewards, and the reduction in willingness to work can be seen as a signal that employees plan to leave the company. If managers do not care about the organization's assessment of their own performance, then the turnover intention has occurred.

Finally, JL has a more significant impact on turnover intentions. Its standardized path coefficient reaches a staggering 0.54 ($p<0.001$). When the manager's JL increases by 1 unit, the turnover intention will increase by 0.54 units. This result gives dedicated support to hypothesis H27. The frequent attention of managers to other job opportunities means that they have turnover intention. This intention reflects the cautious awareness of managers prior to their turnover, that is, their turnover decision was not made rashly, and they were well prepared. Information obtained through search behavior helps it find better jobs in other companies. If managers even do not hide their motivation for finding other jobs, then the turnover is almost inevitable. The reasons for JL are complex. As shown in Table 5-7, in addition to the indirect effects of related factors, organizational factors, BCI, JE, PC and CR all directly lead managers to seek for other job opportunities. For example, CR makes managers feel upset, and the best way to eliminate this feeling is to prepare for turnover. Thus the managers have to search for job information through various ways. The managers with lower PC tend to pay attention to the talent market information frequently when the company is in normal operation. Such employees do not think that frequent job-hopping is unethical behavior.

In addition, the variable of JFC did not pass the significance tests, indicating that the out-of-role performance indicators reported by the managers in this sample have no explanatory power for the turnover intention. Our hypothesis H25 has not been supported by this structural model. This book attempts to explain this in three ways. First, the performance indicators in this sample may have the problem of "self-misrepresentation". Most of the work performance indicators used in the literature are taken from the assessment of supervisors, colleagues, or clients (e.g., Lee et al., 2004), so they have certain explanatory powers for the turnover intention. However, due to limited conditions, it is difficult for us to obtain such objective data. The data obtained by the manager's self-assessment of his performance outside his role may not necessarily reflect this variable, so the significance may be affected. Secondly, from the latent variable correlation matrix shown in Table 5-5, the correlation coefficient between JFC and JSC reaches 0.46. The structural model may face multiple collinearity problems. The explanatory power of JFC on turnover intention variance has been partially covered by the JSC variable. Finally, the managers who have turnover intention may indeed not show a decline in their JFC. That is, managers who are active in off-the-job performance may also have turnover intention. This type of performance may instead be a kind of concealment of their true will. In the next chapter, we try to retest the hypothesis by applying another turnover measurement in the Logit model.

2. Significance of antecedent variables and its influence path

An important consideration in proposing the process model is that the influence of personal, organizational, employer, and work factors on employee turnover is indirect. Managers' perceptions of these factors are not immediately reflected in turnover intention. The aforementioned variables such as JSC and JA play an important intermediary role in it. The structural equation model method has advantages in analyzing such problems. It can simultaneously estimate the complex path among the antecedent variables, the mediating variables, and the explanatory variables. It provides deep insights for understanding the influence mechanism and action path of each factor. The SEM empirical results show that in addition to BLH, BCI, SR and EM, the remaining nine constructs' significance on the overall effect of turnover intentions is supported (see Table 5-8). The following discussion is based on the size of the standardized path coefficients.

The PC has the greatest effect. Its coefficient is -0.40, and is significant at the level of 0.001, strongly supporting our hypothesis H2a. This result shows that the managers' own value of turnover behavior has the most important predictive effect on their turnover intention. It is very difficult for a manager who takes "job-hopping" as capital accumulation to stay in the same organization for a long time. Such individual tendency is a characteristic that employees already had before entering the organization, and it was difficult for the company to change it in the short term. Employees with a low commitment propensity either feel boring in the same company for long time, or take "job-hopping" as a strategy to maintain competitiveness in their careers. They think that working in different companies can help to improve their skills and qualifications (Parker et al., 2015; Connie and Kammeyer-Mueller, 2000). Therefore, do not expect such managers to be truly loyal to the organization. We will further examine the moderating effect of this construct in the next chapter.

The coefficient of OSC variable is -0.11 ($p < 0.05$), and its influence effect ranks second. The factor structure produced by the previous EFA shows that this construct contains five original concepts of organizational returns, salary, organizational conditions, fairness, and organizational attractiveness. Therefore, it can be determined that our hypotheses H4, H5, H6a, H6b, and H8 are strongly supported. Organizational factors have been the focus of the literature on employee attitudes, job performance, and turnover intentions (Ramlall, 2003; Krishnan et al., 2006). The empirical results of this book also show that the organization's own factors play a key role in the turnover of professional managers of small and medium private enterprises. Managers' lower expectations on organizational returns and organizational conditions, lower procedural fairness perceptions and salary satisfaction will lead to higher turnover intentions. The main purpose of the managers is to accumulate and realize their professional capitals (Huang, 2007). If this goal can be achieved in the company will largely determine their retention. It is easy to understand that good incentive system, good development space, and competitive compensation and other organizational factors all contribute to the achievement of managers' career goals. It is further necessary to point out that OSC indirectly affect managers' turnover intentions through other attitude variables such as job satisfaction and organizational commitment (see Table 5-7). That is, managers' perception of relevant organizational factors will not immediately be reflected in their turnover intention.

The coefficient of JP variable is -0.10, and the influence effect ranks third. Although the total effect of this factor is significant at the level of 0.05, it is surprising it's result is opposite to the hypothesis (H12). It reflects that the greater the JP perceived by the manager, the lower the turnover intention. As far as we know, the relationship between JP and turnover given in the literature is not yet clear (Cavanaugh et al., 2000), but discovers on the negative relationship are not very much. One exception is that Cavanaugh et al. (2000)'s empirical study of 1886 sample of American professional managers. The study found that challenging-related self-reported stress is positively related to job satisfaction, and negatively related to job search behavior. Hindrance-related self-reported stress is negatively related to job satisfaction and positively related to job search behavior and turnover. That is, the influence effects of different kinds of JP on the turnover intention are different or even the opposite. This book originally introduced work-challenging variables to capture the negative effects, and to separate the effects of negatively-acting JP. But as the three indicators of workability failed to pass the reliability and validity tests, the SEM model failed to introduce the construct for testing.

Despite this, Cavanaugh et al. (2000) suggest that we may give a possible interpretation of the results. That is, in this research, the elite group of professional managers may have understood the stress as a challenging job stress. Such employees may feel that the perceived high JP means that their responsibility and position are more important, and they are "significant" people for the company. Professional managers mostly have high motivation for success. They often understand the heavier workload as the success of their own profession. That is, only the manager who is appreciated by the boss will bear the burden. Therefore, its perception of job stress adversely affects turnover intention. Of course, this interpretation needs the support of other relevant research. Further empirical analysis may consider introducing the professional manager's individual achievement motivation variable to examine whether it has a regulatory effect on the negative relationship. It is also worth noting that the negative relationship of this total effect mainly functions in direct way. Results in Tables 5-7 and 5-8 indicate that the indirect effects of JP on the turnover intention through the intermediary variables such as JA are positive ($p<0.05$), that is, the greater the work pressure, the worse the JA ($\xi=0.48$, $p<0.001$), and the higher the turnover intention (this indirect effect is 0.07, and is significant at the 0.05 level). However, as the negative direct effect is too large ($\xi=-0.17$, $p<0.001$), the total effect of JP on turnover intentions showed a negative relationship ($-0.17+0.07=-0.10$). This reminds us that if the JP does not lead to a decline in JA, the increase in such pressure will help managers to retain their positions. It is necessary to further study the design of different types of JP indicators in accordance with the recommendations of Cavanaugh et al. (2000), to examine which pressures will lead to a decline in JA, thereby increase the turnover intention, and which pressures will directly reduce the turnover intention.

The total effect of JE variable is -0.09, and is significant at the level of 0.01. It supports our hypothesis H20. This result confirms the effectiveness of this construct, first proposed by Mitchell et al. (2001), in interpreting the turnover variance. It suggests that SME professional managers value the JE a lot. Managers who have "acquaintances" in the organizations or have a better personal relationship with the boss are more reluctant to leave. Nowadays, many companies have begun to pay attention to the relationship between job seekers and existing employees when recruiting new employees. This also proves that the degree of JE is a very important factor. In addition, according to Table 5-7, we find that JE indirectly influences the turnover through mediating variables such as JFC (ξ=-0.13, $p<0.01$) and JL (ξ=-0.16, $p<0.001$). The previous relationship is inconsistent with the hypotheses and common sense. One possible explanation is that managers with high JE feel that they have "acquaintances" in the company, or have a better personal relationship with the employer, even if the performance is poor, they will not be officially punished by the organization. The lack of external restraint makes them dare to indulge themselves. It's found that the deeper the degree of JE, the weaker the managers' working enthusiasm. This finding is different from the conclusions of most Western literature, which reflects the significant influence of the special relationships governance under the Chinese cultural background. Related to this, but differently, it's found that the higher the degree of JE, the stronger the informal binding of "relational" network, and the more reluctant the managers want to go out and find other job opportunities. Therefore, in terms of the overall effect, JE does help to reduce managers' turnover intention.

The total effect of OJ variable is also 0.09 ($p<0.05$), supporting our hypothesis H22, which is consistent with the mainstream conclusions of the turnover literature (Griffeth et al., 2005). It is worth noting that the influence of OJ on turnover intention is straightforward. This shows that even if managers have a higher level of JSC and JFC, once they have better job opportunities, their turnover intention will be directly generated and leave the organization without any precursors. Most of the turnover caused by OJ has undergone processes of rational comparisons, evaluations, and calculations (Maertz and Campion,

2004). Managers do not experience significant changes in JA. For such managers, it is difficult for the company to observe relevant information in advance. Therefore, the turnover caused by OJ may make companies caught off guard.

The total effect of BFT variable is -0.07, but its effect is significant only at the level of 0.10. Hypotheses H17, H18, and H19 receive only slight support. This shows that professional managers of small and medium-sized private enterprises will consider the relevant employer factors in the selection of employment, but the degree of emphasis is not too high. They value the organizational factors more. Compared with the employer's own attractiveness, they think organizational attraction is the most important. These managers have realized that it is not wise to simply tie one's future destiny to someone. The impersonal organization system is more reliable. Therefore, even if the boss personally treats the subordinates somewhat unfairly, or doesn't trust the manager much, but if the organizational conditions are still satisfactory, there is nothing wrong to stay in such a company. Of course, this also reflects that at this stage, managers of private enterprises in China are mostly very rational and their career planning will not be affected by certain individuals. This result shows that, as far as direct influence is concerned, the general conclusion that professional managers in Western companies place more emphasis on the organization's own factors also applies to Chinese private enterprises. This also reflects that Chinese companies and employees have made some progress in the "modernization" process. Despite this, as pointed out above, the employer factor in small and medium-sized private enterprises cannot be ignored, and the structural equation model can only examine the influence of one aspect. We will examine its regulatory effects on relevant organizational factors in the next chapter. At the same time, we will conduct group inspections according to the manager's background characteristics and company characteristics, to test whether this key variable has a different influence on certain types of managers.

The overall effect of CR variable is 0.06 ($p<0.05$). It is in line with the expected result has strongly supported hypothesis H10. This to a certain extent verifies the "impact" effect emphasized in the Lee and Mitchell (1994) model. It shows that professional manager will also be "impacted" due to CR, and thus have the turnover intention. Our structural model also reveals that this factor functions indirectly, which means that CR does not directly lead to turnover. When the manager perceives that the CR is about to occur, he will first search for other jobs. If the collected information indicates that the turnover is more favorable, he will eventually leave the company. CR will make people feel upset, in which situation the managers often look for other jobs. If the organization can't eliminate this mentality of employees, it will inevitably lose a lot of excellent talents in the process of transformation.

The coefficient of JC variable is -0.04 ($p<0.05$), which supports the hypothesis H11. The managerial group, the upper-level employees, values the freedom to control the work process. We believe that, on the one hand, the value orientation of such employees determines that they will regard JC as their own needs. Enjoying higher JC means higher status and more trust. This can be partially proven from the results given in Table 5-7. The correlation coefficient shows that JC has an indirect effect on turnover intentions through JSC ($\xi=0.17$, $p<0.05$), JFC ($\xi=0.18$, $p<0.05$) and JA ($\xi=-0.22$, $p<0.01$). Professional managers are mostly at the top of the talent market. They have higher quality, stronger ability, and are full of self-confidence. If they do not have enough power to control their own work processes, they have no "right to speak" with matters related to themselves. Then, their job satisfaction will inevitably be declined, and loyalty to the organization will also be weakened. On the other hand, JC contributes to the accumulation and improvement of human capital of professional managers, and the development of higher-level management capabilities requires more "discretionary space". Higher JC allows managers to have more room for "free play". This training can improve the ability to adapt to higher management positions, and enhance the "employability" in the market. Therefore, it is easy to conclude that both will affect the final turnover decision of the manager.

The coefficient of JI variable is -0.03 ($p<0.05$). It supports the hypothesis H1a. It shows that the managers' view on work behavior itself and their willingness to work hard will affect their turnover intention. When managers see work as a dispensable thing in their lives, they can easily make a turnover decision when the job is slightly unsatisfactory. From Table 5-7, we can see that higher JI will increase the JSC ($\xi=0.26$, $p<0.001$), increase JFC ($\xi=0.15$, $p<0.05$), and ultimately reduce turnover intention. Employees with high JI regard the work itself as the top priority in life, and as their main source of fun. Under other conditions unchanged, such managers will have higher job satisfaction and organizational commitment. Work enthusiasm is also higher. The importance of having a job makes it gratitude to organizations that can provide him with opportunities to perform work activities (Lance, 1991) and thus has a high degree of commitment (Ravichandan, 2015). In addition, to examine more influence effects of this factor, we will use the Logit model in the next chapter, to test its regulatory effect on the relevant direct antecedent variables.

BLH, BCI, SR and EM have not been validated in the structural model of this chapter. As we pointed out earlier, the effects of BFT variable are only slightly supported ($p<0.10$), and BLH and BCI have not been found to be significant for managers' turnover intentions. This shows that at this stage, the professional managers of small and medium-sized private enterprises do not directly consider the factors of employers when choosing for employment. The most important factors are the organizational factors such as salary, fairness, corporate image, as well as work factors. For example, the BCI is the spiritual reward that bosses give to managers. It's a kind of informal encouragement. While managers do not think that this can replace formal organizational incentives. These results mean that managers are mostly rational decision-makers, and they will not simply link their future and destiny to certain individuals. The appeal of impersonal organizations is even more important. That is, even if the employer's leadership is insufficient, and the manager is not paid special attention by the boss, as long as the company's incentive system and development opportunities are relatively favorable, there is no reason not to stay. Of course, as will be demonstrated by the test of regulatory effects in the next chapter, although employers do not have these direct effects, they will have a regulatory effect on the relationship between organizational factors and turnover intentions, which we cannot easily ignore.

The construct of SR has no effect in this sample, and does not support hypothesis H7. This result shows that managers' choices are more "pragmatic" in nature. If the organizational conditions such as income and development opportunities are attractive enough, even if the SR is not good, the managers do not care. Of course, SR, the "soft" environment appeal, will take longer to realize its value. Shorter employees may not be aware of this. As shown in Table 5-1, the average length of service of middle managers in the sample is less than 3 years. However, employees who stay in the company for a long time will care more and more about the company's interpersonal environment. If an organization wants to retain good talent for a long time, this factor must not be overlooked.

The influence of EM is also not significant, and does not support hypothesis H3a. This means that at this stage, the career development goals of most SME managers are still to be "professional managers". Managers with higher turnover intentions do not think of being self-employed in the future, but think of going to another company. In the next chapter, we will examine how this variable modulates other influencing factors, and will classify them by age and position. In this way to examine whether there are different effects of EM on different categories of managers. The latter results will show that EM has a significant positive impact on turnover intentions for middle and senior managers. This means that high-ranking managers do leave the company under the impulse of self-employment, which verifies the results of our previous investigations and qualitative research.

In addition, the relevant measurement items of career growth opportunities and matching degree, as revealed by EFA, cannot satisfy the validity requirements. Their impact on turnover intentions has not been examined in this study. However, as the relevant hypotheses pointed out in Chapter 4, there is a large body of literature that confirms the predictive power of these two constructs. Therefore, the next step of the study needs to re-design the measurement items in terms of both content validity and convergence effectiveness, to test their effectiveness in predicting the turnover intention of managers.

Summary

In this chapter, the process model of the turnover intention of professional managers, obtained by applying the structural equation model method, shows that the turnover decision of professional managers of small and medium-sized private enterprises follows a certain process and sequence. Managers firstly perceive relevant individuals, organizations, employers, jobs, and other job opportunities. This decline in perceived satisfaction is reflected in job initiatives on job satisfaction, organizational commitment etc., which in turn lead to turnover intention.

The standardized path coefficients given by SEM indicate that JL has a very significant effect on turnover intention of managers; and JA also has a significant impact on turnover intention. In addition, JSC significantly affect JFC and JA. There is no significant relationship between JFC and JA; the relationship between JSC and JL is not significant, indicating that their influence on turnover intention is mainly transmitted indirectly through JA variables. In addition, BCI, JC, JI and SR have significant effect on managers' JSC; BLH, BFT, JC, JI and JE have significant effect on JC; BCI, JP and JC have significant effect on employers' JA; BCI, JC, JE, PC and CR directly affect JL; and JP and OJ have direct and significant effect on turnover intentions.

According to LISREL's influence-effect decomposition, in terms of total effects, apart from JFC, BLH, BCI, SR and EM, the other 12 variables have significant effect on the turnover intention of managers. Among them, JA, JL and OJ affect turnover intention in a direct way;

JP and PC affect turnover intention both directly and indirectly; and all other variables indirectly affect turnover intention.

Chapter 6

Further Empirical Research on the Influencing Factors of Manager Turnover

Based on above results, we further examine some important aspects of influencing factors of manager turnover. The following include robustness tests, moderating effects tests. In addition, although turnover intention is the best predictor of turnover behavior (Murray and Zimmerman, 2005), many studies have found that lots of employees who have shown turnover intention do not actually leave the company (Allen et al., 2005). As empirical studies on the influencing factors of turnover behavior require longitudinal data, it is difficult to conduct investigations on such problem directly. However, the main purpose of the turnover study is to predict and prevent possible turnover. It becomes a key issue that whether the turnover intention is consistent with the actual turnover behavior. In this book, a method under existing research conditions was put forward, to examine the consistency of turnover intention and turnover behavior in the sample.

Robustness Test of Empirical Results

1. Importance and satisfaction degree ranking of influencing factors

As shown in Table 6-1, in terms of direct subjective evaluation of managers, the five factors most important to their job selection are: BLH, BFT, OSC, SR and JFC. In terms of satisfaction degree, only the ranking of managers' perceptions on relevant organizational work factors is given. The five factors with highest satisfaction degree are: BLH, SR, JC, BFT AND OSC.

Table 6-1 The Importance and Satisfaction Degree Ranking of Influencing Factors

Sort by importance				Sort by satisfaction			
Variables	Mean of importance	Standard deviation	Ranking	Variables	Mean of satisfaction	Standard deviation	Ranking
BLH	6.03	1.03	1	BLH	6.18	1.01	1
BFT	6.03	1.07	2	SR	5.50	1.05	2
OSC	5.91	1.03	3	JC	5.41	1.11	3
SR	5.83	0.97	4	BFT	5.23	1.37	4
JFC	5.79	1.10	5	OSC	4.53	1.40	5
JSC	5.76	0.91	6	BCI	4.52	1.40	6
JC	5.72	0.96	7	JP	3.26	1.44	7
BCI	5.43	1.19	8				
JI	5.36	1.21	9				
PC	5.08	1.27	10				
JP	5.02	1.44	11				
EM	4.95	1.60	12				
RA	4.91	1.31	13				
VI	4.84	1.31	14				
OJ	3.45	1.93	15				
JE	2.95	1.93	16				

Note: There is no differential test for the mean ranking in the table, so the statistical significance of this order is not guaranteed.

2. Robustness test based on OLS and Logit model comparison

In order to ensure the reliability of the empirical results, we designed two different indicators to measure the variable of turnover intention in questionnaire (see the questionnaire given in Appendix 2 for details). One is that "I hope to work in the company until retirement" (Q8, Likert 7 Measurement), the other is that "I plan to spend my entire career in the company" (Q28, the answer should be "Yes" or "No"). In the following, we apply the two variables to construct the OLS and Logit Discrete Dependent Variable Models, and directly introduce the mediating variables and the antecedent variables into the test program, respectively to examine the robustness of the related influence effects. Since the model studied here does not consider the mediating effect of related variables, the conclusions may be different from the previous chapter, so the results are only of reference significance. Our main goal is to verify the reliability of the main empirical results of the previous chapter by comparing two different models that use different measure methods.

The construction of OLS model is: $y_i = x_i'\beta + \varepsilon_i$, where y_i is the explained variable, refers to the turnover intention of i (measured by Q8), x_i refers to the relevant influencing factor vector introduced into the model. The effects of direct antecedent variables (that is, the mediating variables in the model of previous chapter) and antecedent variables are examined here.

The construction of OLS model is: $P(Y=1) = \frac{e^{\beta' X}}{1+e^{\beta' X}}$, where Y refers to turnover intention, from the measurement of Q28. $Y=1$ indicates the manager leaves the current job, $Y=0$ indicates the manager doesn't leave the current job. $P(Y=1)$ refers to the probability that an individual 'i' may go to 'turnover'. X is the matrix of relevant influencing factors.

The above two models are estimated using Eviews 5.0 software (see Table 6-2 for related results). It is easy to see that the effects of the two model-related factors are almost identical, which shows that the main empirical conclusions of this book are very reliable, and that the turnover intention reported by managers in the sample shows sufficient internal consistency. What needs to be emphasized again is that the effect of the previous dependent variable is different from that found in the SEM model of the previous chapter. The main reason is that the former does not consider the mediating effect of related variables, and results of structural equation model are more significant for management practice.

Table 6-2 Robustness test results

OLS			Logit		
Variables	Model 1	Model 2	Variables	Model 3	Model 4
Constant term	3.777***	9.260***	Constant term	2.197*	7.145***
JFC	-0.158		JFC	-0.357**	
JSC	-0.206**		JSC	-0.343**	
JA	0.150**		JA	0.253***	
JL	0.619***		JL	0.460***	
OSC		-0.217***	OSC		-0.267**
BLH		0.010	BLH		-0.009
BFT		-0.151*	BFT		-0.267*
BCI		-0.042	BCI		-0.006
JP		-0.063	JP		0.022
EM		0.099*	EM		0.237***
PC		-0.556***	PC		-0.759***
JC		-0.093	JC		-0.005
JI		-0.085	JI		-0.390***
SR		0.058	SR		0.165
OJ		0.092*	OJ		0.139*
JE		-0.110**	JE		-0.122*
CR		0.172	CR		-0.245
Adj. R^2	0.313	0.326	McFad. R^2	0.192	0.293
F stat.	56.737***	19.115***	LR stat.	119.321***	189.888***
N	491	487	N	459	475

Note: "*" indicates being notable at the level of 0.10, "**" indicates being notable at the level of 0.05, and "***" indicates being notable at the level of 0.01 (the same below).

3. The marginal effects of the influencing factors in Logit model

The marginal effect of the corresponding variables on the turnover probability is not shown in model 3 and model 4. It can be calculated by the following formula:

$$\frac{\partial[y|x]}{\partial x}=\frac{e^{\beta' X}}{1+e^{\beta' X}}[1-\frac{e^{\beta' X}}{1+e^{\beta' X}}]\beta \quad (6\text{-}1)$$

Table 6-3 Marginal Effects of Logit Model

Variables	Marginal effects	Standard error
Constant term	0.529	0.278
JFC	-0.086	0.036
JSC	-0.083	0.040
JA	0.061	0.022
JL	0.111	0.021

The marginal effect of an explanatory variable is related to the values and coefficients of all explanatory variables. In order to give specific values, we calculate the relevant marginal effects based on the mean of all direct antecedent variables based on model 3, and the results are listed in table 6-3. Results find that when the manager's JFC increases by 1 unit at the average, the probability of turnover decreases by 8.6 percentage points; for every 1 unit of increase in JSC, the turnover probability decreases by 8.3%; for every 1 unit decline in JA, the probability of turnover increases by 6.1%; for every 1 unit of increase in JL, the probability of turnover increases by 11.1%.

Test of Moderating Effect

1. The moderating effect of personal factors on attitude variables

Logit Discrete Dependent Variable Model is used to examine the moderating effects of related factors. The first type of moderating effect comes from the five personal variables, namely JI, PC, EM, RA and VI. Their moderating effect on the two direct antecedent variables of JA and JL is taken to consideration. Table 6-4 shows the relevant results.

It's shown in table 6-4 that the moderating effect of JI and PC are strongly supported; EM, RA and VI are partially supported. Specific explanations are given below:

Table 6-4 Moderating Effects of Individual Factors

Variables	Model 1	Model 2	Model 3	Model 4	Model 5
C	0.727	0.648	0.439	0.447	2.265*
JSC	-0.247	-0.280*	-0.177	-0.210	-0.382**
JFC	-0.196	-0.151	-0.203	-0.171	-0.324**
JA	1.055***	0.225***	1.487***	0.246***	0.108
JL	0.432***	1.059***	0.387***	1.317***	0.449***
JA*JI	-0.149***				
JL*JI		-0.113***			
JA*PC			-0.226***		
JL*PC				-0.172***	
JA*EM					0.028
McFad. R^2	0.208	0.213	0.234	0.249	0.192
LR stat.	128.527***	131.903***	144.856***	154.115***	118.4232***
N	456	456	456	456	455

Table 6-4 Moderating Effects of Individual Factors (Continued)

Variable	Model 6	Model 7	Model 8	Model 9	Model 10
C	2.482**	1.618	2.225*	1.945*	2.085*
JSC	-0.389**	-0.325**	-0.360**	-0.319**	-0.335**
JFC	-0.350**	-0.289*	-0.341**	-0.328*	-0.332**
JA	0.244***	0.685***	0.249***	0.581***	0.252***
JL	0.214*	0.445***	0.458***	0.437***	0.610***
JL*EM	0.047***				
JA*RA		-0.086**			
JL*RA			-0.001		
JA*VI				-0.067*	
JL*VI					-0.037
McFad. R^2	0.200	0.198	0.189	0.195	0.193
LR stat.	123.649***	122.375***	116.752***	120.611***	119.269***
N	455	456	456	456	456

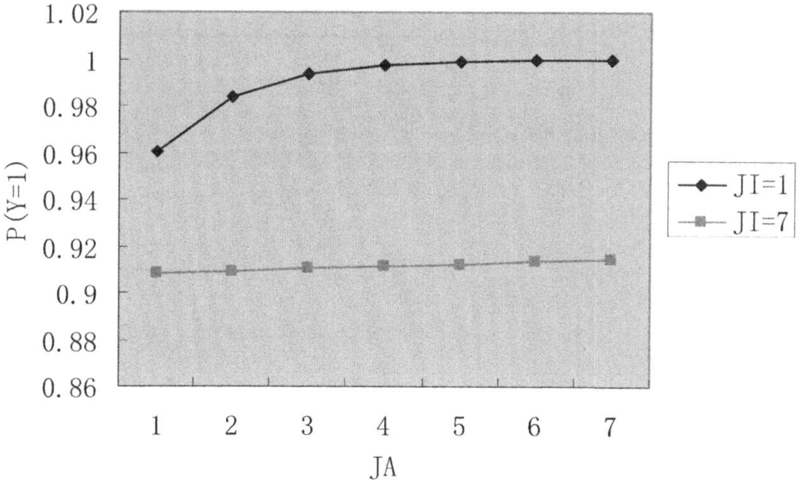

Figure 6-1 Moderating Effect of JI on JA (-)

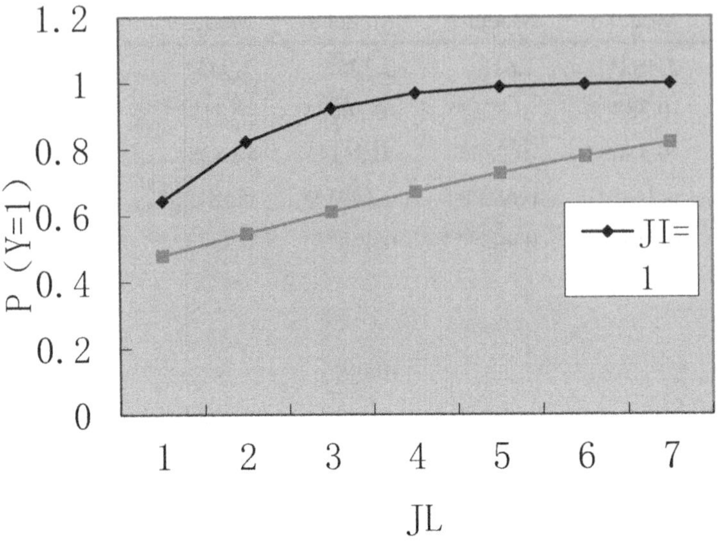

Figure 6-2 Moderating Effect of JI on JL (-)

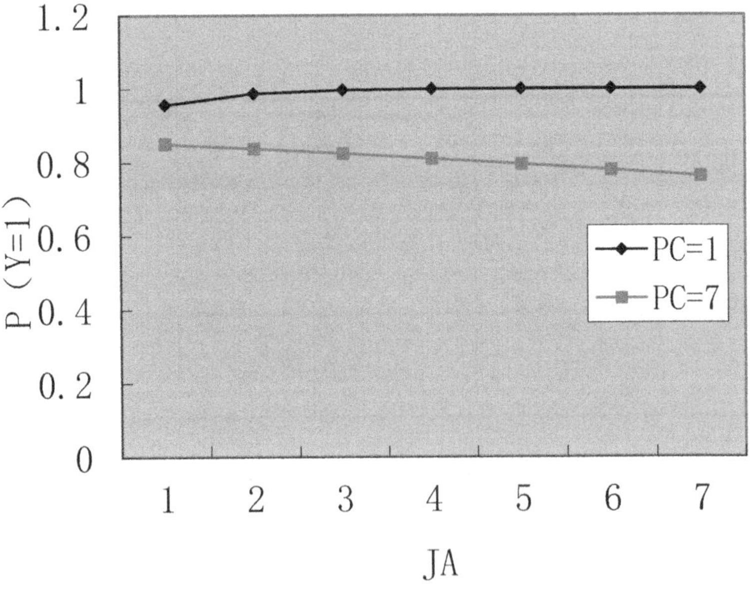

Figure 6-3 Moderating Effect of PC on JA (-)

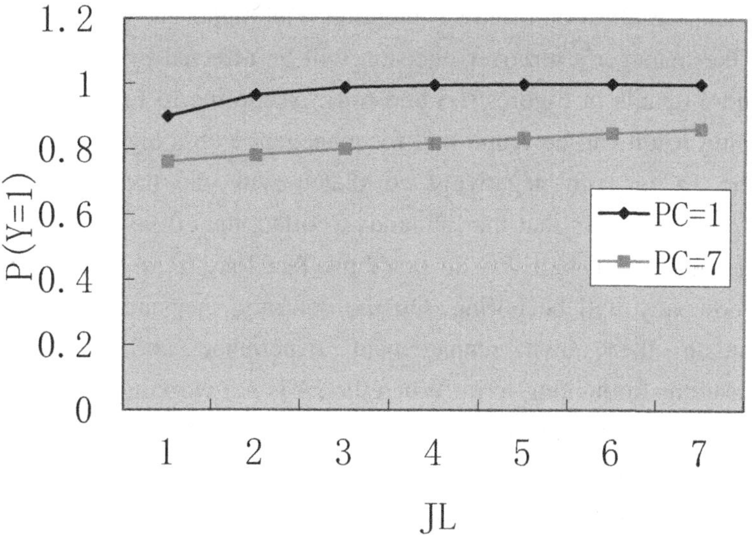

Figure 6-4 Moderating Effect of PC on JL (-)

The moderating coefficient of JI on the relationship between JA and turnover intention is -0.149, and on the JL is -0.113. Both are consistent with the hypotheses, and both are notable at the 0.01 level, supporting the hypothesis of H1b. This result shows that JI not only has a direct impact on the turnover intention of managers, but also eases the relationship between JA, JL and turnover, that is: the higher the JI, the less likely the managers with poorer JA and high JL will resign (see more details in Figures 6-1 and 6-2). The reason is that the highly involved managers regard work as the top priority in their lives. Their main pleasure comes from the work itself. Therefore, even if some other reasons may worsen their JA, and they might start to find other jobs. In the end they are likely not to leave the current job. The fear of unemployment of such managers sometimes offsets the dissatisfaction brought about by other factors.

The moderating coefficient of PC on JA is -0.226, and on JL is -0.172. Both are consistent with hypotheses, and both are notable at the level of 0.01, strongly supporting the hypothesis H2b. This result shows that PC tends to mitigate the effect of the related direct antecedent variables on turnover intention. The higher the PC, the less likely the manager's turnover decision will be affected by JA and JL (see more details in Figures 6-3 and 6-4). According to Figure 6-3, a surprising result can be found that for managers with a high degree of PC, the JA is even negatively correlated with the probability of turnover. This shows that the PC tends to offset the effect of declined JA. Managers with high PC do not think that long-term work in the same company will be boring. On the contrary, they are willing to accumulate their own management experience and personnel qualifications in the long-term. When the JA is not working well, even if they are interested in looking for OJ, their unwillingness to "move" will urge them to act cautiously. Not a last resort, such managers will not easily leave their long-serving company.

The moderating coefficient of EM on JA is not that much notable, but on JL is 0.047, which is in line with expectations and is notable at the level of 0.01. This result has partially supported the hypothesis H3b. Results show that EM increases the sensitivity of the relationship between JL and turnover intention, that is, for managers with strong EM, once they plan to seek OJ, their turnover probability will greatly increase (compared to managers with lower EM) (see more details in Figure 6-5). The main reason for this result lies in that if the manager JSC is reduced due to the organization, the employer, or the work factors, which inspires him to look for OJ, then, even if no better job is found, as the manager has already had plans to start their own businesses, they may eventually resign. In addition, results also show that EM does not aggravate the positive correlation between JA and turnover intentions, that is, managers with strong EM do not resign more rashly because of poor JA.

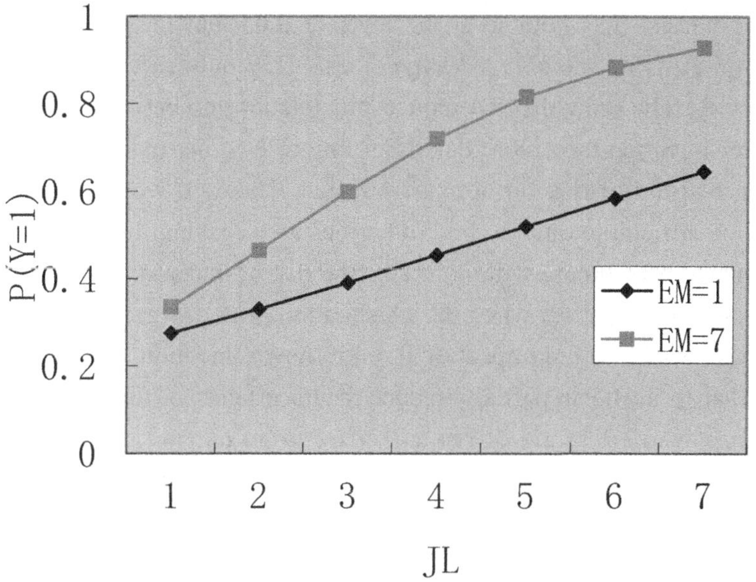

Figure 6-5 Moderating Effect of EM on JL (+)

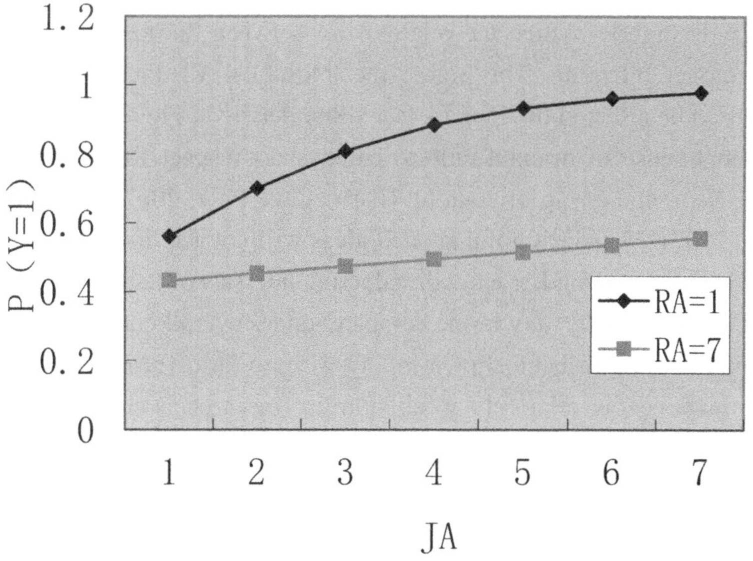

Figure 6-6 Moderating Effect of RA on JA (-)

The moderating coefficient of RA to JA is -0.086, consistent with the hypothesis. It is notable at the level of 0.05, but the moderating effect on JL is not notable. The hypothesis H29 only receives partial support. Results show that RA reduces the relationship between JA and turnover intention (see more details in Figure 6-6), ie, managers who are more afraid of risk do not easily resign. They are worried that it would be difficult to quickly find other jobs after leaving the company. Only managers who are willing to take the risk of uncertainty can dare to try other possibilities when the JA situation goes down. In addition, RA does not reduce the impact of JL on turnover intention, which may mean that JL itself can partially reduce the uncertainty of future events. Managers who are afraid of risk also dare to go out for a try. Future studies need to further distinguish which specific factors offset the impact of RA, and to reveal more deeply the interaction between RA and JL.

The moderating coefficient of VI to JA is -0.067, consistent with the expectation, but it is only notable at the level of 0.10. At the same time, its moderating effect on JL is not notable. Therefore, the hypothesis H28 is only slightly supported. Results show that the degree of VI will slightly reduce the relationship between the manager's JA and turnover intention. The higher the traditional VI, the less likely they are to be affected by their JA (see more details in Figure 6-7). The traditional sense of oriental culture emphasizes respect for authority, collectivism, and group orientation (Farh et al., 1997, 2007; Chen and Aryee, 2007). Managers holding such ideas will not act "individualism" when they are in poor JA. He will value the interests of the company's group, and eventually stay in the company under overall consideration. This finding has not been shown in any western turnover model. This result, however, is relatively weak. Further research is necessary to continue to examine its moderating effects, especially for those managers who are older and have more traditional ideas.

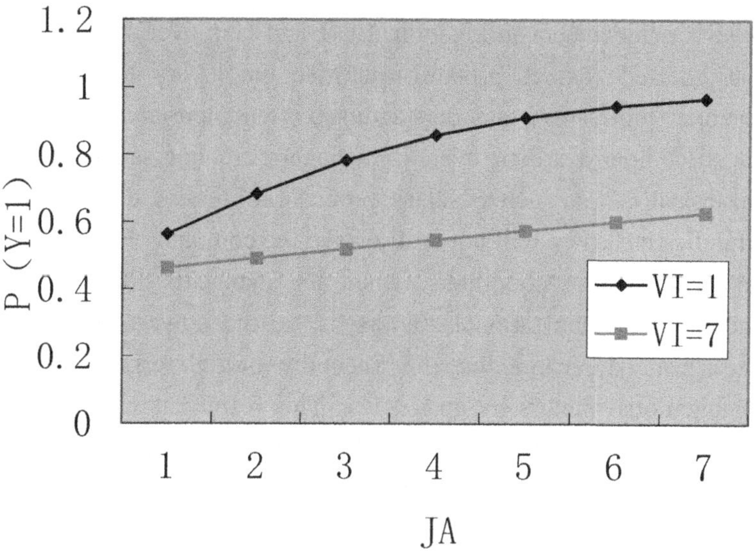

Figure 6-7 Moderating Effect of VI on JA (-)

2. Moderating effect of employers' factors on organizational factors

The moderating effect of BLH, BFT and BCI (Employers' Factors) on OSC (organizational factors) is examined in this research. The results presented in table 6-5 show that the moderating effects of BLH and BFT on organizational factors are empirically supported. The moderating effect by BCI is not notable.

Two of the three employers' factors have a notable moderating effect on organizational factors. The hypothesis H30 is fully supported. First, the moderating coefficient for employer leadership is 0.291, consistent with the hypothesis. It is notable at the 0.05 level. Results show that employers' leadership can weaken the negative relationship between organizational factors and turnover intention. This means that the stronger the self-employment leadership of employers in small and medium-sized private enterprises, the less likely they are to be affected by organizational factors (see more details in Figure 6-8). Based on the factor structure given in the previous chapter, this construct includes the related test items of three primary variables, respectively employer's achievement motivation, BLH and employer's honesty. It can be inferred that if private enterprise employers have strong achievement motivation and outstanding entrepreneurial ability, and follow strict honesty, then even if managers are not satisfied with organizational factors such as salary, procedural fairness, development opportunities etc., they will not easily leave the company. From Figure 6-8 under the same conditions, when the managers feel that the satisfaction of organizational factors is at the lowest level, the employer leadership can reduce the probability of high turnover caused by organizational factors by up to 40%. This result has not yet been there in the western turnover model. In the social context where the market system is relatively complete and the individualism tradition prevails, the employer's own characteristics will not have a material impact on the subordinate's rational decision. The interests of the latter may be protected by the rules and regulations of the law, organization rules, and contracts and do not have to tie this on some individuals.

Table 6-5 Moderating Effects of Employers' Factors

Variables	Model 1	Model 2	Model 3
C	15.390***	10.363***	7.636***
OSC	-2.122**	-0.962 **	-0.377
BLH	-1.278**	-0.015	-0.012
BFT	-0.260*	-0.806**	-0.261*
BCI	-0.013	0.001	-0.125
JP	0.035	0.038	0.024
EM	0.238***	0.238***	0.237***
PC	-0.781***	-0.794***	-0.762***
JC	-0.015	-0.007	-0.002
JI	-0.434***	-0.420***	-0.394***
SR	0.173	0.126	0.168
OJ	0.137*	0.145**	0.139*
JE	-0.094	-0.124*	-0.121*

Variables	Model 1	Model 2	Model 3
CR	-0.208	-0.210	-0.240
OSC* BLH	0.291**		
OSC* BFT		0.132***	
OSC* BCI			0.025
McFad. R^2	0.300	0.298	0.293
LR stat.	194.788***	193.000***	190.048***
N	475	475	475

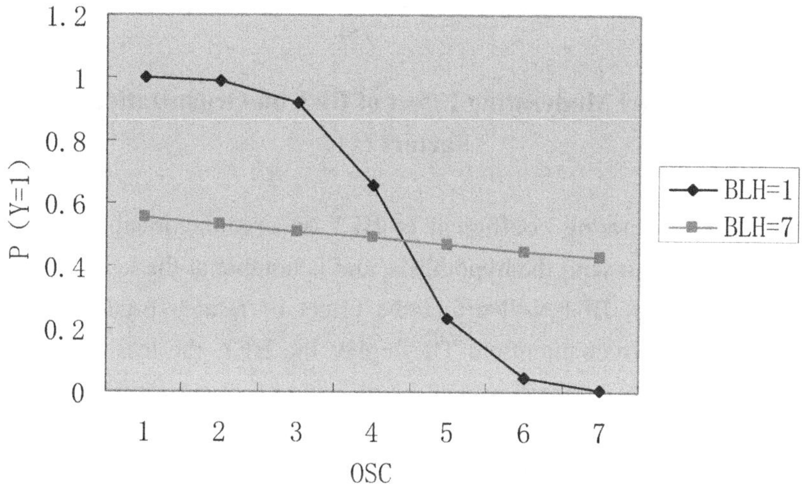

Figure 6-8 Moderating Effect of BLH on Organizational Factors (+)

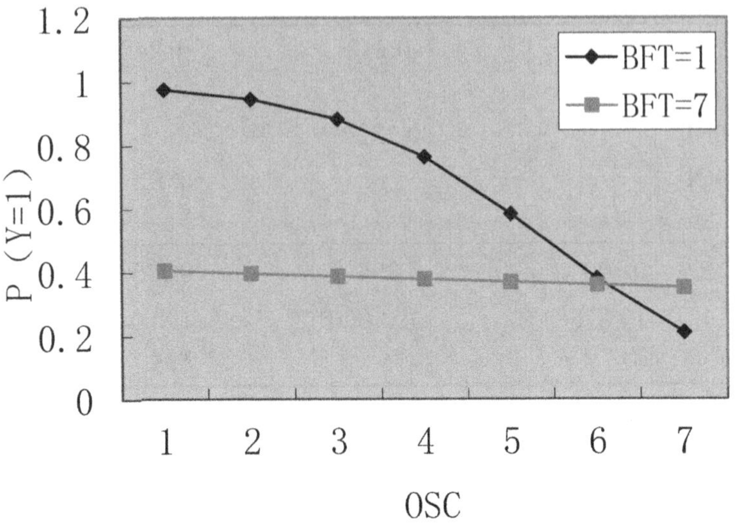

Figure 6-9 Moderating Effect of BFT on Organizational Factors (+)

The moderating coefficient of BFT on organizational factors is 0.132, consistent with the hypothesis, and is notable at the level of 0.01 It indicates that BFT will affect the effect of related organizational factors on turnover intention. The higher the BFT, the less likely the manager's turnover decision is to be affected by organizational factors (see more details in Figure 6-9). Even if the manager perceives that certain organizational factors are not attractive enough, he will receive some psychological compensation from the sense of fairness and trust given by the boss. As can be seen from Figure 6-9, BFT can reduce the probability of turnover by up to about 60%. This shows that employers can indeed play an important role in preventing manager turnover.

Findings have shown some obvious management implications. It means that there are many ways for small and medium-sized private enterprises, which have significant gaps with large enterprises or foreign-funded enterprises in terms of salary, development space, and corporate image, to enhance their attractiveness. If the business owner does have a desire to do an excellent job, then by improving his entrepreneurial ability and integrity management, while trusting his subordinates, the disadvantages of his organizational attractiveness will be offset by the attractiveness of the employer. And excellent managers will not go away when they are not satisfied.

Grouping Regression Results

1. Regression results grouped according to demographic background

Table 6-6 Regression Results Grouped by Population Background

Variables	Group by gender		Group by marriage		Group by age		Group by work position
	Female	Male	unmarried	Married	<30	≥30	Grassroots
C	4.969**	7.715***	5.833***	10.775***	6.105***	9.155***	5.680***
OSC	-0.385*	-0.304*	-0.402***	-0.143	-0.288**	-0.233	-0.435**
BLH	0.584*	-0.161	-0.085	0.486	0.193	0.058	0.132
BFT	-0.710***	-0.072	-0.025	-0.988***	-0.198	-0.976***	-0.116
BCI	-0.186	0.173	-0.001	-0.163	-0.097	0.303	-0.182
JP	-0.118	0.094	-0.070	0.323*	-0.013	0.261	-0.265*
EM	0.181	0.377***	0.195*	0.233	0.161	0.296*	0.199
PC	-0.701***	-0.880***	-0.682***	-1.150***	-0.769***	-1.075***	-0.752***
JC	0.216	-0.163	-0.087	-0.006	-0.044	0.001	-0.040
JI	-0.382*	-0.424**	-0.296*	-0.308	-0.487***	0.039	-0.256
SR	0.441*	-0.015	0.335	-0.251	0.372*	-0.335	0.484**
OJ	0.213	0.142	0.214**	0.099	0.093	0.273*	0.191
JE	-0.038	-0.101	0.009	-0.163	0.003	-0.099	-0.147
CR	-0.414	-0.092	-0.145	-0.649	-0.095	-0.787	0.108
McFad. R^2	0.256	0.367	0.227	0.465	0.253	0.468	0.242
LR stat.	58.53***	148.70***	78.36***	121.57***	101.36***	100.54***	67.22***
N	173	294	275	192	306	156	221

Table 6-6 Regression Results Grouped by Population Background (Continued)

Variables	Group by work position	Group by total length of service		Group by length of service in current company		Group by education	
	Middle and senior	<5 years	≥5 years	<2 years	≥2 years	< undergraduate	≥undergraduate
C	9.162***	5.441***	8.431***	6.120***	9.266***	6.072***	8.641***
OSC	-0.018	-0.407**	-0.136	-0.259	-0.320*	-0.101	-0.518**
BLH	-0.061	0.659**	-0.353	0.359	-0.375	0.200	-0.333
BFT	-0.751***	-0.397	-0.268	-0.340	-0.227	-0.306*	-0.287
BCI	0.390*	-0.183	-0.017	-0.247	0.350*	-0.056	0.161
JP	0.331**	-0.255	0.248*	-0.115	0.203	0.099	-0.187
EM	0.266**	0.196	0.222*	0.240*	0.138	0.232**	0.305**
PC	-0.925***	-0.638***	-0.911***	-0.672***	-1.055***	-0.691***	-0.843***
JC	0.172	0.035	0.155	-0.139	0.145	0.031	-0.205
JI	-0.491**	-0.699***	-0.173	-0.319*	-0.554***	-0.537***	-0.215
SR	-0.377	0.434*	-0.157	0.201	0.223	0.068	0.476*
OJ	0.098	0.241*	0.116	0.258**	0.039	0.116	0.206
JE	-0.053	-0.167	-0.067	0.010	-0.231**	-0.102	-0.096
CR	-0.715	0.195	-0.414	-0.328	-0.194	-0.325	-0.193
McFad. R^2	0.428	0.298	0.354	0.277	0.375	0.283	0.322
LR stat.	141.61***	76.82***	122.56***	85.12***	116.92***	108.25***	78.75***
N	239	200	250	231	225	276	188

Table 6-6 shows the Logit regression results after the samples are grouped according to the demographic background. Here, only the effects of factors that influence organizations, individuals, employers, and work are examined, so these variables are directly introduced into the model. According to the results in the table, in addition to OSC, PC, and JI, the influence of other factors in each group is not consistent.

Relatively speaking, females are more likely to value employers' factors such as BLH, BFT, and the "soft" environmental appeal like the company's SR; while males are less sensitive to these factors, and EM is a crucial factor affecting male managers' turnover intention. This means that companies need to pay attention to managers' different preferences based on gender differences. Strengthen corporate culture and enhance interpersonal interactions, to improve the company's SR. This is necessary to attract outstanding female managers; at the same time, there must be sufficient space within the company for male managers to play their entrepreneurial spirit. Otherwise, they will leave the organization because they have other opportunities.

Results grouped by marital status indicate that organizational conditions, entrepreneurial motives, and OJ are the main factors that are considered by unmarried managers during the turnover decision process; employer equity and trust and job pressure (+) are significantly affecting married managers. The reason for this discrepancy is that unmarried managers are mostly in the early stages of their career development, their career choices are still in an unstable period, the career prospects are not yet clear, and the more "real" realistic conditions the company issues are more likely to attract them. In addition, most of the unmarried managers have joined the company not long ago. Their sense of belonging and loyalty to the organization has not yet been established. Once other companies give more favorable material conditions, or there are opportunities for self-employment outside the company, they will resign without hesitation. Relatively speaking, married managers do not care much about these visible temptations. They are more concerned about whether the boss treats subordinates fairly and are willing to believe in themselves. There is an important managerial implication here, that is, when arranging the company's core positions, it can be appropriately tilted toward married people. In addition, we have also found that job pressure will increase the turnover intention of married people, which is different from the results of the previous chapter's full-sample process model. This may be related to the increase in the burden of family affairs on married managers. With other conditions remain unchanged, such employees are even more reluctant to bear higher job pressure.

Results of grouping by age show that managers under the age of 30 pay more attention to organizational conditions and SR; managers over the age of 30 value more for BFT. EM and OJ also have a significant impact on their turnover intentions. Comparing the results by grouping according to the marital status, it tells that younger and unmarried professional managers really value organizational factors such as pay, development space and procedural fairness; while older and married managers tend to choose job mainly based on employers' factors such as BFT. This needs to attract the attention of entrepreneurs. When designing related professional manager turnover management measures, it is necessary to treat different types of managers differently, and to meet the special needs of various managers as far as possible under the premise of minimizing the total cost. In addition, results find that EM and OJ also have an impact on the turnover decision of older managers. This indicates that for managers who have already accumulated certain career development, they may want to try their own business at the peak of their career, to seek a career breakthrough.

Results of grouping by work position show that in the company, grassroots managers pay more attention to OSC and the company's SR; while middle and senior managers pay more attention to employers' factors such as BFT, BCI etc. Meanwhile, EM significantly affects the turnover intention of middle and senior employees. Compared with the previous analysis, due to the low level of work position, it is difficult for grassroots managers to get in touch with the boss frequently. In the early stage of their career development, grassroots managers are less likely to value employers' factors. Instead, they are more concerned with organizational factors such as the salary, organizational systems, and development prospects. In contrast, middle and senior managers have opportunities to communicate with their bosses frequently. Employers' personal accomplishments and their appreciation and care for themselves can have a major impact on their turnover. What's more, the EM of middle and senior managers also significantly affects their turnover intentions. Once they have the impulse to start a business, they can transform entrepreneurial enthusiasm into actual action. Based on these findings, it can be concluded that if SMEs want to retain talented senior managers, it is not enough to rely solely on salary, position, and other material attractions. The entrepreneur's own capabilities may be even more important.

According to the grouped regression results for the total length of service, relatively short-term (<5 years) managers value organizational conditions, BLH, SR, and OJ. For those employees who have extensive work experience, JP and EM make it easier for them to generate turnover intentions. This is like the result of grouping by age, and the reason is nearly the same.

Results of grouping by the length of service in current company show that new employees (less than 2 years) will mainly consider OJ and entrepreneurial possibilities when making turnover decisions, while older employees (more than 2 years) care more about factors like OSC, BCI and JE. One possible explanation can be that new employees have not formed the sense of belonging and loyalty to the organization in the company, and their other links with the company (JE) have not yet been established, so once there are other better job opportunities, or there is the possibility of self-employment, they will show a higher turnover intention. Relatively speaking, older employees with longer service years have developed a sense of belonging (if the organization does have enough attractiveness). They have learned whether the boss will appreciate himself and care about his own interests. Meanwhile, they have already established links with other members of the company. Therefore, their turnover decisions are more susceptible to these factors. If the manager is satisfied with this perception, he will not resign in spite of many other better job opportunities. Here, the management refers to that the best strategy for retaining new employees is to allow him to quickly recognize the company's competitive advantage in the labor market, and make him difficult to find other better alternatives quickly. The strategy to retain old employees in the company is more complicated. The manager already has a full understanding of the company and the external labor market, only when the organizational conditions are attractive and the boss also shows enough concern and care, these managers will be willing to stay in the company for a long time. Of course, the personal relationship established by working long hours in the company can also play a role in preventing them from turnover.

Results of grouping by education indicate that relatively low-educated managers pay more attention to BFT when make turnover decision, while high-educated managers (undergraduate and higher) pay more attention to OSC and company atmosphere. EM has a significant effect on the turnover intention of both parties. The reason for this is difficult to tell. Further research is needed to examine differences in other characteristics caused by educational levels, and then to explain the role of education in moderating relevant factors.

2. Regression results grouped by company characteristics

Table 6-7 Regression Results Grouped by Company Characteristics

Variables	Group by asset size		Group by fixed number of years of the company	
	＜40 million	≥40 million	＜10years	≥10years
C	9.976***	5.902***	6.431***	8.861***
OSC	-0.386	-0.265*	-0.317*	-0.157
BLH	-0.287	0.145	0.027	-0.087
BFT	-0.064	-0.290	-0.318*	-0.043
BCI	-0.046	0.058	-0.103	0.172
JP	-0.328*	0.194*	-0.080	0.140
EM	0.276*	0.225**	0.271**	0.204
PC	-0.729***	-0.781***	-0.676***	-0.889***
JC	-0.139	0.008	0.016	-0.093
JI	-0.124	-0.547***	-0.397**	-0.425**
SR	-0.037	0.226	0.354*	-0.349

Variables	Group by asset size		Group by fixed number of years of the company	
	<40 million	≥40 million	<10years	≥10years
OJ	0.080	0.192**	0.095	0.238**
JE	-0.128	-0.103	-0.024	-0.149
CR	-0.102	-0.407	-0.306	-0.309
McFad. R^2	0.279	0.319	0.254	0.377
LR stat.	48.51***	143.21***	79.27***	112.72***
N	132	326	233	217

It shows in the Table 6-7 that in grouped regression by asset size, JP, EM and PC have notable impact on the turnover intention of all kinds of managers, while OSC, JI and OJ only have notable impact on the turnover intention of managers of larger companies. The reason lies in that the organizational conditions of small companies are not superior to other companies. Employees are already very aware of this before they enter the organization. Once they choose to come to such small companies, they will not excessively consider the organizational factors. Unless there is a lack of PC and a strong EM, or there is too much JP, otherwise they not resign from the company. Relatively speaking, larger companies can improve their organizational conditions to increase their attractiveness. If the salary, development space, and human capital investment they offer are lower than the manager's expectation, the manager will understand it as that the company treat unfairly to him. Therefore, employees will compare the conditions provided by the company with other companies during the turnover decision process. This result means that larger enterprises need to improve and maintain the attractiveness of the organization. Otherwise, once other companies have created better conditions, the situation for managers who are not treated well in current company may easily result in "job-hopping".

Results of grouping by fixed number of years of the company show that managers of shorter-established companies (<10 years) are more likely to be influenced by OSC, BFT, EM, and SR in the process of turnover decision, while managers of longer-established companies (≥10 years) are less sensitive to these factors, whose turnover decision is mainly affected by OJ. New businesses are generally small and weak in strength, but they are full of vigor and vitality. Managers of such companies have already learned about this before they enter. Once they choose to work in this company, it means either they prefer to work in start-ups, or they do not have enough capacity to enter long-established companies. In this case, they may not consider the impact of OJ when he is choosing a job for the second time. On the contrary, long-established companies have been in operation for many years. If its conditions are inferior to other companies, this means that their development prospects are pessimistic. Therefore, managers are more concerned about the attractiveness of other companies when they make turnover decisions. In addition, managers in start-up companies have more contact with the bosses. The employee knows very well whether the employer trusts him or not, and has a deep understanding of the boss's behavior and abilities. If they think their ability is not inferior to the boss, they may start their own business under the drive of EM.

3. Management implications

The above results are of great significance to management practices.

First, the problem of professional manager turnover in SMEs is different for different individuals or different companies. It is not possible for companies to adopt the same set of measures to manage the turnover of all managers. It is sensible to deepen understanding, treat differently, and truly "target" the retention of managers.

Second, individuals with different demographic characteristics have different preferences in the turnover decision process, and companies can design an early warning mechanism of manager turnover based on the population information they have mastered. In this mechanism, the company can adjust job arrangements as appropriate according to the turnover possibility, so as to retain managers of important positions.

Third, as demographic information and individual variables have predictive power for managers' turnover, the company can initially determine the turnover probability when the employee enters the organization. Therefore, employers can make comprehensive evaluations based on relevant organizations, work, and personal information, and recruit only the most suitable employees. For the best talents in the labor market, if companies do not have confidence in retaining them in the future, then they don't need to waste too much effort on them during the recruitment phase.

Finally, small and medium private enterprises are not naturally unattractive. For a certain type of manager, small enterprise has an advantage instead. If the employer in small enterprises has grasped the employees' preferences and expectations, and give full play to his own skills, small and medium-sized private enterprises are also competitive in the battle for talent.

Predicting Effect of Turnover Intention on Turnover Behavior

1. Research meaning and methods

Although turnover intention is the best predictor of turnover behavior (Murray and Zimmerman, 2005), many studies have found that lots of employees who have shown turnover intention do not actually leave the company (Allen et al., 2005). Existing literature shows that the explanatory power of turnover intention on turnover behavior rarely exceeds 10%-15% (Griffeth et al., 2000; Hom and Griffeth, 1995). As empirical studies on the influencing factors of turnover behavior require longitudinal data, it is difficult to conduct such continuous investigations. Therefore, most of the turnover documents are based on turnover intention, and indirectly examine the influencing factors affecting turnover behavior. This study can help employers to predict several important effect variables to some extent. However, the main purpose of the turnover study is to predict and prevent possible turnover. It becomes a key issue that whether the turnover intention is consistent with the actual turnover behavior.

In this book, a method under existing research conditions was put forward, to examine the consistency of turnover intention and turnover behavior in the sample. First, respondents were asked to report their perception on related organization, employer, work, and other factors in previous company. Evaluating information on previous company from the managers who have had prior turnover experience was collected, and then was combined to current manager's perception of relevant variables in current company. In this way, variance analysis method can be used to study the statistical difference in perception of related variables between managers who have turnover intention (i.e., managers who want to leave the company now, hereinafter referred to as the A-type manager) and managers who have turnover experience (i.e., managers who have left the previous company, hereinafter referred to as the B-type manager). If the perception of relevant factors does not show a systematic difference between the two, it can be initially assumed that the prediction of turnover intention is highly consistent with turnover behavior.

This study tries to use the Logit Discrete Variable model to directly test the influencing factors of turnover behavior. It compares the relevant results with turnover intention model to determine whether the prediction effects of the two are consistent. Specifically, managers who have worked continuously in the company for more than four years are set as "at work" (for the current company), and their relevant perception variables on the current company are measured. Managers with turnover experiences are set as "out of work" (for the former company), and the relevant perceived variables on the former company are measured. A sample of this can be used to test the factors affecting the turnover behavior. Although this act may face the recall biases pointed out by Kammeyer-Mueller et al. in 2005, under existing conditions, it is of certain reference value to compare this conclusion with the relevant conclusion (total effect) in the structural equation model. Based on this, it can be determined that if the turnover behavior is consistent with the prediction of turnover intention.

2. ANOVA

Table 6-8 shows the descriptive statistics for the main antecedent variables. Table 6-9 gives the results of ANOVA. Table 6-10 shows the test results of variance homogeneity. From the results of ANOVA, except for OSC, BCI and JP, other mean values of factors perception show significant differences between the A-type and B-type managers ($p<0.05$). According to the comparison of these mean values (refer to Table 6-8), combined with the action direction of related factors from the SEM turnover model, we try to test: whether the relevant influencing factors which can predict turnover intention can also predict turnover behavior?

Table 6-8 Descriptive Statistics of Related Factors Perception of Current and Previous Company

Variables		N	Mean	Std. Dev.	Std. Err.	95% Confidence Interval for Mean Low. Bound	Upp. Bound
OSC	0[a]	283	4.047	1.343	0.080	3.890	4.204
	1	408	4.251	1.448	0.072	4.110	4.392
	Total	691	4.167	1.408	0.054	4.062	4.272
BLH	0	282	5.887	1.131	0.067	5.755	6.020
	1	406	5.078	1.308	0.065	4.950	5.205
	Total	688	5.410	1.300	0.050	5.312	5.507
BFT	0	283	4.725	1.403	0.083	4.561	4.889
	1	405	4.400	1.446	0.072	4.259	4.541
	Total	688	4.534	1.436	0.055	4.426	4.641
BCI	0	283	4.165	1.348	0.080	4.007	4.323
	1	405	4.376	1.415	0.070	4.238	4.514
	Total	688	4.289	1.390	0.053	4.185	4.393

Variables		N	Mean	Std. Dev.	Std. Err.	95% Confidence Interval for Mean	
						Low. Bound	Upp. Bound
JP	0	283	3.474	1.356	0.081	3.316	3.633
	1	406	3.597	1.312	0.065	3.469	3.725
	Total	689	3.546	1.331	0.051	3.447	3.646
JC	0	283	5.098	1.143	0.068	4.964	5.232
	1	406	4.883	1.301	0.065	4.756	5.010
	Total	689	4.971	1.242	0.047	4.878	5.064
SR	0	283	5.209	1.087	0.065	5.081	5.336
	1	408	4.734	1.312	0.065	4.606	4.861
	Total	691	4.928	1.246	0.047	4.835	5.021
OJ	0	284	2.729	1.774	0.105	2.522	2.936
	1	404	3.906	2.215	0.110	3.689	4.123
	Total	688	3.420	2.123	0.081	3.261	3.579
JE	0	283	2.297	1.762	0.105	2.091	2.503
	1	405	2.607	1.932	0.096	2.419	2.796
	Total	688	2.480	1.869	0.071	2.340	2.620
CR	0	282	0.727	0.446	0.027	0.675	0.779
	1	360	0.578	0.495	0.026	0.527	0.629
	Total	642	0.643	0.479	0.019	0.606	0.681

Note: a and "0" refer to sample of managers who have turnover intention in current company, relevant statistics are based on perception of the current company; "1" refers to sample of managers who have had turnover experience, and related statistics are based on perception of the former company

Table 6-9 ANOVA Results from Consistency Test of Turnover Intention and Turnover Behavior

		Sum of Squ.	df	Mean Squ.	F	Sig.
OSC	Betw. Groups	6.940	1	6.940	3.511	0.061
	Within Groups	1361.879	689	1.977		
	Total	1368.819	690			
BLH	Betw. Groups	109.136	1	109.136	71.122	0.000
	Within Groups	1052.669	686	1.535		
	Total	1161.805	687			
BFT	Betw. Groups	17.625	1	17.625	8.639	0.003
	Within Groups	1399.527	686	2.040		
	Total	1417.152	687			
BCI	Betw. Groups	7.433	1	7.433	3.861	0.050
	Within Groups	1320.674	686	1.925		
	Total	1328.107	687			
JP	Betw. Groups	2.494	1	2.494	1.409	0.236
	Within Groups	1216.395	687	1.771		
	Total	1218.889	688			
JC	Betw. Groups	7.721	1	7.721	5.033	0.025
	Within Groups	1053.921	687	1.534		
	Total	1061.642	688			
SR	Betw. Groups	37.673	1	37.673	25.104	0.000
	Within Groups	1033.980	689	1.501		
	Total	1071.652	690			
OJ	Betw. Groups	231.054	1	231.054	55.294	0.000
	Within Groups	2866.549	686	4.179		
	Total	3097.603	687			
JE	Betw. Groups	16.070	1	16.070	4.625	0.032
	Within Groups	2383.645	686	3.475		
	Total	2399.715	687			
CR	Betw. Groups	3.519	1	3.519	15.661	0.000
	Within Groups	143.797	640	.225		
	Total	147.316	641			

Table 6-10 Variance homogeneity test

Var.	Levene Statistic	df1	df2	Sig.
OSC	2.617	1	689	0.106
BLH	9.064	1	686	0.003
BFT	1.282	1	686	0.258
BCI	2.221	1	686	0.137
JP	0.063	1	687	0.802
JC	7.008	1	687	0.008
SR	12.170	1	689	0.001
OJ	27.689	1	686	0.000
JE	7.730	1	686	0.006
CR	61.248	1	640	0.000

OSC is an important predictor of turnover intention. The mean value of A-type managers is 4.047, which means that managers who are less satisfied with OSC, below the mean value, are likely to show willingness of turnover. Correspondingly, the mean value of B-type managers is 4.251, which means that for managers who have left the former company, their satisfaction with it is below the mean value. ANOVA shows that there is no significant difference between them on the mean value level of 0.05. The variance homogeneity test in Table 6-10 also guarantees the reliability of this result. Therefore, it can be argued that OSC has the same predictive effect on turnover intention and turnover behavior.

In terms of BFT, the mean value for A-type managers is 4.725, for B-type managers is 4.400. They have notable difference on the level of 0.05. Results show that managers whose satisfaction coefficient on BFT is less than 4.725, they show more turnover intention, and this intention to be converted into an actual turnover behavior will require a lower degree of satisfaction (<4.400). If other conditions remain the same, and a manager's perception degree of BFT lies between these two values, the manager will show out turnover intention, but in the end the manager may not have real turnover behavior. The management implications of this discovery are that once employees' JA is found to be declining, and they are frequently concerned with information from other companies, the company should take relevant measures as soon as possible, to stop them taking actual turnover behavior. The mean value differences of the following variables can be similarly analyzed.

The perception of JP has no significant difference between A-type and B-type managers. This means that it has the same interpretation effect on turnover intention and turnover behavior. This variable has passed the variance homogeneity test, so this result is reliable.

As for JC, the mean value of the A-type managers (5.098) is higher than the B-type managers (4.883), and the difference is notable at the 0.05 level. This shows that JC can predict whether a manager has turnover intention, but may not be able to predict the turnover behavior. As the ANOVA of this variable does not pass the variance homogeneity test, the result may not be reliable.

As for OJ, the mean value of A-type managers is 2.729, lower than the 3.906 of B-type managers, and is notable a 0.05 level. This result shows that the perception of OJ, which can induce the incumbent manager to generate turnover intention, does not necessarily lead to the final turnover behavior, unless the perception is increased to more than 3.906. This variable does not pass the variance homogeneity test, so this ANOVA result is not necessarily reliable.

As for JE, the mean value of the A-type managers (2.297) is lower than the B-type managers (2.607), and is notable a 0.05 level ($p<0.05$). This result means that managers who have a JE level of less than 2.297 will not only show their turnover intention, but they are also very likely to realize this intention. In the statistical sense, as long as the value is less than 2.607, the turnover behavior will happen. This shows that there is consistency in turnover intention and turnover behavior, but this result does not pass the variance homogeneity test, so it is not necessarily reliable.

As for CR, the mean value of the A-type managers (0.727) is higher than the B-type managers (0.578). If the CR in a company triggers a manager turnover, the change is likely to prompt eventual turnover behavior. There is consistency between turnover intention and turnover behavior, but it should be noted that this result has not passed the variance homogeneity test.

In conclusion, when predict turnover intention and turnover behavior, only OSC and JP show a reliable consistency. That is, if a certain professional manager reports the perception of relevant factors, and it can predict the turnover of employees, then, the manager is very likely to turn to turnover behavior. Although the JE and CR also show consistency, due to failure to pass the variance homogeneity test, the result may not be reliable. The ANOVA results for the other three factors are also unreliable. Therefore, the hypothesis H31 is only partially supported. The next section uses the Logit model for further investigation.

3. Logit regression model

Table 6-11 shows the Logit regression results with the dependent variables of turnover intention and turnover behavior. It indicates among the 7 significant variables, only BLH, OJ, JE reflect consistency in the two models. This again proves the hypothesis H31 is only partially supported. It is also worth noting that the variables that show consistency in the regression model are not the same as those given by ANOVA. Therefore, our analysis is not necessarily reliable. Longitudinal data should be applied to conduct more rigorous study on influencing factors of turnover behavior.

Table 6-11 Comparison of Logit Regression Results

Explanatory variables	Explained variables	
	Turnover intention	Turnover behavior
C	5.766***	6.216***
OSC	-0.289***	0.095
BLH	-0.286*	-0.807***
BFT	-0.338***	-0.057
BCI	-0.023	0.377***
JP	0.084	-0.038
JC	-0.142	-0.320***
SR	0.019	-0.211*
OJ	0.139**	0.303***
JE	-0.145**	-0.124**
CR	-0.008	-0.234
McFad. R^2	0.187	0.231
LR stat.	123.186***	124.787***
N	483	477

Summary

This chapter first examines the robustness of econometric model, two different measures of turnover intention are used, OLS and Logit models are introduced to examine the reliability of the model. Results show that the significance of the two influencing factors in two models is almost identical, which indicates that the main empirical conclusions of this book are very reliable. In the sample, the turnover intention reported by managers shows sufficient internal consistency. The process model and factor model given earlier provide a reliable basis for proposing practical management recommendations. Also based on the Logit mode, the marginal effect of relevant factors on turnover intention is calculated. The results clearly reflect the direct influence of the four mediating variables on turnover intention.

The moderating effect test has examined two types of effects. One is the moderating effect of individual factors on attitude variables, and the other is the moderating effect of employers' factors on organizational factors. Results of the first type of effect test show that the moderating effect of the two personal variables, JI and PC, has been strongly supported. Effect of EM, RA and VI has only been partially supported. This means that personal factors play a very important role in the relationship between related organizations, jobs, employers, attitude variables and turnover intention. Organizations can apply certain human resources measures (such as recruitment, induction training, organizational socialization process, etc.) to reduce turnover rate.

The second type of moderating effect test shows that BLH and BFT have moderating effect on the relationship between organizational factors and turnover intention, while the moderating effect of BCI is not notable. This means that managers' perception of employers' own factors will affect the moderating effects of other factors. This is beneficial to small and medium-sized private enterprises, which have significant gaps in terms of salary, development space, and corporate image with large-scale enterprises or foreign-funded enterprises. There are many ways to improve their attractiveness. If the employers do have a desire to do a great job, improve their entrepreneurial ability and integrity management, while at the same time trust their subordinates, then the disadvantages will be offset by their attractiveness, and managers will not easily go away.

Results of grouping regression based on population statistics show that relatively speaking, females value more of the "soft" environmental attraction such as BLH, BFT, and SR, while males have a low sensitivity on these factors. EM is an important factor affecting male managers' turnover intention. OSC, EM and OJ are the key considerations for unmarried managers in the process of making turnover decisions. BFT and JP (-) significantly affect married managers. Managers under the age of 30 pay more attention to OSC and SR. For managers over the age of 30, they pay more attention to BFT, and EM and OJ also have a significant impact on their turnover intention. Grassroots managers pay more attention to OSC and SR; while middle and senior managers care more about employers' factors such as BFT and BCI. EM also significantly affects the turnover of middle and high-level employees. Managers with a short working experience (<5 years) pay more attention to OSC, BLH, SR and OJ. For employees with rich work experience, JP and EM make it easier for them to leave their jobs. New employees in the company (<2 years) will mainly consider OJ and start-up possibilities when leaving a job, while older employees (more than 2 years) who have a longer service age in the company, will be more concerned with OSC, BCI, JE etc. Less-educated managers care more about BFT, while highly-educated managers (undergraduate and higher) pay more attention to OSC and SR when making turnover decisions, and EM has a significant impact on both of them.

Results of grouping by company characteristics find that JP, EM and PC have significant effects on managers of different company sizes. OSC, JI and OJ only have significant influence on the turnover intention of managers in large companies. Managers of shorter-established companies (<10 years) are more likely to be affected by OSC, BFT, EM and SR, and managers of longer-established companies (≥10 years) are less sensitive to these factors, whose turnover decisions are mainly influenced by OJ.

In the last part, the predictive effect of turnover intention on actual turnover behavior is studied. It is important to carry out this research. Although turnover intention is the best predictor of turnover behavior (Murray and Zimmerman, 2005), there are also many studies that found that many employees who have shown turnover intention do not eventually leave the job (Allen et al., 2005). Therefore, it's importing to make clear that if the turnover intention will be translated into actual turnover behavior? And will a manager who shows a higher turnover intention really leave? Longitudinal data are needed to test it.

It is difficult to obtain such data under existing conditions, so the book conceived a method to try to examine it. The results comparison of ANOVA and Logit model shows that the consistency of turnover intention and turnover behavior is only partially supported, but as pointed out in the text, due to limited conditions, this analysis here is not rigorous enough, so the relevant results only have reference value. A more reliable study of the relationship between turnover intention and turnover behavior requires the use of longitudinal data.

From this chapter and the empirical analysis of the previous chapter, most of the research hypotheses are empirically supported. Table 6-12 summarizes the relevant results.

Table 6-12 Empirical Supporting Status for All Hypotheses

Hypotheses	Empirically supported or not	Hypotheses	Empirically supported or not	Hypotheses	Empirically supported or not
H1a	Supported	H9	Not be tested	H21	Not be tested
H1b	Supported	H10	Supported	H22	Supported
H2a	Supported	H11	Supported	H23	Supported
H2b	Supported	H12	Supported (-)	H24	Supported
H3a	Not supported	H13	Not be tested	H25	Not supported
H3b	Partly supported	H14	Not supported	H26	Supported
H4	Supported	H15	Not supported	H27	Supported
H5	Supported	H16	Not supported	H28	Partially supported
H6a	Supported	H17	Supported	H29	Partially supported
H6b	Supported	H18	Supported	H30	Supported
H7	Not supported	H19	Supported	H31	Partially supported
H8	Supported	H20	Supported		

Chapter 7

Economic Explanation on the Turnover of Professional Managers

The process and causes of the turnover of professional managers have been empirically examined in previous chapters, that is, the voluntary turnover decision of professional managers is influenced by many people, organizations, employers, and jobs in reality. Therefore, it seems it is very easy to propose corresponding governance mechanisms and measures for private enterprises. If the significant variables given by the model are improved, it is sufficient to improve the relevant influencing factors, to increase the attractiveness of the organization, and thus retain the excellent professional managers. However, the problem is far from simple. The actual SMEs need to consider the cost of doing so while trying to enhance their attractiveness. Sometimes it is optimal to maintain the status quo. For example, increasing remuneration packages to retain professional managers will directly increase personnel costs. If a manager with turnover intention stay in the company, the expected benefits are not sufficient to offset its salary costs. Then the business owner will consider it as a trade-off. It is not worthwhile to raise salary for this manager. Therefore, on the one hand, professional managers attach immense importance to those factors that we pointed out above. If their perceptions are not satisfactory, the turnover intention will inevitably be enhanced. On the other hand, companies believe that improving these factors will "get more out of gain", and maintain more turnover intention will be more favorable.

Therefore, the question that needs further exploration is: Why do managers value these factors regarding their personal welfare? Why are business owners not willing to improve these factors as much as possible to reduce managers' turnover intention, and prefer to maintain this equilibrium? Is there a way to break this equilibrium and achieve a "win-win" relationship between enterprises and managers? In this chapter we will apply rigorous economic analysis tools, refer to research results in sociology, social psychology and other related fields, and try to answer it theoretically.

The analysis will show that most private enterprises have such profound economic and social roots to maintain such equilibrium, where employers value managers' ability and loyalty, and managers place importance on positions and monetary returns. The turnover of professional managers and the family-based business management is equilibrium between managerial abilities and loyalty information asymmetry. The adverse selection caused by asymmetric information makes it difficult for professional managers to enter the core management groups of private enterprises, and the operation of the enterprises is degraded to a closed mode dominated by family members. Most of the family-clan business researchers in the past only described the phenomenon of family-owned business, and to some extent proved the advantages and disadvantages of family-style management. This is far from enough, and we still need to find a way to solve related problems. Since the family model is a kind of equilibrium, it is necessary to find the economic and social reasons that support this "inefficient" equilibrium first, and then on this basis, it is necessary to propose countermeasures to change the equilibrium to help retain professional managers and achieve the "win-win" match between private entrepreneurs and professional managers.

Specifically, this chapter will be based on the two-dimensional space matching between private enterprises and professional managers. Under the hypothesis of information asymmetry, it proves that the turnover of professional managers and the familization of private enterprises is equilibrium. It will show that only by changing the reasons behind the support of the equilibrium, can the "familism predicament" be breached under the condition that the private enterprise and the professional manager participate in the restraint and incentive compatibility constraint. In addition, the interaction between private enterprises and managers on this basis will be introduced, and then a three-period dynamic information disclosure model will be established. This model means that information disclosure caused by mutual interaction can alleviate information asymmetry to some extent, to improve the equilibrium in the static model. But as we will see, Pareto optimal perfect match is difficult to achieve. This means that business owners need to be very cautious when they consider abandoning the familism model and introduce many external management resources to adopt a modern company management system.

Two-dimensional Space Matching between Private Enterprises and Professional Managers

1. The particularity of the human capital transaction between Chinese private enterprises and professional managers

The human capital transactions between Chinese private companies and professional managers are not entirely based on instrumental contracts. Unlike companies in Western contract societies, Chinese private companies and even overseas Chinese companies involve more issues related to personal conduct in the process of introducing professional managers. The goal of the company is to find professional managers who are talented and loyal. Only those managers with superior abilities and good loyalty will be entrusted with important tasks and occupy important positions. Those with outstanding abilities but misbehaving managers have become the main "keep away" targets for business owners (Zheng, 1995). Correspondingly, the pursuit of Chinese professional managers in enterprises also has its own specific features. Although ordinary managers in Western societies also consider positions and power when pursuing their own professional success (Herriot and Pemberton, 1994), professional managers in China appear to be considering more. In addition to pursuing salary gains, the level of the ranks, the distance from the core, the importance of positions, and so on are all important considerations.

As the motivations and needs of both sides of the human capital transaction include special dimensions, the market trading rules that are prevalent in the Western world are difficult to apply to transactions between Chinese employers and professional managers. Although theorists and practitioners have noticed this problem either intentionally or unintentionally, but frankly, we still know little about it. There is no systematic theory that can explain the unique phenomena of Chinese companies such as clan patterns, clan predicaments, parenting styles, and pan-familization. In order to find efficient Chinese enterprise management model (Chu, 2000, p479), such a theory is indispensable.

Classical market theory sees human capital transactions as an exchange of similar elements such as capital and land. The core point is that in equilibrium, the labor force just gets its marginal product value as compensation. Although it is not explicitly pointed out, as production is related to the productivity of the labor force, this theory implies that the real object of human capital transactions is the workers' ability to complete production tasks - the services of the production process, while the employer's payment is the market price of labor. This theory excludes the specificity of the transaction of human capital transactions and other factors, and incorporates human capital transactions into classical price theory.

With the introduction of human capital theory, people have noticed that the labor force and other factors of production are not the same after all. It has the characteristics of heterogeneity and marginal return. And because the labor force is attached to the "living" human body, the knowledge, skills, health, morality, reputation, and social relations and other factors will all affect their supply and demand. Human capital not only requires investment to be accumulated, but also needs to be motivated to obtain its services (Zhou, 1996). The theory of human capital has taken note of the particularity of human capital transactions, focusing on the resulting property rights characteristics, subjective initiative, and the transaction costs of human capital transactions within the company (Zhang, 2001). This helps us understand Chinese private enterprises and occupations. The nature of human capital transactions between managers has certain significance. However, it is important to point out that transactions based on the characteristics of human capital are always carried out under the guarantee of the western contract society. Formal and informal institutional environments make it possible for the human capital transactions of senior managers in the Western world to be completed in a sound market. The elements involved in the transaction are also mainly the manager's ability and the company's currency payment. The transaction between private enterprises and professional managers in China is obviously not so simple. It is more specific in many aspects.

The relational characteristics of China society have resulted in the complexity of transactions and cooperation between individuals at various levels of relationship (Fei, 2005). The private entrepreneurs of the "embedded" social system must pay attention to the influence of "relationships" when they hire employees. Here, because "people on their own side are reliable", when there are not enough "people on their own side" in a company, the introduction of external management resources becomes the only way for the company to continue to grow (Li, 2002). However, due to lack of general trust (Fukuyama, 1998; Li, 2002, etc.), employers have doubts about "outsiders" such as professional managers. In addition to considering the outsiders' capabilities, private enterprises need to consider the moral integrity and loyalty (Zheng, 1995; Huang, 2004), after all, "outsiders are not reliable".

It is necessary to specify this point. Many studies on family-clan businesses in China have talked about the employers' trust in professional managers. What needs to be emphasized is that compared to Western companies, the reason of why has trust been a problem faced by Chinese private companies, is that managers' individual behavior cannot be achieved through external formal or informal systems, and internal monitoring systems are well-constrained, managerial position occupation (Chu and Liu, 2005) and malicious betrayal (Zhang, 2002) occur from time to time. Due to differences in the level of social development and cultural traditions, China's formal systems such as legal systems, credit systems, and informal social networks can hardly guarantee the professional conduct of managers. However, internal control systems are often difficult to truly prevent them in advance. As a result, employers of private enterprises can only rely on the expectation of managers' individual cultivation. Here, Eastern cultural traditions require individuals to "build from the inside out" to cultivate their body and mind, and then the concept of "family, rule, and peace" has a very significant impact on modern society (Liang, 2005). Entrepreneurs cannot restrain the managers' behavior by the outside pressure. Instead, they can only hope that the managers' own moral character is noble. Therefore, the human capital transaction between Chinese private enterprises and professional managers has one more dimension: loyalty. The core nature of this dimension is that it is difficult to observe and measure beforehand and only through actual interaction can partial understanding be achieved.

From a professional manager's point of view, their goal for transaction is also different from that of Western society managers. In addition to pursuing monetary gains, Chinese managers also value their position and power in the company. Of course, we are not saying that managers in Western society do not pursue positions of authority and status. We mean that this is particularly evident in Chinese managers, and there is a profound social and historical reason. First, feudalism of thousands of years has created the "official-level" consciousness in people's minds. "Officer" with high positions and power is a symbol of dignity, status, and reputation. "Being an officer" is a "a matter of face" (Huang, 2004). As this consciousness being reflected in the company, managers excessively pursue high positions. Secondly, the aforementioned relationship-oriented features of Chinese society make professional managers from the outside look for ways to enter the "internal," and preferably become members of the family or the Pan family. Being in a key position can bring the employee closer to the core of the family, and to a certain degree be the "people of their own side". Finally, the incompleteness of the macro-micro system has led managers with certain real powers to gain direct control gains. Some managers believe that even if the nominal income is not high, if the position and power are high and strong enough, the hidden income is also very substantial.

In summary, we can use the dimensions of loyalty (l) and ability (a) to characterize the quality of professional managers. This is the demand of private companies for professional managers. The two dimensions of status (s) and remuneration (r) are used to describe the return that the enterprise gives to the professional managers. This is reflected in the goal and needs of professional managers to conduct human capital transactions (see Figure 7-1). It should be noted that the "s" variable is a broad concept. It is a comprehensive indicator that includes the dimensions of the rank hierarchy, work importance, distance to the core, size of real power, level of secrecy, etc. (Zheng, 1998; Chen, 1998). The two two-dimensional spaces formed by this setting are used to study the matching issue between private enterprises and professional managers.

2. Match between private enterprise and professional manager

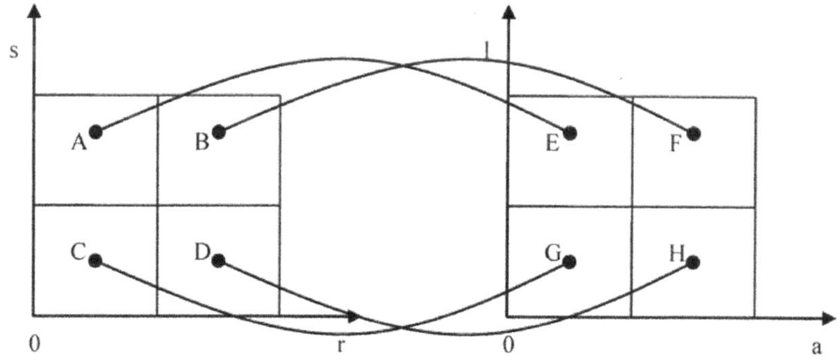

(a) The return of professional managers (b) The quality of professional managers

Figure 7-1 Two-dimensional Space Matching in Professional Managers' Human Capital Transactions

For ease of analysis, we temporarily divide the professional managers' quality and return space into four regions (Figure 7-1). In the reporting space, A-zone refers to giving managers lower income, but allows them to stay in higher positions; B-zone means high salary and high positions; C-zone means low salary and low positions; D-zone means high salary and low positions. In the quality space, in accordance with the classification process and category archetypes of Zheng (1995), the managers in the E-zone are relatively loyal but lack of ability. They are suitable to serve as the "eye liner" of the employer. The managers in the F-zone not only have superior capabilities, but also are loyal to the employer. They can be the "business partner" of the employer. The managers in the G-zone are not capable enough and have low loyalty. They can only be regarded as the "edge persons" of the company. The managers in the H-zone have good capabilities, but not loyal. They are possible to "betray" employers at any time, and are the objects of "keep away" in the company.

Based on the above analysis, it is easy to understand that when employers of private enterprises hire external professional managers, they will arrange corresponding positions and remuneration according to the quality of professional managers. In general, the most important and core positions will only be open to those loyal and honest managers, as these posts are related to the company's lifeline. Those managers who are not capable enough but are highly loyal to the boss will get some positions that are closer to the family-clan core. Even if their remuneration is not high, the psychological feeling of being close to the boss is also a excellent job incentive. Managers with outstanding ability, but not enough loyalty, generally do not get higher positions. On the contrary, they will be guarded from time to time. Usually, employers will only use high salary as an incentive. As for those managers who lack capacity and complain all day, they are only the marginal figures of the company. These people bear the brunt of the layoffs (Zheng, 1995). This series of matching relations is represented by the arc connection in Figure 7-1.

Obviously, employers' consideration of their optimal return arrangement based on their own interests depends on the full information hypothesis, that is, the employer must know which zone of the professional space a certain professional manager belongs to. However, the reality is not the case. Employers do not fully understand the manager's ability or even his loyalty. This asymmetry of information will make it difficult to achieve the aforementioned optimal matching. As a result, on the one hand, employers don't believe in "outsiders" when information is incomplete, which makes them not dare to easily open important positions to outside professional managers. On the other hand, managers with high loyalty and capacity prefer the position and power of the company. If they are not satisfied with position and power, they will leave. What's more, the information asymmetry of capabilities will also limit its monetary income. As a result, the operation of private enterprises is returned to the governance mode, which is fully controlled by the family. The most important positions are left to the "trustworthy" ones, and some less-important positions are given to those who are "edge people". This idea is modeled below.

Adverse Selection Process in Human Capital Transactions of Professional Managers

1. Basic settings

For mathematical analysis, we first make some preliminary settings for the model. As mentioned above, the quality of professional managers is characterized by two dimensions: loyalty and ability. In the coordinate system shown in Figure 7-2, there is a certain substitute relationship between the requirements of the managers for the loyalty and ability. This is represented by the company's indifference curve $J = J(l, a)$, but when l is too low, the two are irreplaceable. Extremely unfaithful managers have no value in the eyes of employers. This is easy to understand because an unfaithful manager may pose a great threat to the company.

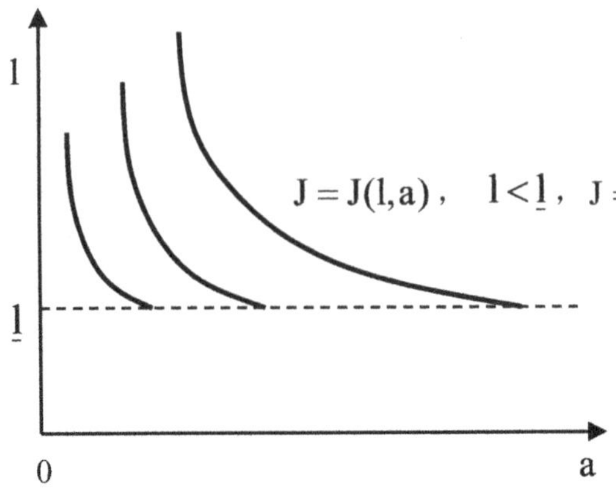

Figure 7-2 Preference of Private Enterprises in Quality Space

Correspondingly, we give the manager's indifference curve in the return space of Figure 7-3 ($\pi = \pi(r,s)$), and the return curve that the company gives managers $B(r,s)$. As we will see, this return curve is given by the employer based on the value function of the manager ($J(l,a)$), and the joint probability distribution of professional manager loyalty and ability, which forms the constraints faced by managers. The manager will solve the following questions:

$$\underset{r,s}{\mathrm{Max}}\, \pi(r,s)$$

$$\text{s.t. } B(r,s) \le E \qquad (7\text{-}1)$$

It is worth noting that, corresponding to the previous analysis, the positions and returns in the returns curve provided by the company can only be replaced within a certain range ($s < \bar{s}$). For some managers, even if only a very low salary is required, the employer will not compensate for high positions. On the contrary, for those "trustworthy" outstanding managers, the company will them both higher position and higher pay.

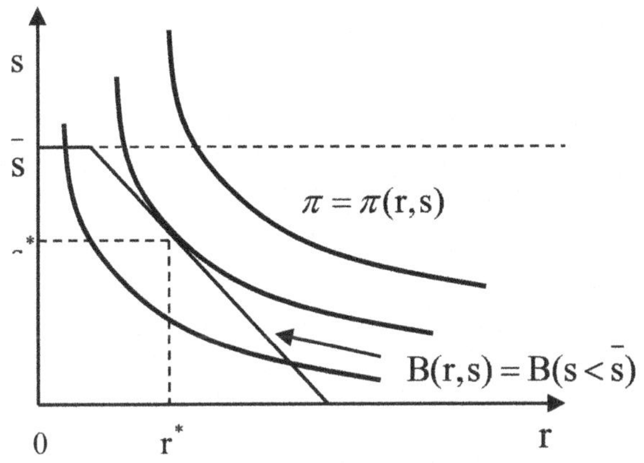

Figure 7-3 Issue of Manager's Maximization in the Return Space

2. Adverse selection model

Now we specifically analyze the adverse selection in the process of introducing professional managers into private enterprises. Suppose employers are facing a group of employable professional managers at the first period. Because of the asymmetric information, employers do not know their true qualities, and only know that they obey a joint probability distribution ($f_0(l,a)$). Professional managers have complete information about their own quality. In order to reach a transaction, the employer provides the manager with a return curve ($B(r,s) = E$). For convenience, we assume that the E-zone is the expectation of value function ($J(l,a)$) based on distribution ($f_0(l,a)$).

$$E_0[J(l,a)] = \int_{-\infty}^{+\infty} \int_{-\infty}^{+\infty} J(l,a) f_0(l,a) dl \cdot da \tag{7-2}$$

Now managers solve the following problems:

$$\underset{r,s}{\mathrm{Max}}\, \pi(r,s)$$

$$\text{s.t.} \quad B(r,s) \le E_0[\cdot] \tag{7-3}$$

Get the best choice of managers from the above formula: (r^*, s^*), the indirect utility of managers is expressed as

$$\pi_0^* = \pi(r^*, s^*) \tag{7-4}$$

(7-4) means that if a manager works for the company, he will get total utility (π_0^*) from remuneration (r^*) and status (s^*). If the manager leaves the office, it will retain its utility

$$\pi_e = \pi_e(l,a) \tag{7-5}$$

As the manager has complete information about his own qualities, the usefulness of his retention may be determined. It is not difficult to see that this reserved utility is related to other job opportunities, self-employment and leisure preferences, etc. In short, we assume that managers always know the effectiveness of the post-employment. At this time, professional managers make the following decisions:

$$\begin{cases} \pi_0^* < \pi_e \longrightarrow \text{Post-employment} \\ \pi_0^* \ge \pi_e \longrightarrow \text{In-service} \end{cases} \tag{7-6}$$

Assume that the company fully understands the above decision structure of the manager. Therefore, in the second period, the employer knows that the manager who remains in the company definitely satisfies the formula (7-6), and the collection of managers facing the company becomes:

$$\Theta_1 = \{l, a | \pi_e(l, a) \leq \pi_0^*\} \tag{7-7}$$

The a priori joint probability distribution ($f_0(l, a)$) needs to be modified as follows:

$$f_1(l, a | \Theta_1) = \frac{f_0(l, a)}{F[\pi_e(l, a) \leq \pi_0^*]} \tag{7-8}$$

Employers having incomplete information at this time need to adjust the return curve given to the delisting manager, that is, the B is:

$$E_1[J(l, a)] = \iint_{\Theta_1} J(l, a) f_1(l, a | \Theta_1) dl \cdot da \tag{7-9}$$

Based on formula (7-9), the constraint line of the second period of retained manager ($B(r, s) = E_1[\cdot]$) is formed. In general, conditional expectations ($E_1[\cdot]$) will be adjusted downwards, that is: $E_1[\cdot] < E_0[\cdot]$, so the constraints faced by managers are tightened, and they maximize the indirect utility after selection ($\pi_1^* < \pi_0^*$). Managers who retain their utility ($\pi_e \in (\pi_1^*, \pi_0^*]$) will leave at the end of the second period. Therefore, by the third period, the company's manager collection will become:

$$\Theta_2 = \{l, a | \pi_e(l, a) \leq \pi_1^*\} \tag{7-10}$$

The joint probability distribution continues to be revised to $f_2(l, a | \Theta_2)$. This series of adjustments will continue until $E_n[\cdot] = E_{n-1}[\cdot]$. The final equilibrium is defined by:

$$E^*[J(l,a)|\pi_e(l,a) \le \pi^*(r^*,s^*)] = E^*\left|\left\{\underset{r,s}{\operatorname{argmax}}[\pi(r,s)] = (r^*,s^*), s.t.B(r,s) = E^*\right\}\right. \quad (7\text{-}11)$$

Since we have not made any restrictions on the corresponding functions and probability distributions in (7-11), it can be expected that the results of adverse selection may have multiple equilibrium. However, if there is information asymmetry between the employer and the professional manager regarding the quality of the manager, Pareto optimal perfect match equilibrium will hardly appear. To make the above analysis more specific and easier to understand, we will use the specific function form for further study below.

3. Further study of the adverse selection model

To analyze the adverse selection model in detail, we do these simple settings. We set the value function of the professional manager as: $J(l,a) = l + a$. The utility function takes the form of Cobb-Douglas: $\pi(r,s) = s^\gamma \cdot r^{1-\gamma} (\gamma \in (0,1))$. The retained utility of the professional manager after turnover is: $\pi_e(l,a) = \delta(l+a)$, here, $\delta \in (0,1)$ can be interpreted as the degree of depreciation of the human capital after turnover. The return curve provided by the employer to the manager (manager's budget constraint line) takes a linear form: $B(r,s) = s + \alpha r = E[\cdot](\alpha > 0)$. In addition, we assume that random variables loyalty (l) and ability (a) are independent of each other, and $f_0(l) \sim N(\mu_l,1)$, $f_0(a) \sim N(\mu_a,1)$, so $f_0(l,a) = f_0(l) \cdot f_0(a)$.

With the above settings, it is easy to calculate the returns that the company provides to professional managers in the first period.

$$E_0[J(l,a)] = \int_{-\infty}^{+\infty}\int_{-\infty}^{+\infty}(l+a)\cdot f_0(l)\cdot f_0(a)dl\cdot da$$

$$= \int_{-\infty}^{+\infty} \int_{-\infty}^{+\infty} l \cdot f_0(l) \cdot f_0(a) dl \cdot da + \int_{-\infty}^{+\infty} \int_{-\infty}^{+\infty} a \cdot f_0(l) \cdot f_0(a) dl \cdot da$$

$$= \mu_l + \mu_a \qquad (7\text{-}12)$$

So managers will solve the following questions

$$\underset{r,s}{\mathrm{Max}}\, \pi(r,s) = s^{\gamma} \cdot r^{1-\gamma}$$

$$\text{s.t. } s + \alpha r \le \mu_l + \mu_l \qquad (7\text{-}13)$$

According to the Kuhn-Tacker condition, the solution to the problem (7-13) is:

$$s^* = \gamma \cdot (\mu_l + \mu_a),\ r^* = \frac{1-\gamma}{\alpha} \cdot (\mu_l + \mu_a) \qquad (7\text{-}14)$$

The indirect utility of professional managers is:

$$\pi_0^* = s^{*\gamma} \cdot r^{*(1-\gamma)} = \frac{\gamma^{\gamma}(1-\gamma)^{1-\gamma}}{\alpha^{1-\gamma}} \cdot (\mu_l + \mu_a) \qquad (7\text{-}15)$$

Now the manager makes the turnover decision according to the structure given in (7-6), and when calculated retention utility of professional manager (according to their own real qualities) is $\pi_e(l,a) = \delta(l+a) > \frac{\gamma^{\gamma}(1-\gamma)^{1-\gamma}}{\alpha^{1-\gamma}} \cdot (\mu_l + \mu_a)$, he will leave the company. This leads to a collection of retained managers becoming:

$$\Theta_1 = \{l,a \mid \pi_e(l,a) \le \pi_0^*\} = \left\{ l,a \,\middle|\, \delta(l+a) \le \frac{\gamma^{\gamma}(1-\gamma)^{1-\gamma}}{\alpha^{1-\gamma}} \cdot (\mu_l + \mu_a) \right\}$$

(7-16)

The expected returns of the in-service managers in the second period are given based on the probability distribution ($f_1(l,a|\Theta_1)$). In our model setting, this return is:

$$E_1[J(l,a)] = \iint_{\Theta_1} (1+a)\frac{f_1(l,a|\Theta_1)}{F[l,a|\Theta_1]} dl \cdot da$$

$$= \mu_l + \mu_a - \frac{2\int_{-\infty}^{+\infty} \phi(n)\cdot\phi[\lambda(n)]dn}{\int_{-\infty}^{+\infty} \phi(n)\cdot\Phi[\lambda(n)]dn} \quad (7\text{-}17)$$

(See Appendix 1)

In the above formula, $n = a - \mu_a$, $\lambda(n) = \dfrac{\pi_0^* - \delta(\mu_l + \mu_a - n)}{\delta}$,

$\phi(\cdot)$ and $\Phi(\cdot)$ are respectively the probability density function and cumulative distribution function of the standard normal distribution. It is easy to see that the returns given by the company in the second period:

$$E_1[\cdot] < \mu_l + \mu_a = E_0[\cdot]$$

Under the new constraints, the indirect utility of managers who stayed in the second period from positions and benefits is:

$$\pi_1^* = \frac{\gamma^\gamma (1-\gamma)^{1-\gamma}}{\alpha^{1-\gamma}} \cdot E_1[\cdot] < \pi_0^* \quad (7\text{-}18)$$

Therefore, managers who retain their utility in the range $(\pi_1^*, \pi_0^*]$ will leave at the end of the second period. By the third period, the remaining manager collection becomes:

$$\Theta_2 = \{l,a|\pi_c(l,a) \le \pi_1^*\} = \left\{l,a \middle| \delta(1+a) \le \frac{\gamma^\gamma(1-\gamma)^{1-\gamma}}{\alpha^{1-\gamma}} \cdot E_1[\cdot]\right\} \subset \Theta_1$$

(7-19)

This adverse selection process will continue until the equilibrium is achieved. It can be expected that with the commencement of this process, fewer and fewer managers will be left and the quality will become lower and lower. In the equilibrium implementation defined by the formula (7-11), the private business owners will face low-quality managers. These managers either have low abilities or have insufficient loyalty, or both are relatively inferior. The result is that the core positions are again returned to the "trustworthy" family-clan members (possibly with insufficient ability). Professional managers with comparatively outstanding capabilities are always "wandering" on the edge of the core of corporate power. Private enterprises have to suffer "familyism dilemma" again and operate below the border of production possibility.

Interaction between Employers and Professional Managers: Information Disclosure and Dynamic Matching

The foregoing analysis builds on the hypothesis of asymmetric information between employers and professional managers. If considering that the interaction between the two parties can reduce the degree of incomplete information, and some managers have enough patience to wait until the company fully understands them and then give appropriate return arrangements (jobs and salaries), then the difficulties caused by the aforementioned adverse selection can be alleviated. Here we use a three-period dynamic information disclosure model to describe this process. The analysis will show that the existence of interactive information disclosure can indeed improve the match between private enterprises and professional managers.

1. Basic settings

Let's start with some settings. Previous studies have assumed that employers with incomplete information know beforehand, that the quality of managers obeys a joint probability distribution ($f_0(l,a)$). For the sake of analysis, here we directly assume that the employer knows that the value of the manager's quality to the company

($J(l,a) = l + a = q$) obeys the normal distribution, ie, $q \sim N(\mu, \sigma_q^2)$, assume that $\mu > 0$. Correspondingly, the current retention effect of professional managers is $\pi_e = \delta \cdot q (\delta \in (0,1))$.

It is assumed that the interactive process is carried out in three phases. In the first period, the enterprise determines the return to the manager ($\pi_1^* = E_0[\cdot]$) according to the prior probability distribution of manager's quality ($f_0(q)$). The manager compares the value of post-employment and on-service under the return constraint, to decide whether to leave or no. The solution to the problem is to retain the $\bar{\pi}_1$, and the manager leaves the company when the utility gained in the current period is less than the value.

By the second period, employers observed information through interactions with retained professional managers ($y = q + \varepsilon$), among them the noise $\varepsilon \sim N(0, \sigma_\varepsilon^2)$, from which the distribution of q is deduced ($f_1(q|y)$). Then use the revised probability distribution to calculate the return to the manager in the second period, the professional manager makes the turnover decision according to the same procedure.

In the third period, the information on the quality of retained managers is fully disclosed through further interactions. The remaining managers achieved an optimal match, that is, the arrangement of positions and salaries according to the classification group given in Figure 7-1.

2. Model

Following Ljungqvist and Sargent's (2000) approach, we have used a adverse analysis program to examine this model.

In the third period, the company fully grasps the manager's quality information, so according to our settings, the total effect of the current period of the manager's stay is $\pi_3^* = q$. If the manager's discount rate is $\beta \in (0,1)$, till to the third period, the value of the optimal decision that can be continued is $V_3(q)$, then the total utility of the company that remains in the company for the current period and beyond can be expressed as $q + \beta V_3(q)$. Correspondingly, we use V_1 to show the value of the manager in the first period facing the return given by the company and making the corresponding optimal decision. In this way, the Bellman equation is:

$$V_3(q) = \text{Max}\{q + \beta V_3(q), \delta q + \beta V_1\} \qquad (7\text{-}20)$$

The solution to this problem is the optimal policy, that is, optimally retain the decision of $\bar{\pi}_3$. The implication is $\bar{\pi}_3$ similar to π_e in the third section of the model. Managers compare it with the effectiveness of keeping on position $\pi_3^* = q$, and to decide whether to leave.

$$V_3(q) = \begin{cases} q + \beta V_3(q) = \dfrac{q}{1-\beta} & q \geq \bar{\pi}_3 \\ \delta \cdot q + \beta V_1 & q < \bar{\pi}_3 \end{cases} \qquad (7\text{-}21)$$

$\bar{\pi}_3$ Can be defined by:

$$\bar{\pi}_3 + \beta V_3(\bar{\pi}_3) = \delta \cdot \bar{\pi}_3 + \beta V_1 \tag{7-22}$$

That is: $\bar{\pi}_3 = \dfrac{(1-\beta)\beta}{1-\delta+\delta\beta} \cdot V_1$

The optimal strategy means that the higher the V_1 (determined by other job opportunities, self-employment value, leisure preferences, etc.), the higher the $\bar{\pi}_3$ (The critical level of the manager's retention), that is, other conditions remain the same, the higher the manager's turnover intention.

Now back to the second period. Through interactions with professional managers, employers observe information about the quality of managers ($y = q + \varepsilon$) and form probability inferences. For the reservation utility $\bar{\pi}_1 > \pi_1^*$ in the end of the first period, those managers have already left the company. The collection of on-the-job managers is: $\Theta = \left\{ q \middle| \bar{\pi}_1(q) \le \pi_1^* \right\}$, so the probability distribution of their quality is:

$$f_1(q|y,\Theta) = \frac{f_1(q|y)}{P(q \in \Theta)} \tag{7-23}$$

In this formula, $f_1(q|y)$ is the normal distribution density function. Using Kalman filter or LS regression method, the mean (μ_1) and variance (σ_1^2) of the conditional distribution are:

$$\mu_1 = \mu + \frac{\sigma_q^2}{\sigma_q^2 + \sigma_\varepsilon^2}(y - \mu) \tag{7-24}$$

$$\sigma_1^2 = \frac{\sigma_q^2}{\sigma_q^2 + \sigma_\varepsilon^2}\sigma_\varepsilon^2 \qquad (7\text{-}25)$$

Based on the distribution in formula (7-23), enterprises can determine the return paid to the manager in the second period, namely:

$$\pi_2^* = \int_\Theta q \cdot \frac{f_1(q|y)}{P(q \in \Theta)} dq \qquad (7\text{-}26)$$

As the form of $\overline{\pi}_1(q)$ is very complex, it is very difficult for us to get a simple inequality that represents the collection ($\Theta = \left\{q \middle| \overline{\pi}_1(q) \le \pi_1^*\right\}$), so the result of formula (7-26) is difficult to calculate specifically. For further analysis, we tentatively assume that $\overline{\pi}_1(q)$ is a monotonically increasing function. In this way, the inequation $\overline{\pi}_1(q) \le \pi_1^*$ can be rewritten into an inverse function: $q \le \overline{\pi}_1^{-1}(\pi_1^*)$, so:

$$\pi_2^* = \mu_1 - \sigma_1 \cdot \frac{\phi(\eta)}{\Phi(\eta)} \qquad (7\text{-}27)$$

(See Appendix 1)

$\eta = \dfrac{\overline{\pi}_1^{-1}(\pi_1^*) - \mu_1}{\sigma_1}$, the Bellman equation is:

$$V_2(q) = \text{Max}\left\{\pi_2^* + \beta V_3(q), \delta q + \beta V_1\right\} \qquad (7\text{-}28)$$

The optimal strategy for this problem is to determine the utility of retention ($\overline{\pi}_2$), which results in:

$$V_2(\pi_2^*) = \begin{cases} \pi_2^* + \beta V_3(q) & \pi_2^* \geq \overline{\pi}_2 \\ \delta \cdot q + \beta V_1 & \pi_2^* < \overline{\pi}_2 \end{cases} \qquad (7\text{-}29)$$

$\overline{\pi}_2 = \delta \cdot q + \beta V_1 - \beta V_3(q)$. It is easy to see that the optimal strategy here is positively related to the value faced after turnover (V_1), and negatively related to the value of continuing to stay ($V_3(q)$).

Similarly, we can easily write down the Bellman equation of the professional manager selection problem in the first period, that is:

$$V_1 = \mathrm{Max}\left\{\pi_1^* + \beta \cdot \int V_2(\pi_2^*) g(\pi_2^* | q) d\pi_2^*, \delta q + \beta V_1\right\} \qquad (7\text{-}30)$$

Formula (7-30) needs detailed explanation. First, $\pi_1^* = \int q \cdot f_0(q) dq = \mu$, it is the employer's current return to the manager based on the prior probability distribution ($f_0(q)$) of the professional manager's quality. Second, the value function $V_2(\pi_2^*)$ is defined by formula (7-29). Finally, $g(\pi_2^* | q)$ is the inference from the professional manager that the probability distribution of the second-stage retention return (π_2^*) is formed based on his true quality (q). As π_2^* is related to the observed information $y = q + \varepsilon$, it is actually a conditional distribution of the function y. The economic implications here are that if the manager considers himself to be of higher quality, he will expect that the information the employer observes through interaction will be beneficial to him, that is, $y > \mu$. According to formula (7-24), this shows $\mu_1 > \mu$, which means without considering the turnover in the first period, the conditional mean value of the manager's quality will be larger than the mean value calculated based on prior probability in the first period. This indicates that interactive information does help to distinguish managers of different qualities, to some extent alleviate the aforementioned problems of adverse selection, and form turnover equilibrium.

Based on the formula (7-30), we can draw the optimal strategy for the managers in the first period ($\bar{\pi}_1$), and:

$$V_1 = \begin{cases} \pi_1^* + \beta \cdot \int V_2(\pi_2^*) g(\pi_2^* | q) d\pi_2^* & \pi_1^* \geq \bar{\pi}_1 \\ \delta q + \beta V_1 = \dfrac{\delta q}{1-\beta} & \pi_1^* < \bar{\pi}_1 \end{cases} \qquad (7\text{-}31)$$

$\bar{\pi}_1$ is defined by:

$$\bar{\pi}_1 + \beta \cdot \int V_2(\pi_2^*) g(\pi_2^* | q) d\pi_2^* = \frac{\delta q}{1-\beta} \qquad (7\text{-}32)$$

At this point, we have completed the description of the dynamic information disclosure model. We will then make specific analysis of related issues to reveal more useful implications.

3. Further analysis

Further investigations will be made based on the previous section and the third section of the adverse selection model. The main result is the following proposition, which is the core result of this chapter.

Proposition: *In the first period, for professional managers with any quality (q), the best strategy for turnover decisions is* $\bar{\pi}_1 < \pi_e$*, the probability of staying is* $P(\pi_1^* \geq \bar{\pi}_1) > P(\pi_1^* \geq \pi_e)$.

(See Appendix 1)

This proposition shows that if there is a dynamic information disclosure process, then in the first period, when the manager is making turnover decision, the critical level of leaving or staying – the optimal strategy $\overline{\pi_1}$ is less than the critical level when there is no information disclosure process – preserve utility in the current period $\pi_e = \delta q$ (can be seen as the optimal strategy in the adverse selection model). This result means that if the interaction between the employer and the manager can provide information about the quality of the employer, the professional manager will be more likely to stay (even if he did not get the return value that should be obtained), and stay to the third period, when the information is fully disclosed, to achieve an complete mating, that is, the probability of staying $P(\pi_1^* \geq \overline{\pi_1}) > P(\pi_1^* \geq \pi_e)$. Therefore, companies understand and grasp the full range of information of the managers through variety ways, and make career management for them. This will make those truly outstanding managers feel that their talent will not be buried and stay in the company temporarily.

How to Retain Professional Managers

As proved by the adverse selection model in Section 3 of this chapter, due to the there are new dimensions in the human capital transactions between private enterprises and professional managers, there is a vital information asymmetry problem in the transaction process, which leads to Pareto optimal double-dimensional space matching difficult to achieve, and the governance of private enterprises has returned to the closed family-clan model. The "familism predicament" is hard to break through. As shown in the fourth section, from the perspective of professional manager's turnover decision, if there is information disclosure mechanism during the introduction of professional managers in private enterprises, then the aforementioned problems can be partially alleviated. The key point here is that managers who have enough patience to wait will expect that the continuous replenishment of information will help the company to understand the true self, so as to get a proper return at some time in the future. This expectation supports him to make decision to stay in the current period. If this decision-making structure is also known to the enterprise, the company will also expect that the remaining manager will have higher quality, and will appropriately increase the return to the on-the-job managers. This approach on one hand can directly improve the balance of adverse selection; on the other hand, it can further improve managers' expectations and form a virtuous circle. Therefore, the inefficient balance of adverse selection can be alleviated to some extent.'

Now from the perspective of employers, we further analyze the significance of the information brought about by the interaction between the company and professional managers. The analysis will show that the existence of information disclosure can not only reduce the turnover intention of professional managers, but also help companies to distinguish professional managers according to the observed information, in order to implement differential treatment, to achieve a certain degree of separating equilibrium

In the first period, the employer calculates the return to the professional manager based on the prior probability distribution, that is, $\pi_1^* = \int q \cdot f_0(q)dq = \mu$, this is the same as the adverse selection model. Of course, the aforementioned propositions have shown that, even in the case of information disclosure, even if the same returns are obtained, the manager's turnover intention will be lower, because at this time $\bar{\pi}_1 < \pi_e$

In the second period, the return in the adverse selection model is:

$$E_2[\cdot] = \mu - \sigma_q \cdot \frac{\phi(\lambda)}{\Phi(\lambda)} \qquad (7\text{-}33)$$

We can easily get the above result according to the formula (7-27). Correspondingly, according to the formula (7-24), (7-25), and (7-27), the information disclosure model returns the enterprise's payment as (with $\overline{\pi}_1(q)$ under the monotonically increasing assumption):

$$\pi_2^* = \mu_1 - \sigma_1 \cdot \frac{\phi(\eta)}{\Phi(\eta)} = \mu + \frac{\sigma_q^2}{\sigma_q^2 + \sigma_\varepsilon^2}(y - \mu) - \sigma_1 \cdot \frac{\phi(\eta)}{\Phi(\eta)} \qquad (7\text{-}34)$$

Comparing (7-33) and (7-34) above, it shows that if the employer observes a large enough value of y from a manager in the second period, then the value of π_2^* is maybe higher than $E_2[\cdot]$ or even μ. The return will be relatively higher, even higher than μ in the first period. Since the conditional distribution of y is related to the true qualities of managers (q), it means that managers with higher quality are more likely to be observed higher levels of y from their employers, thereby be given higher returns. On the contrary, if the actual quality of the manager is low, the employer will have a higher probability to observe a lower y in the second period, and the return for the professional manager may be revised downwards, even less than $E_2[\cdot]$ in the adverse selection model. Therefore, through the process of information disclosure, employers can, to some extent, distinguish managers with different real qualities and implement differential treatment.

It is also worth noting that the observed amount of information of y has an important value here. Under the normal distribution assumption, the amount of information can be measured by the variance of the quality (σ_q^2)and the variance of the noise (σ_ε^2). Consider the extreme situation $\sigma_\varepsilon^2 = 0$,where the observed information does not have "noise", then (7-34) becomes $\pi_2^* = y$. This means that what is observed of y is the true quality (q) of professional managers, that is, the complete symmetry of information is achieved. Of course, this is just a special case of the above model.

As for the third period, the full disclosure of information has been achieved under our setup. According to the previous results, the managers who are still on-job at this time will be able to achieve an ideal two-dimensional space match.

Summary

Although many theoretical and empirical studies have shown that the "family-clan governance model" is lack of efficiency. It's not conducive to the company's better use of external management resources. The reality, however, is that a large number of private enterprises still commonly adopt this system. This is confusing. A large number of existing studies on the professional managers' turnover of family-clan businesses cannot provide satisfactory explanations. This study attempts to systematically study this issue from the perspective of the interests of employers and professional managers.

Our analysis shows that the turnover of professional managers and the familization of private enterprise systems have deep economic and social roots. In the two-dimensional space where the employers emphasize on managers' ability and loyalty, and managers emphasize on positions and currency returns, the family system, which exclude external professional managers, is an equilibrium concerning managerial abilities and loyalty information asymmetry. The adverse selection in private enterprises makes it difficult for the employer to enter the company's core management group, and the operation of the enterprises is degraded to the closed mode dominated by family members. On this basis, this study proposes that only by changing the economic and social reasons supporting this inefficient equilibrium, can the "familism dilemma" be possible to break through, under the conditions of satisfying both the private enterprises and professional managers' participation in restraint and incentive compatibility constraints.

In addition, we have further introduced the interaction process between private enterprises and managers, and established a three-phase dynamic information disclosure model. Through the analysis of this model, we find that compared to complete information asymmetry, the process with information disclosure helps to reduce the turnover intention of managers. At the same time, dynamic processes may discriminate managers of different qualities, and achieve a certain degree of separating equilibrium, which alleviates the problem of inefficient equilibrium caused by information asymmetry. The policy implications of this model are obvious. Strengthening the communication between employers and professional managers, taking care of and understanding managers comprehensively, and implementing good career management will help both parties realize the ideal "win-win" match. Finally, we also provide some specific management suggestions based on the main conclusions of this study. These suggestions are given around solving information asymmetry and reducing professional manager's retention utility.

Chapter 8

Conclusions and Suggestion

Analysis of this study shows that the active employee turnover model based on the Western background, and domestic related research on general enterprises, cannot be used to explain the turnover of professional managers of small and medium-sized private enterprises in China. It is necessary to construct and validate new turnover process models and factor models. Using a combination of theoretical and empirical research methods, this study conducts rigorous empirical tests on the turnover process of professional managers of small and medium-sized private enterprises based on actual survey data, and makes further economic analysis on the specificity of this issue. Based on this, the related turnover management suggestions are proposed. The main conclusions are as follows.

Main Conclusions

1. Direct, indirect and moderating effects of the factors affecting turnover intention

Study finds that in terms of total effect, factors that have a significant impact on turnover intentions include: JSC, JA, JL, OSC, BFT, JP, JC, JE, JI, PC, OJ and CR. Among them, JA, JL, and OJ have a direct impact on the turnover intention; JP and PC influence turnover intention both directly and indirectly; other significant variables have an impact on turnover intention through indirect ways. These results are in summarized in Figure 8-1.

The test of the moderating effect of personal factors finds that: (1) Manager' JI and PC have a role in regulating the relationship between JA, JL and turnover. Managers with higher JI regard work as the top priority in life, and their main pleasure comes from the work itself. Therefore, even if other reasons lead to a decline in their JA and the idea of JL, they will not ultimately leave. Managers with higher PC do not think that long-term work in the same company will be boring. On the contrary, they are willing to accumulate their own management experience and personnel qualifications in the long-term. When they are in low JA condition, even they are interested in finding other job opportunities. Their unwillingness to "move" will force them to act cautiously. Not a last resort, such managers will not easily leave their long-serving company. (2) Manager' EM has a moderating effect on JL. The study of the factors affecting the general employee turnover in the West rarely examines the effects of EM. The finding in this study can be added to this. We have found that if the level of JSC of the manager is reduced by the organization, employer, or work factors, which inspires the manager to look for OJ, even if a better job is not found, the manager who has a strong incentive to start a business may eventually leave. (3) RA and VI have moderating effects on JA. Managers who are more afraid of risk will not easily resign if they are in poor JA, because he fears that it will be difficult to quickly find other jobs after leaving the company. This is very easy to understand, and only managers who are willing to take the risk of uncertainty can dare to try other possibilities when the situation goes down. A manager with a strong traditional attitude does not act "individualism" when his work is in poor condition. He will value the interests of the company's group and will stay in the company under the consideration of the overall situation. This result directly indicates the noteworthy influence of the Chinese cultural tradition on making personal turnover decisions. The mainstream turnover literature in the West has not tested the moderating effect of this variable. The aforementioned findings regarding the role of personal factors in regulation have important management implications. The prior identification of these personal characteristics helps the organization to take measures after the fact to reduce the turnover intention of managers.

An examination of the moderating effects of employers has revealed that: (1) Employer leadership has a moderating effect on the relationship between organizational factors and turnover intention. If the private enterprise employer has a strong motivation for success, outstanding entrepreneurial ability and strict integrity, then even if the manager is not satisfied with organizational factors such as salary, procedural fairness, and development opportunities, he will not easily leave because he has confidence in the boss himself. Employer leadership can reduce the probability of high turnover resulting from organizational factors by up to 40%. (2) BFT has a moderating effect on the relationship between organizational factors and turnover intention. When more fairness and trust are addressed to the manager, the manager's turnover decision will less likely be affected by organizational factors. Even if the manager perceives that certain organizational factors are not attractive enough, he will receive some psychological compensation from the sense of fairness and trust given by the boss. This employer factor can reduce up to 60% of the turnover intention caused by the lack of attractiveness of the organization. This shows that employers indeed play a key role in preventing the turnover of managers. These moderating effects are summarized in Figure 8-1. As far as the author is aware, the empirical results on the moderating role of employers have not yet been there in the Western turnover model. In the social context where the market system is relatively complete and the individualism tradition prevails, the employer's own characteristics will not have a material impact on the subordinate's rational decision. The interests of the employees may be protected by the rules and regulations of the law, organization rules, and contracts. They don't have to tie this on some individuals. However, in today's Chinese society, managers have to consider the influence of the boss' own factors in the decision-making process. This discovery of the study provides a new perspective on the cross-cultural comparison of relevant turnover models.

According to demographic background grouping regression results, women value more on employer factors such as BLH, BFT etc., and "soft" environmental attraction like the company's SR. Men are less sensitive to these factors. EM is a crucial factor affecting male manager' turnover intention. OSC, EM and OJ are the key considerations for unmarried managers in the process of making turnover decisions. BFT and JP have a significant impact on married managers. Managers under the age of 30 pay more attention to OSC and SR; managers over the age of 30 pay more attention to BFT. EM and OJ also have a significant impact on their turnover intention. Grassroots managers pay more attention to OSC and SR; while middle and high-level managers pay more attention to employer' factors such as BFT, BCI etc. At the same time, EM also significantly affects the turnover intention of middle and high-level employees. Managers with a short working life (<5 years) pay more attention to OSC, BLH, SR and OJ. For employees with a rich work experience, JP and EM make it easier for them to leave their jobs. New employees (<2 years) in the company will mainly consider OJ and entrepreneurial possibilities when leaving a job, while older employees (more than 2 years) who have a longer service age will be more concerned with OSC, BCI and JE. Less-educated managers (junior college and below) pay more attention to BFT when leaving a job, while highly-educated managers (undergraduate and higher) pay more attention to OSC and SR, and EM has a significant impact on both.

The empirical results obtained by grouping company characteristics show that apart from JP, EM and PC that have a significant impact on managers of different scales, OSC, JI, and OJ only have a significant effect on the turnover intention of large-scale enterprise managers. In addition, managers of shorter-established companies (<10 years) are more likely to be affected by OSC, BFT, EM, and SR in the turnover decision process; and for managers of older companies (≥10 years), they are less sensitive to these factors, whose turnover decisions are mainly influenced by OJ.

2. Four-stage model for the formation process of turnover of professional managers

According to the process model obtained by applying the structural equation model method, the process of generating turnover intentions of professional managers proceeds in a certain order. It first perceives relevant individuals, organizations, employers, jobs, and other job opportunities. This decline in perceived satisfaction is reflected in attitude changes such as JSC, JFC etc., which in turn leads to manager' decline in JA and the idea of JL, and finally the idea of turnover. The validated process model has strong explanatory power to the turnover variance, and its relative fit index CFI reaches 0.97, which is satisfactory.

In the first stage of the formation process of turnover intention, manager' perception of BCI, JC, JI and SR significantly influence the JSC. The higher the degree of JI, the higher the manager's perceived level of SR, BCI and JC, and the higher the degree of JSC. In addition, BLH, BFT, JC, JI and JE significantly affect JFC. That is, whether managers are willing to actively work for the organization are affected by relevant individuals, employers, work, and relationship factors. These perceivable variables ultimately influence the manager's turnover intention through the intermediary effects of attitude variables such as JSC, JFC etc.

In the second stage, perceived variables such as JSC, BCI, JP, and JC directly affect the manager's JA. Whatever the reason, whether managers are full of work enthusiasm, whether they can get satisfaction from their job, and whether they are emotionally loyal to the company have a significant impact on their JA, and the latter is a direct predictor of turnover intention. At the same time, whether the employer cares and encourages himself, whether the work is overstressed, and whether he can have enough autonomy to complete the task also has a direct impact on the manager's JA. BCI, JC, JE, PC and CR have a direct impact on JL. If employers don't care about their subordinates, the subordinates will inevitably seek other job opportunities. The manager's lower JC and JE, as well as CR will also lead to the idea of searching for other jobs. Finally, managers with lower PC do not think that long-term expectation is a good thing in a company, and it has been their customary behavior to constantly pay attention to the information of other companies.

In the third stage, JP, OJ, JL and JA have a direct impact on the manager's turnover intention. JA and JL play a role in the conduction mechanism of the turnover process. If managers do not care about the organization's evaluation of their work performance, and even do not hide their motivation to find other job opportunities, then the turnover is almost inevitable. At the same time, the JP here also influences the turnover decision, by conveying information about if it is an "edge person" in the organization. For managers already have other job opportunities, their turnover decision will not be directly affected by any intermediate factors. Most of these turnovers have undergone rational calculation procedures. Managers suddenly resign without showing any change in psychological attitude. Companies are often caught off guard.

In the fourth stage, the manager's turnover intention has been created.

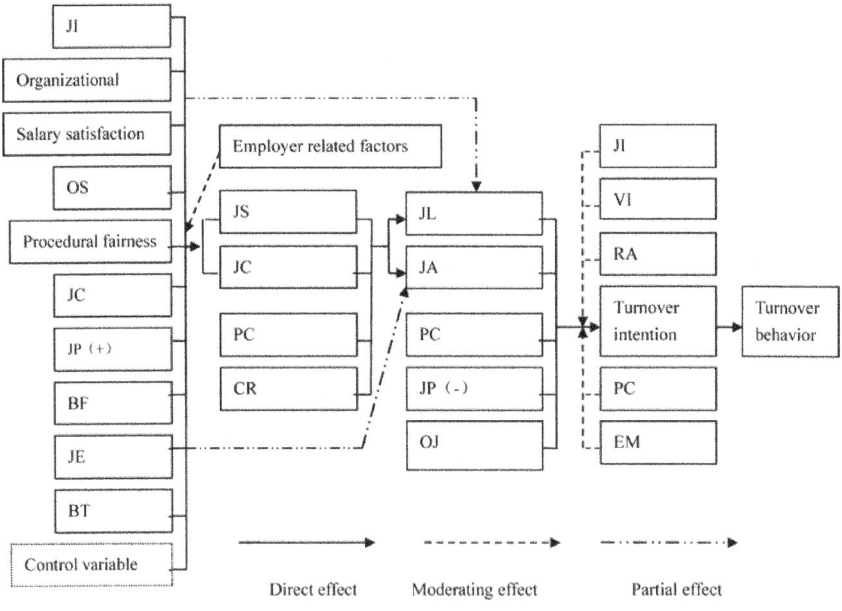

Figure 8-1 Verified Turnover Process Model and Factors Model

3. Economic explanation of professional manager turnover

According to the economic analysis of the turnover of professional managers, in the two-dimensional space, where employer values managerial competence and loyalty, and the manager values jobs and currency return, the family system that excludes external professional managers is equilibrium of asymmetries in capabilities and loyalty information. The adverse selection, in the process of introducing professional managers in private enterprises, makes it difficult for the manager to enter the core layer of the enterprise, and the operation of the enterprise is degraded to the closed mode dominated by family members. Through the introduction of the dynamic information disclosure model, analyzed through the process of interaction between private enterprises and managers, we find that the dynamic process of information disclosure helps to reduce the turnover intention of managers, compared with the complete information asymmetry situation. This mechanism helps enterprises to distinguish managers with different qualities in the market, to achieve a certain degree of separation and equilibrium, which also eases the problem of inefficient balance caused by information asymmetry. At the same time, this study also finds that in the double two-dimensional space given by the model, information asymmetry related to competence and loyalty cannot be eliminated, and Pareto optimal matching is difficult to achieve. Therefore, private business owners need to be cautious when they consider abandoning the family model, and introduce a large amount of external management resources, to adopt a modern company management system.

Management Suggestions for Turnover of Professional Managers

1. Administrative measures for the formation process of professional manager turnover intention

The turnover process model in this study shows that professional managers of small and medium-sized private enterprises experience complex factors, such as perceptions of relevant factors, changes in JSC, changes in JFC, decline in JA, idea of JL and turnover intentions. Enterprises can take different measures in accordance with the priorities of these different stages, to address the problem of the turnover of professional managers. In the previous discussion of empirical results, we have put forward some suggestions for governance based on related findings. In order to more systematically propose an overall coordinated governance mechanism, this chapter further provides relevant suggestions based on the time sequence of the manager's decision-making process, and various aspects of the company's HRM system.

2. Related factors perception stage

According to our model, the starting point for manager turnover decisions is their perception of factors such as self, organization, employer, work, and other job opportunities. If evaluation of these factors leads to a deterioration of their work attitude, then the entire process of turnover will be start up.

From Table 5-8, the manager's JI, JE and PC significantly affect their turnover intention (total effect), that is, the perception of these factors will eventually be reflected in their decision to leave or not. However, as mentioned above, since these factors mainly depend on the characteristics of managers themselves, it is very difficult for companies to make changes. Therefore, what the organization can do is to identify such features through certain screening methods during the recruitment phase, to consider the possibility of turnover during the job placement, and take early response measures. The core position is best not to be assigned to managers who have a low degree of JI and JC. Often, managers with higher levels of JI, PC and JE do not easily initiate turnover decision-making procedures under some insignificant "impact". On the contrary, company management needs to pay attention to those employees who have had a lot of turnover experiences. Such employees like "job hopping" and do not think that working in the same company for a long time is beneficial to their career development. For them, the decline in JA and the idea of JL can easily be converted to turnover (see the moderating effect in Table 6-4).

Second, managers' perceptions of OSC, CE etc. will ultimately significantly affect their turnover intentions. Therefore, if companies want to maintain managers' high JSC and JFC at the initial stage, so as to dispel their turnover intentions, then, efforts to improve their organizational appeal are the most important (the empirical results show that its total effect is in the second place). Specific measures include: improving organizational conditions such as work environment, management system, corporate image, etc.; improving the company's return system and creating more room for staff development; improving the company's procedural fairness in relation to people; ensuring the external competitiveness and internal fairness of the company's compensation level. In addition, for companies facing organizational changes, they need to pass on favorable information about the future of the company to their employees through internal communication, publicity, and raising revenue expectations, so that they are still willing to stay after being "impacted". Because corporate change will create turbulence and uncertainty for employees, if management cannot dispel people's concerns, the organization will lose a lot of talented people in the process of transformation.

In terms of employers' factors, only BFT has a significant impact on managers' turnover intentions. Of course, the results of the test of moderating effects in Table 6-5 show that BFT and BLH have moderating effect on related organizational factors. Therefore, through improving measures such as improving the fairness of leaders, raising the level of their own integrity, giving employees full confidence, and strengthening their own leadership, the leaders of the company can not only directly increase the initiative of managers, thereby reducing their turnover intentions. It can also ease the effect of organizational factors on turnover intention. If business owners want to increase the attractiveness of the company, they need to start from their own. By improving their entrepreneurial ability and honest management, and trusting their subordinates, the disadvantage of its organizational attractiveness will be offset by the attractiveness of the employers themselves. In this way, the excellent managers will not easily leave.

In terms of the perception of work factors, the results in Table 5-8 indicate that the greater the JP and JC, the less likely the managers are to leave. This means that managers are willing to take on heavier work burdens, shoulder greater job responsibilities, and hope that companies will give themselves more freedom to play. If companies want to retain those truly outstanding talents, they must entrust them with important tasks, and believe that they will work hard for the interests of the company. In general, managers with a stronger sense of responsibility value organizations' emphasis on their value. If they are only a dispensable "edge person" in the company, then even if other conditions are favorable, such managers will also choose to leave, as he needs a wider space to display his talent and realize his own life value.

Finally, the perception of other job opportunities also has a significant effect on managers' turnover intentions. This finding reminds employers notice the trends of managers who are interested in information about other job opportunities. This may be an important precursor to their turnover. It is also worth noting that this factor will directly affect their turnover intention. This indicates that even if the manager's job satisfaction, organizational commitment, and JFC are at an elevated level, once a better job opportunity is available, the manager's intention to leave will be directly generated, and they will leave the organization without any precursors. For such managers, it is very difficult for the company to observe relevant information in advance, to be able to respond. Therefore, the turnover caused by other job opportunities may surprise companies. For core positions, companies need to take protective measures in advance. Once the relevant managers resign, the organization will have a counter plan, and will not face difficulties in unguarded situations. What's more, businesses also need to review their attractiveness at any time, based on the status of the labor market, to reduce the probability of professional manager turnover.

3. Working attitude changes stage

Table 5-8 shows that managers' job satisfaction and organizational commitment have a significant negative effect on their turnover intentions. As pointed out in the previous analysis, many people, organizations, jobs, and other factors will affect the degree of satisfaction and commitment. Therefore, once the professional manager is affected by the perception of the relevant factors in the previous stage, it reduces the degree of job satisfaction and organizational commitment, and then the organization needs to take certain remedial measures to regain the working attitude of the managers. That is, if the company has other measures that can improve the manager's JFC and JA, then the negative effect of the decrease in satisfaction and commitment, caused by the perception of the relevant antecedent variables, may partially offset the negative impact on the turnover intention.

There are numerous studies in the literature that have proposed measures to improve employee job satisfaction (Brief and Weiss, 2002; Lance, 1991), such as leaders, work team characteristics, physical settings, organizational returns and penalties system, results of organization return, size of work area, fairness of reward system, relationship with colleagues, role pressure compensation, etc. At the same time, measures to increase the employee's organizational commitment have also been examined by many studies, such as organizational support (POS) (Rhoades et al., 2001), perceptions of other job opportunity attractions (Lance, 1991), mentoring (Payne and Ann, 2005), organizational socialization (Griffeth et al., 2000) and so on.

The empirical study also finds that perceived variables such as BCI, JC, JI, SR can significantly affect JSC (see Table 5-7). Therefore, companies need to keep abreast of changes in their employees' work attitudes. If they find that there are signs of decline in JSC, they need to further analyze what factors led to the situation, and then restore employers' work attitudes, and stop them from turnover. Of course, the company can also take other measures that can help improve JSC, and at this stage, it can stop managers from making turnover decisions.

4. Decline in JA and formation of JL stage

According to the process model in this study, JA and JL have a significant impact on managers' turnover intentions, and JA is directly affected by OSC, BCI, JP, JC and JE. As the decline in JA and formation of JL are direct antecedent variables for managers to generate a final turnover idea, once the employee's decision-making process of turnover enters this stage, it is very difficult for the company to prevent its turnover intention. In the process of previous interviews, many private enterprise employers also have told us that by observing the JA of employees, we can roughly determine whether they intend to go.

The measures that organizations can take at this stage include: 1. Making face-to-face communication and exchanges, and understanding in depth the main reasons leading employees to be in this condition. 2. Addressing relevant issues in a targeted way (such as salary increase, promotion, job conversion, etc.). If the company itself is indeed difficult to solve these problems, then it is very necessary to convince the work. 3. Getting prepared for manger turnover, so as to reply to possible adverse impacts to the company.

As shown in Table 6-4, five personal variables, JI, PC, EM, RA and VI have a moderating effect on JA and JL. Therefore, if a manager who has a higher degree of JI, PC, RA, and VI, and a lower degree of EM, even if he shows a poor JA and a strong JL, he will not eventually turn it into turnover intention. This shows that if an organization recruits many employees with such characteristics, through a certain selection process, during the recruitment phase, it will be more able to prevent them from turnover.

5. Turnover intention formation stage

Existing literature shows that in general, turnover intention is one of the best predictors of actual turnover behavior (Schwepker, 2001; Murray and Zimmerman, 2005). Therefore, employees who show high turnover intention will very likely leave the organization. It is very difficult for an organization to retain employees who have already demonstrated the idea of leaving at the last minute, especially those managers who claim to resign.

Some companies may take special measures against individual managers who want to resign, in order to appease their mentality, and try to call them back as far as possible, but this is usually difficult to achieve. The managers who have formally resigned usually have gone through long and careful consideration. Moreover, if they continue to stay, the boss and colleagues will have bad impression on them, which is extremely unfavorable for the long-term development of managers. For companies, special retention strategies may lead other managers to follow suit, and eventually undermine the organization's human resources management system. Therefore, most companies may not take too many retention measures, and would rather to focus their attention on finding alternatives.

Sure, the standardization and systematization of the company's management system will help the organization resist the fluctuations, caused by possible personnel changes. The turnover of a certain manager will not have a significant impact on the normal operation of the company. Therefore, the improvement of the company's management system should be regarded as a very important part of the manager's management mechanism of turnover.

Governance Measures throughout the Entire HRM System

1. Recruitment procedures

The model in this study provides an important revelation for managerial drain management. The governance mechanism and measures are a systematic and comprehensive system. In order to retain outstanding professional managers for a long time, the company's entire human resources management system needs to pay attention to this.

As mentioned above, individual psychological characteristics such as JI and PC affect managers' turnover intentions, but these psychological characteristics are often determined before employees enter the company, and it is very difficult for organizations to make changes. Therefore, the best way is to use the screening process to identify those employees who have high levels of JI and PC, and use them as candidates for further investigation. The company will be in a more favorable position when it comes to managing the turnover of employees with a higher degree of JI and PC.

In addition, studies have found that personal resume information and demographic background help predict their future turnover probability (Murray and Zimmerman, 2005; Griffeth et al., 2000), such as length of service, age, marital status, work experience, etc. Therefore, companies can collect relevant information during the recruitment phase, and based on this, the future turnover probability estimates for various types of managers are provided for reference for further personnel arrangements.

Companies that have taken effective measures during the recruitment phase to effectively reduce the employee's turnover probability include: Price Waterhouse Coopers, Northwestern Mutual Life, Leo Burnett, Cisco Systems, Disney World, Intel, etc. (Zhang, 2006). This empirically proves the importance of the recruitment process for the governance of turnover issues of managers.

2. Employment contract

The analysis of the previous chapters shows that when managers make turnover decisions, they will fully consider relevant benefits and job conversion costs. In order to reduce the probability of turnover, when signing a labor contract with an employee, the company can appropriately increase the clauses, which help increase the earnings and conversion costs. Such contracts include post-remuneration, deferred bonuses, retirement plans, etc. (Lazear, 1998). This measure has strong operability. Enterprises can prevent managers from irresponsible turnover before the establishment of labor relations.

Employment contract has two crucial functions in preventing the turnover of professional managers.

First, it can act as a screening tool, screening employees who have a higher degree of JI and PC, and who are more likely to be loyal to the company. Since those managers who do not plan to serve the company for a long time have lower expected returns, under such contracts than those offered by other companies, such managers will not accept the contract. The manager who accepts this contract must expect higher returns than other contracts. Therefore, it can be expected that those who intend to enter the company should have a high degree of JI and PC, and are willing to be loyal to the company. The employment contract serves as a screening tool here.

Second, the employment contract directly increases the income from job retention and job conversion costs. Items such as post-payment compensation and deferred bonuses delay the employee's immediate labor compensation until later in the career period. If managers leave before the payment period arrives, their losses will be very heavy. The clauses such as compensation for breach of contract directly stipulate the price that the employee needs to pay for the early termination of the labor contract. If the benefits provided by other job opportunities are insufficient to offset this cost, the manager will not rush to leave under the temptation.

3. Induction training and organization socialization

The first impression of new employees on the company is critical to their future career development. For excellent companies, they usually attach significant importance to the management of employees, while in the stage of entering the company, in the human resources management system. Induction training and organizational socialization are among the most important aspects. On the one hand, it provides support for junior employees with lesser qualifications, and advice on careers and personal development, to help them better adapt to future work. A manager who has confidence in his company's future will inevitably be less willing to leave. On the other hand, induction training and organizational socialization can increase employees' initial perceived satisfaction with relevant aspects of the company. Because the cognitive process has a selective perception characteristic, the initial evaluation of the company by the manager will affect the subsequent level of perception. If the initial evaluation is high, even if some unsatisfactory areas are discovered later, he will give a certain degree of understanding and tolerance, and will not easily translate this perception into worsening work attitudes, and then angrily leaving.

In addition, by organizing the socialization process, new employees can acquire the ideas, behavioral orientation, and knowledge, which are necessary to become members of the organization (Payne and Ann, 2005). A key element of this socialization is the understanding and acceptance of organizational goals and values. Research shows that employees who can share organizational goals and values will have a higher degree of emotional commitment to the organization, and this will reduce their turnover intention (Griffeth et al., 2000).

4. Job design and position arrangement

Our model shows that JP and JC have an important influence on the turnover intention of managers. For managers at a higher level in the workplace, the more challenging the company is to provide them with work, the greater the room for freedom given, and the more willing the manage is to remain in the company for an extended period of time.

Companies that have successfully reduced the probability of employee turnover through job design and position arrangement include General Electric, AES, and Ritz Cariton, etc. The main measures include providing more decision-making opportunities and allowing them full freedom when arranging positions. The effect achieved is very obvious (Zhang, 2006).

5. Organization and employer attraction

Organizational factors are the core factors affecting the turnover intention of managers. Employer factors have also been found to play a key role in the corresponding turnover decision-making process. Improving the attractiveness of organizations and employers in the company's HR system, is a crucial step in managing employee turnover.

Existing studies have pointed out that increasing the attractiveness of organizations and employers can be based on professional development opportunities and space, salary, organizational fairness, and the integrity of employers (Huang, 2007). Further measures include improving manager's expectations for the company's development prospects, building a harmonious internal and external network of companies, ensuring timely promotion, conducting a series of career guidance and vocational training, etc. (Zhang and Huang, 2007), and comprehensively enhancing the comprehensive attraction of the company through systematic organization and career management (Zhang et al., 2007).

Results also find that the companies' efforts in terms of organizational conditions, compensation systems, fair procedures, and space for development will help improve managers' perceptions, improve their satisfaction and commitment, and ultimately reduce their turnover intention. For managers with strong entrepreneurial motivation, it is more important for the enterprise to create a relaxed internal entrepreneurial environment, so that his entrepreneurial spirit can be fully played within the company. Otherwise, once the manager finds a right chance, he will resign from the current company and start up his own business.

Of course, as we pointed out in Chapter 7, when organizations do these efforts, they will face a trade-off between costs and benefits. However, for a very good managerial talent, it is worthwhile for the organization to pay a certain price.

6. Career planning and retirement

Managers enter the company to achieve their own career goals (Huang, 2007). Whether this goal can be achieved in the company will greatly affect the decision to continue their retention. Companies that can guide their employees in long-term career planning and help them achieve the plan will inevitably attract better professional managers.

Companies can take various measures to help managers' career development, such as: internal career promotion channels, sustainable development work, help employees to clarify their career development goals, encourage employees to locate their career development direction, and provide adequate on-job training Opportunities, etc. (Zhang, 2006).

Finally, retirement and pension plans in the company's human resources management system also help prevent managers from turnover (Lazear, 1998). Although the mandatory old-age insurance plan is not affected by the flow of managers, the special retirement policies of many companies stipulate the consequences of early turnovers. Therefore, in order to prevent the turnover of managers, it is important to design appropriate terms in retirement policy to increase the cost of their turnover. Employees have to consider the impact of this factor, when deciding whether to spend the entire career in this company.

7. Governance recommendations based on economic analysis on turnover

According to the economic analysis of the turnover of professional managers, if there is information asymmetry, the ideal match between professional managers and private enterprises is difficult to achieve. The truly capable and loyal managers cannot get the positions that can play a good role. The important posts have to be closed to the outside world. The core position that controls the company's operations is occupied by family members. With the expansion of company scale and the aggravation of management tasks, this family-controlled operation and management model will become increasingly inefficient, and it is necessary to break through the difficulties of familyism (Li, 2002). According to relevant results, the following specific recommendations are delivered:

First, make full use of intermediary companies of professional managers. Since the core of the problem lies in the information asymmetry about the quality of professional managers, so long as we overcome the incompleteness of this information beforehand, we can largely overcome the problem of inefficient balance. Talent agency companies (eg, headhunters, etc.) can play this role. They can provide companies with enough information to reduce the blindness of introducing professional managers. In general, an intermediary company hold various aspects of professional managers' information, including competence, loyalty, moral cultivation, work experience, past behavior, etc. Although it is impossible to be complete, this information can indeed reduce the degree of information asymmetry between employers and managers to some extent, and ease the impact of adverse selection.

Second, make use of social networks. Information about the quality of professional managers is likely to spread through social networks (especially those professional managers of better capability). Therefore, if the employers are fully embedded in social networks, such as chambers of commerce, clubs, entrepreneurs' associations, etc. (Granovetter, 1985), then the information about the quality of a manager can be learned from a variety of sources. This can reduce the asymmetry of information beforehand.

Third, improve the psychological cost of turnover. As the model analysis shows, when the manager obtains indirect utility from the firm π^* less than the retention utility π_c, he will leave. By shaping the corporate culture, increasing the value of identity, and strengthening the sense of belonging of professional managers, etc., the psychological cost of turnover can be increased, and retention utility π_c can be reduced. In this way, companies can expect the quality of managers who remain on the job to be not too bad, and trust them appropriately. The strengthening of trust can further increase the psychological cost of turnover, consolidate the psychological contract between the employer and the manager (Rousseau, 1990), and increase his loyalty, which will form a virtuous cycle. In fact, we have discovered that many companies have done so. A company with a good corporate culture, a harmonious company environment will not worry about the turnover issue of professional managers.

Fourth, implement "Loyalty Management". The above analysis indicates that for Chinese private enterprises, the loyalty of managers is of great value. Therefore, it is necessary to implement management for loyalty, which means both to maintain the loyalty of already loyal managers and to improve the loyalty of managers who are inclined to betray. According to the theory of social exchange (Blau, 1966), the social relationship between individuals is often strengthened through "courtesy demands reciprocity" and mutual trust etc. This is especially true for Chinese society (Huang, 2004; Fei, 2005). Therefore, business owners can increase their interaction and with managers, treat people sincerely (Fan and Zheng, 2000), and gradually let those loyal professional managers remain loyal. This kind of management that internalizes "outsiders" and turns them into "owners" can alleviate the adverse selection problem to some extent.

Fifth, implement career management of on-job managers (Sturges, 2005), understand managers' information comprehensively, and achieve separation equilibrium. Since management resources are major asset of the company, it is necessary to take good care of it. If there is a lack of attention to the managers, then those good managers will most probably leave and leave those less capable managers staying in the company.

Sixth, implement the institutionalization, standardization and transparency of company management. The main reason why private enterprises are concerned that professional managers may be unfavorable to them, is not that the manager cannot perform due diligence, but that those managers who are in positions of responsibility will use the company resources they control to seek private gains, and ultimately harm the company (Zhang, 2002; Chu and Liu, 2005). There is a lack of external institutional constraints, such as lack of legal control, social pressure, etc. In the situation where the external institutional environment cannot be changed immediately, the risk caused by low professional manager loyalty can be reduced through institutionalization, standardization, and transparency of management. Once the obscure areas of management have been eliminated, an effective and clear system of powers and responsibilities and a monitoring system have been established. Even managers who are not loyal to themselves are afraid to act rashly, and must behave according to the rules.

The above countermeasures help to alleviate the adverse selection problem in the process of professional managers' human capital transactions. In fact, many overseas Chinese companies and domestic private enterprises have already done so, and their effectiveness can be verified. Despite this, we still cannot fully overcome the consequences of information asymmetry. In the Chinese society that pays much attention to "relational governance" (Chen, 1998), many private entrepreneurs think that the loyalty of "outsiders" is difficult to verify after all, and that "family-clan members" are always reliable.

Main Contributions of This Research

First, based on the influencing factors examined in the existing research, this study introduces new influencing variables from the perspectives of cultural background differences, specialties of small and medium-sized enterprises and professional managers, and makes up for the turnover of managers of small and medium-sized private enterprises in China. In the context of Chinese culture, we test the mature model of turnover factors in the West, compare the similarities and differences between them, determine the commonality and specificity of the relevant models, and enrich existing turnover documents through cross-cultural comparison.

Second, based on the Chinese cultural background, we have introduced employer-related factors as important explanatory variables and moderating variables for managers' turnover intention. The empirical results show that the turnover decision of the professional manager is indeed affected by the employer factors. The business owner can improve the satisfaction of the manager through his own efforts, and offset the negative influence caused by other aspects. This discovery can bring inspiration to the turnover of managers of SMEs, and to a certain extent, it advances the progress of research on organizational behavior in the context of Chinese culture.

Third, based on qualitative research, this study has fully considered the personal characteristics of Chinese managers, such as career goals, achievement motivation, commitments, and job involvement etc. It proposes and verifies the process model of turnover intention formation from the following aspects: perception of relevant factors, change of work attitude, job search intention, and final turnover. It clarifies the relationship between different paths and phases given by different existing process models.

Forth, this study confirms the role of personal factors, such as JI, PC, EM, RA, and VI etc., in moderating the relevant attitude variables. It validates the role of employer factors in the moderating of organizational factors. This result helps companies find effective management measures for manager turnover.

Fifth, when domestic related researches put forward mechanisms and countermeasures, for managing the turnover of professional managers, most of them are based on individual factors and stages, and the proposed recommendations are not targeted and systematic. To overcome this deficiency, we understand the turnover decision of professional managers as a "process" consisting of a series of complex phases. Based on the process model obtained from the empirical test, the pre-prevention and post-event governance measures for turnover of professional managers are established for different stages and paths of the process. We also put forward related turnover management suggestions, from various aspects such as recruitment, employment contracts, training, job design etc., which has improved existing human resource management theory from the perspective of turnover management.

Sixth, based on the results of relevant studies in sociology, social psychology, and other disciplines, this study applies an adverse selection model and a dynamic matching model, to strictly provide a lack of management resources for private enterprises in China. It gives economic explanations on the turnover of professional managers and the family-oriented governance model. This explanation touches on the essence of the family-owned enterprise problem, emphasizes the essential difference between the Chinese family-owned enterprises and the western family-owned enterprises, and deepens the understanding of the existing research on the family-owned enterprise in China.

Seventh, this study provides enterprise managers with a set of assessment tools, concerning employees' perceptions, work attitudes, on- job status, and career goals etc. It helps organizations to understand the psychological status and subjective performance of on-job managers and predict their future trends, to better manage and use existing human resources. SME owners can design specific human resource management measures on the basis of managers' assessments, and achieve the goal of persistent management resources management by referring to relevant governance proposals proposed by us.

Research Limitations and Further Research Directions

First, due to the limited research conditions, the explanatory variables used in the empirical study are turnover intentions rather than turnover behaviors, although this is a widespread practice in the mainstream turnover literature. It is necessary to verify the turnover process model and factors model by collecting longitudinal data and using actual turnover behavior. This is the direction of further research.

Second, the sample of this study comes from questionnaires collected at a certain point of time. This type of cross-section data centralizes the antecedent, mediating, moderating and explanatory variables at the same time. The resulting process model is difficult to fully verify the cause-and-effect relationship between managers' turnover decision-making stages. Therefore, the next step in the research needs to measure the relevant variables at multiple time points, to obtain a progressive relationship in the turnover decision process.

Third, although we have avoided the common method variance (CMV) problem as far as possible in the design of the scale, according to the recommendations of the management literature, it must be recognized that most of the measured objects are psychological perception and subjective attitude variables. It is difficult to overcome the problem completely. The solution has to rely on objective measures of longitudinal data and related variables.

Forth, the sample of this study mainly came from Province. Therefore, when applying the relevant conclusions to SMEs in other regions, it is necessary to consider its locality and particularity. Of course, the next study can simply extend the scope of investigation to the whole country.

Fifth, the exploratory factors analysis, which we conduct before the formal empirical test, re-organizes the organization-related factors and employer-related factors into a few factors. The empirical results are not conducive to revealing in detail the effects of these factors on the impact of turnover. Further studies need to reconstruct constructs with higher discriminatory validity, in order to examine in more detail, the effects of specific organizational factors and employer factors.

Appendix 1: Some Proofs for the Chapter 7

1. Proof of formula (7-17)

Under the settings of specific function form and distribution in text, it is easy to get

$$E_1[J(l,a)] = \iint_{\Theta_1} (l+a)\frac{f_1(l,a|\Theta_1)}{F[l,a|\Theta_1]}dl \cdot da$$

$$= \iint_{\delta(l+a)\le\pi_0^*} (l+a)\cdot\frac{f_1(l|\Theta_1)\cdot f_a(a|\Theta_1)}{F[l,a|\Theta_1]}dl \cdot da \qquad (7\text{-A-1})$$

$F[l,a|\Theta_1]$ in above formula is give by following

$$F[l,a|\Theta_1] = P[\delta(l+a) \le \pi_0^*]$$

$$= \iint_{\delta(l+a)\le\pi_0^*} f_0(l)\cdot f_0(a)dl \cdot da$$

$$= \iint_{\delta(l+a)\le\pi_0^*} \phi(l-\mu_l)\cdot\phi(a-\mu_a)dl \cdot da \qquad (7\text{-A-2})$$

Let $m = l - \mu_l$, $n = a - \mu_a$, (7-A-2) can be written as

$$\iint_{\delta(m+n)\le\pi_0^*-\delta(\mu_l+\mu_a)} \phi(m)\cdot\phi(n)dm \cdot dn = \int_{-\infty}^{+\infty} dn \int_{-\infty}^{\lambda(n)} \phi(m)\cdot\phi(n)dm$$

$$= \int_{-\infty}^{+\infty} \phi(n)\cdot\Phi[\lambda(n)]dn \qquad (7\text{-A-3})$$

$\lambda(n)=\dfrac{\pi_0^*-\delta(\mu_1+\mu_a-n)}{\delta}$. According to same logic we can have following results:

$$E_1[J(1,a)]=\iint\limits_{\delta(m+n)\le\pi_0^*-\delta(\mu_1+\mu_a)}(m+n)\frac{\phi(m)\cdot\phi(n)}{F[1,a|\Theta_1]}dm\cdot dn+$$

$$\iint\limits_{\delta(m+n)\le\pi_0^*-\delta(\mu_1+\mu_a)}(\mu_1+\mu_a)\frac{\phi(m)\cdot\phi(n)}{F[1,a|\Theta_1]}dm\cdot dn$$

$$=\iint\limits_{\delta(m+n)\le\pi_0^*-\delta(\mu_1+\mu_a)}\frac{m\phi(m)\cdot\phi(n)}{F[1,a|\Theta_1]}dm\cdot dn+\iint\limits_{\delta(m+n)\le\pi_0^*-\delta(\mu_1+\mu_a)}\frac{n\phi(m)\cdot\phi(n)}{F[1,a|\Theta_1]}dm\cdot dn+$$

$$(\mu_1+\mu_a)\cdot\frac{\int_{-\infty}^{+\infty}\phi(n)\cdot\Phi[\lambda(n)]dn}{F[1,a|\Theta_1]}$$

$$=(\mu_1+\mu_a)\cdot\frac{\int_{-\infty}^{+\infty}\phi(n)\cdot\Phi[\lambda(n)]dn}{F[1,a|\Theta_1]}+\frac{\int_{-\infty}^{+\infty}\phi(n)dn\int_{-\infty}^{\lambda(n)}m\phi(m)dm}{F[1,a|\Theta_1]}\qquad(7\text{-A-}4)$$

$$+\frac{\int_{-\infty}^{+\infty}\phi(m)dn\int_{-\infty}^{\lambda(m)}n\phi(n)dn}{F[1,a|\Theta_1]}$$

Insert （7-A-3）into（7-A-4）, we get

$$E_1[J(1,a)]=\mu_1+\mu_a-\frac{2\int_{-\infty}^{+\infty}\phi(n)\cdot\phi[\lambda(n)]dn}{\int_{-\infty}^{+\infty}\phi(n)\cdot\Phi[\lambda(n)]dn}<E_0[J(1,a)]=\mu_1+\mu_a$$

This is just the result in text.

2. Proof of formula（7-27）

In term of the settings in text, the return of the second stage is

$$\pi_2^*=\int_{\Theta}q\cdot\frac{f_1(q|y)}{P(q\in\Theta)}dq$$

Under the hypothesis of monotone increasing of $\overline{\pi_1}(q)$, let

$\eta = \dfrac{\overline{\pi_1}^{-1}(\pi_1^*) - \mu_1}{\sigma_1}$, $x = \dfrac{q - \mu_1}{\sigma_1}$, above formula can be expressed as

$$\pi_2^* = \int_{-\infty}^{\overline{\pi_1}^{-1}(\pi_1^*)} q \cdot \frac{f_1(q|y)}{F[q \le \overline{\pi_1}^{-1}(\pi_1^*)]} dq$$

$$= \int_{-\infty}^{\eta} \sigma_1 \cdot x \frac{\phi(x)}{\Phi(\eta)} dx + \int_{-\infty}^{\eta} \mu_1 \cdot \frac{\phi(x)}{\Phi(\eta)} dx$$

$$= \sigma_1 \cdot \frac{\int_{-\infty}^{\eta} x\phi(x)dx}{\Phi(\eta)} + \mu_1 \cdot \frac{\int_{-\infty}^{\eta} \phi(x)dx}{\Phi(\eta)}$$

$$= \mu_1 - \sigma_1 \cdot \frac{\phi(\eta)}{\Phi(\eta)} \qquad (7\text{-A-5})$$

3. Proof of Proposition

According to the result from text, we have

$$\pi_c - \overline{\pi_1} = \delta q - \frac{\delta q}{1-\beta} + \beta \cdot \int V_2(\pi_2^*) g(\pi_2^*|q) d\pi_2^*$$

$$= \frac{-\beta\delta q}{1-\beta} + \beta \cdot \int_{-\infty}^{+\infty} \text{Max}\{\pi_2^* + \beta V_3(q), \delta q + \beta V_1\} g(\pi_2^*|q) d\pi_2^*$$

$$= \frac{-\beta\delta q}{1-\beta} + \beta \cdot \int_{-\infty}^{\overline{\pi_2}} (\delta q + \beta V_1) \cdot g(\pi_2^*|q) d\pi_2^* + \beta \cdot \int_{\overline{\pi_2}}^{+\infty} [\pi_2^* + \beta V_3(q)] \cdot g(\pi_2^*|q) d\pi_2^*$$

$$\ge \frac{-\beta\delta q}{1-\beta} \cdot \left\{ \int_{-\infty}^{\overline{\pi_2}} g(\pi_2^*|q) d\pi_2^* + \int_{\overline{\pi_2}}^{+\infty} g(\pi_2^*|q) d\pi_2^* \right\} + \frac{\beta\delta q}{1-\beta} \cdot \int_{-\infty}^{\overline{\pi_2}} \cdot g(\pi_2^*|q) d\pi_2^* +$$

$$\beta \cdot \int_{\overline{\pi_2}}^{+\infty} [\pi_2^* + \beta V_3(q)] \cdot g(\pi_2^*|q) d\pi_2^*$$

$$=\int_{\bar{\pi}_2}^{+\infty}[\beta\pi_2^* + \beta^2 V_3(q) - \frac{\beta\delta q}{1-\beta}]\cdot g(\pi_2^*|q)d\pi_2^*$$

（7-A-6）

In accordance with（7-21）, $V_3(q)=\text{Max}\left\{\frac{q}{1-\beta},\delta q+\beta V_1\right\}$,

consequently,

(1) When $q \geq \bar{\pi}_3$, $V_3(q)=\frac{q}{1-\beta}$, then

$$\bar{\pi}_2 = \delta q + \beta V_1 - \frac{\beta q}{1-\beta} \geq \frac{\delta q}{1-\beta} - \frac{\beta q}{1-\beta} = \frac{(\delta-\beta)q}{1-\beta} \qquad (7\text{-A-}7)$$

We can get the following inequality:

$$\int_{\bar{\pi}_2}^{+\infty}[\beta\pi_2^* + \frac{\beta^2 q}{1-\beta} - \frac{\beta\delta q}{1-\beta}]\cdot g(\pi_2^*|q)d\pi_2^* > \int_{\bar{\pi}_2}^{+\infty}[\beta\bar{\pi}_2 + \frac{\beta^2 q}{1-\beta} - \frac{\beta\delta q}{1-\beta}]\cdot g(\pi_2^*|q)d\pi_2^*$$

$$\geq \int_{\bar{\pi}_2}^{+\infty}[\beta\frac{(\delta-\beta)q}{1-\beta} + \frac{\beta^2 q}{1-\beta} - \frac{\beta\delta q}{1-\beta}]\cdot g(\pi_2^*|q)d\pi_2^* = 0$$

That is

$$\pi_e - \bar{\pi}_1 > 0 \qquad (7\text{-A-}8)$$

(2) When $q < \bar{\pi}_3$, $V_3(q)=\delta q+\beta V_1$, then

$$\bar{\pi}_2 = \delta q + \beta V_1 - \beta V_3(q) = (\delta q + \beta V_1)(1-\beta)$$

This inequality is established:

$$\int_{\bar{\pi}_2}^{+\infty}[\beta\pi_2^* + \beta^2(\delta q + \beta V_1) - \frac{\beta\delta q}{1-\beta}]\cdot g(\pi_2^*|q)d\pi_2^*$$

$$> \int_{\overline{\pi}_2}^{+\infty} [\beta \overline{\pi}_2 + \beta^2 (\delta q + \beta V_1) - \frac{\beta \delta q}{1-\beta}] \cdot g(\pi_2^* | q) d\pi_2^*$$

$$= \int_{\overline{\pi}_2}^{+\infty} [\beta (\delta q + \beta V_1)(1-\beta) + \beta^2 \delta q + \beta^3 V_1 - \frac{\beta \delta q}{1-\beta}] \cdot g(\pi_2^* | q) d\pi_2^*$$

$$\geq \int_{\overline{\pi}_2}^{+\infty} [\beta (\delta q + \beta \frac{\delta q}{1-\beta})(1-\beta) + \beta^2 \delta q + \beta^3 \frac{\delta q}{1-\beta} - \frac{\beta \delta q}{1-\beta}] \cdot g(\pi_2^* | q) d\pi_2^*$$

$$= 0$$

That is

$$\pi_e - \overline{\pi}_1 > 0 \qquad (7\text{-}A\text{-}9)$$

In the end, through combining the results of (1) and (2), we conclude: $\overline{\pi}_1 < \pi_e$, and

$$P(\pi_1^* \geq \overline{\pi}_1) > P(\pi_1^* \geq \pi_e)$$

This is just the result we want to prove.

Appendix 2: Questionnaire

Evaluation Table of Corporate Appeal for Professional Managers

This form is used to determine the attractiveness of a company to professional managers. We guarantee that personal data will not be disclosed to any individual or department in any form.

I. Basic Information

Gender	Male ( ) Female ( )	**Marital status**	Unmarried ( ) Married ( )
Age	( )	**Position**	High-level ( ); Mid-level ( ); Grassroots ( )
Total working years	( ) years	**Length of service in this company (accurate to the month)**	( ) years+ ( ) months
Education	High school and below ( ); Junior college ( ); Undergraduate ( ); Graduate and above ( )		
Company size (total assets)	40 million or less ( ); 40 million -400 million ( ); 400 million or more ( )		
Years of operation	( ) years	**How many companies have you worked for before you came to this company?**	( )

II. Occupational Attitude (In the third column, "1" means "completely disagree", and "7" means "completely agree"; the fourth column shows the importance of various factors to the employees' long-term work in the company. "1" refers to "very unimportant", "7" refers to" very important")

Items	Descriptions	Level of Agreement	Degree of Importance
Q1	Q1_1:　I like the job	1……7	1……7
	Q1_2:　I am passionate about my work	1……7	1……7
	Q1_3:　I can get satisfaction from my job	1……7	1……7
	Q1_4:　I am generally satisfied with my work	1……7	1……7
Q2	Q2_1:　The current work has important implications for my professional development	1……7	1……7
	Q2_2:　I have a strong sense of belonging to the company	1……7	1……7
	Q2_3:　I am proud to work for this company	1……7	1……7
Q3	Q3_1:　The boss is very satisfied with my performance	1……7	1……7
	Q3_2:　I often put extra effort for the company	1……7	1……7
	Q3_3:　I often help my colleagues do work outside the scope of my duties	1……7	1……7
Q4	Q4_1:　I will take the initiative to safeguard the interests of the company	1……7	1……7
	Q4_2:　Even without supervision, I will do my best to complete the work	1……7	1……7
	Q4_3:　I feel honored for the company's achievements	1……7	1……7
Q5	Q5_1:　I am bored with my job	1……7	
	Q5_2:　I sometimes feel sorry for working in this company	1……7	

III. Career Preferences

Items	Descriptions	Level of Agreement
Q6	Q6_1: This company is a good place for talents	1……7
	Q6_2: I would like to recommend a friend to work for the company	1……7
	Q6_3: I hope to work in the company for a minimum of five years	1……7
Q7	Q7_1: I rarely pay attention to information about other job opportunities	1……7
	Q7_2: I have no interest in other job opportunities	1……7

Items	Descriptions	Level of Agreement
Q7	Q7_3: I will ont find other jobs in the next three years	1……7
Q8	Q8: I hope to work in the company until retirement	1……7

IV. Evaluation of organizations, jobs and employers

Items	Descriptions	Level of Agreement	Degree of Importance
Q9	Q9_1: The company has a sound incentive system	1……7	1……7
	Q9_2: Employees have good development opportunities and space in the company	1……7	1……7
	Q9_3: Employees have the opportunity to get higher pay in the company	1……7	1……7

Q10	Q10_1: Company compensation is competitive in the industry	1……7	1……7
	Q10_2: The company has just compensation system	1……7	1……7
	Q10_3: I am generally satisfied with my salary	1……7	1……7
Q11	Q11_1: The company's work environment and cultural atmosphere are good	1……7	1……7
	Q11_2: The company management system is perfect	1……7	1……7
	Q11_3: The company has bright development prospects	1……7	1……7
	Q11_4: The company has Good social image	1……7	1……7
Q12	Q12_1: The relationship between the company's superior and subordinate relations is harmonious	1……7	1……7
	Q12_2: The relationship between employees is harmonious	1……7	1……7
	Q12_3: The relationship between company employees and outsiders is harmonious	1……7	1……7
Q13	Q13_1: When the company has a major event, it will inform relevant personnel	1……7	1……7
	Q13_2: High-level decision-making will seek opinions from relevant personnel	1……7	1……7

	Q13_3：Company decision-making process considers employee needs and benefits	1……7	1……7
Q14	Q14_1：Employees have the opportunity to learn new knowledge and skills in the company	1……7	1……7
	Q14_2：Work experience in this company helps improve work ability	1……7	1……7
	Q14_3：The company provides full vocational training and rotation opportunities	1……7	1……7
Q15	Q15_1：I can control my own work process	1……7	1……7
	Q15_2: I have an influence on matters related to me at work	1……7	1……7
	Q15_3: I usually participate in decisions related to my work	1……7	1……7
Q16	Q16_1：My job responsibilities are blurred	1……7	1……7
	Q16_2：Different supervisors will ask for conflicting job requirements	1……7	1……7
	Q16_3：My work load exceeds the range I can afford	1……7	1……7
	Q16_4：I can't get enough work support	1……7	1……7

Q17	Q17_1: I often have extra work to do	1……7	1……7
	Q17_2: My job responsibilities are significant	1……7	1……7
	Q17_3: I have a larger jurisdiction	1……7	1……7
Q18	Q18_1: Leaders are proud of my achievements	1……7	1……7
	Q18_2: Leaders often care about my personal welfare	1……7	1……7
	Q18_3: Leaders value my contribution to the organization	1……7	1……7
Q19	Q19_1: The boss has a strong entrepreneurial ability	1……7	1……7
	Q19_2: The boss's management style is very agreeable	1……7	1……7
	Q19_3: The boss is very charismatic	1……7	1……7
Q20	Q20_1: The boss maintains integrity with business partners	1……7	1……7
	Q20_2: The boss usually fulfills his promise to his employees	1……7	1……7
	Q20_3: The company strictly abides by various laws and regulations	1……7	1……7
	Q20_4: Boss cares about corporate social responsibility	1……7	1……7

Q21	Q21_1: The boss just treats all subordinates	1……7	1……7
	Q21_2: The boss respects the rights of employees	1……7	1……7
	Q21_3: The boss treats all employees equally	1……7	1……7
Q22	Q22_1: The boss strongly hopes to make the company strong and long-lasting	1……7	1……7
	Q22_2: The boss regards work as the most important thing in life	1……7	1……7
	Q22_3: The boss has a strong dedication	1……7	1……7
Q23	Q23_1: I am introduced to the company by acquaintance	1……7	1……7
	Q23_2: I have a very good personal relationship with my boss	1……7	1……7
	Q23_3: I have a good relationship with the company	1……7	1……7
Q24	Q24_1: In the company I can give full play to my talent	1……7	1……7
	Q24_2: I am very adaptable to corporate culture	1……7	1……7
	Q24_3: I agree with the boss's personal values and company philosophy	1……7	1……7
	Q24_4: In general, I match with the company in all aspects	1……7	1……7

Q25	Q25_1：If I leave the company, I will find a better job	1……7	1……7
	Q25_2：Someone can help me find other jobs	1……7	1……7
	Q25_3：I now have other job opportunities	1……7	1……7
	Q25_4：For better work I can go elsewhere	1……7	1……7
Q26	Q26_1: The boss believes that employees will consciously safeguard the interests of the company	1……7	1……7
	Q26_2：The boss is willing to speak to his subordinates and sincerely communicate	1……7	1……7
	Q26_3：The boss gives full authority to each management position	1……7	1……7
Q27	Q27：Is the company undergoing or will undergo major organizational changes or adjustments?	Yes ( )	No ( )
Q28	Q28：I plan to spend my entire career in the company	Yes ( )	No ( )

V. Personal Career Orientation

Items	Descriptions	Level of Agreement	Degree of Importance
Q29	Q29_1: Work is my main pleasure	1……7	1……7
	Q29_1: Work is a top priority in my life	1……7	1……7
	Q29_1: My life and work are inseparable	1……7	1……7
Q30	Q30_1: I will try my best to avoid risks and avoid responsibility	1……7	1……7
	Q30_1: I prefer to work with stable income and low risk	1……7	1……7
	Q30_1: I prefer to work in my own familiar job	1……7	1……7
Q31	Q31_1: In case of dispute, the higher-level should make decisions	1……7	1……7
	Q31_1: Avoiding mistakes is best done in accordance with senior guidance	1……7	1……7
	Q31_1: Employees should try to listen to boss' decisions and work arrangements as much as possible	1……7	1……7
Q32	Q32_1: I am willing to work for a company for a long time	1……7	1……7
	Q32_1: Long-term work in a company helps to accumulate qualifications	1……7	1……7

Q32	Q32_1： Long-term in a company is not monotonous	1……7	1……7
Q33	Q33_1： I will consider starting a business throughout my career	1……7	1……7
	Q33_1：If conditions are ripe, I will consider starting my own business	1……7	1……7
	Q33_1： In the near future I may start my own business	1……7	1……7

If you have worked in other companies before you come to the company, please answer the following questions about the situation of former company.

VI. Related Situation of Former Company ("1" means "totally disagree", "7" means "totally agree")

Items	Descriptions	Level of Agreement
P1	P1_1： The company is a good place to play talent	1……7
	P1_2： I would like to recommend friends to work for the company	1……7
	P1_3： I hope to work in this company for a minimum of five years	1……7
P2	P2_1： Former company has a sound incentive system	1……7
	P2_2： Employees have good development opportunities and space in the former company	1……7
	P2_3： Employees in the former company have the opportunity to obtain higher remuneration	1……7

P3	P3_1: Former company compensation is competitive in the industry	1……7
	P3_2: The pay system in the former company is just	1……7
	P3_3: I was generally satisfied with my salary	1……7
P4	P4_1: The former company's working environment and cultural atmosphere is good	1……7
	P4_2: The former company management system is perfect	1……7
	P4_3: There is bright prospects for the former company's development	1……7
	P4_4: The former company has good corporate social image	1……7
P5	P5_1: there is good relationship between the previous company's superior and subordinate	1……7
	P5_2: There is good relationship between employees in former company	1……7
	P5_3: There is good relationship between employees and external personnel in former company	1……7
P6	P6_1: Related personnel will be informed when major events occur in previous companies	1……7
	P6_2: High-level decision-making will seek opinions from relevant personnel	1……7
	P6_3: Former company decision-making process considers employee needs and benefits	1……7

P7	P7_1: Former company's decision-making process considers employee needs and benefits	1……7
	P7_2: The work experience in former company helps improve capability	1……7
	P7_3: Former company provides full career training and rotation opportunities	1……7
P8	P8_1: I can control my own work process	1……7
	P8_2: I have an influence on matters related to me at work	1……7
	P8_3: I usually participate in decisions related to my work	1……7
P9	P9_1: In the former company, my job responsibilities are blurred	1……7
	P9_2: Different supervisors will ask for conflicting job requirements	1……7
	P9_3: My work load exceeds the range I can afford	1……7
	P9_4: In the former company, I have difficulty getting enough work support	1……7
P10	P10_1: I often have extra work to do	1……7
	P10_2: My job responsibilities are significant	1……7
	P10_3: I have a larger jurisdiction	1……7
P11	P 11_1: Former company leaders are proud of my achievements	1……7
	P 11_2: Former company leaders often care about my personal welfare	1……7
	P 11_3: Former company leaders value my contribution to the organization	1……7

P12	P 12_1：Former company boss has strong entrepreneurial ability	1……7
	P 12_2：The management style of the former company boss is agreeable	1……7
	P 12_3：Former company boss has great leadership	1……7
P13	P 13_1: Former company boss maintains integrity with business partners	1……7
	P 13_2：Former company boss often honors their commitment to their employees	1……7
	P 13_3：The former company strictly abides by various laws and regulations	1……7
	P 13_4：Former company boss cares about corporate social responsibility	1……7
P14	P 14_1: Former company bosses treat all subordinates impartially	1……7
	P 14_2：The boss respects the rights of employees	1……7
	P 14_3：Former company boss treats all employees equally	1……7
P15	P 15_1：The former boss strongly hopes to make the company strong and long-lasting	1……7
	P 15_2：The former boss regards work as the most important thing in life	1……7
	P 15_3：Former company boss has strong dedication	1……7

P16	P 16_1：I was introduced to the former company by acquaintances	1……7
	P 16_2：I have a good personal relationship with the former company boss	1……7
	P 16_3：I have a very good personal connections in former company	1……7
P17	P 17_1：In the former company I can give full play to my talent	1……7
	P 17_2：I adapt well to the former corporate culture	1……7
	P 17_3：I agree with former company boss's personal values and company philosophy	1……7
	P 17_4：In general, I match with the former company in all aspects	1……7
P18	P18_1：I could find a better job if I left the company	1……7
	P18 _2：Someone could help me find other jobs	1……7
	P18 _3：I already had other job opportunities when I left	1……7
	P18 _4：I could go elsewhere for better work	1……7
P19	P19 _1：Former company boss believes that employees will consciously safeguard the interests of the company	1……7
	P19 _2: Former company boss is willing to speak to his subordinates and sincerely communicate	1……7
	P19 _3: Former company boss gives full authority to each management position	1……7

P20	P20：Has the former company experienced major organizational changes or adjustments?	Yes ( ) No ( )
P21	P21：What was the initial reason that prompted you to leave the previous company?	Personal reasons （ ）； Employer factors （ ）； Corporate organizational factors （ ）; Human relations（ ）; Work factors （ ）； Other reasons：____________
P22	P 22：Your working experience in the previous company was：（ ） years +（ ） months	

Appendix 3: LISREL Program for Confirmatory Factor Analysis (CFA)

```
TI CFA4
DA NI=54 NO=456 MA=KM
RA FI='...'
SE
1 2 3 4 5 6 7 8 9 10 11 12 13 14 15 16 17 18 20 21 22 23 24 25 26 19 27
28 29 30 31 32 33 34 35 36 37 38 39 40 41 42 43 44 45 46 47 48 49 50
51 52 53 54
MO NX=54 NK=18 TD=SY
LK
OSC SR JC JP BCI BFT BLH JE OJ JI PC EM CR JSC JFC JA JL
TOVL
FR LX(1,1) LX(2,1) LX(3,1) LX(4,1) LX(5,2) LX(6,2) LX(7,2) LX(8,3)
LX(9,3) LX(10,3)
FR LX(11,4) LX(12,4) LX(13,4) LX(14,4) LX(15,5) LX(16,5) LX(17,5)
LX(18,5) LX(19,6) LX(20,6) LX(21,6)
FR LX(22,6) LX(23,7) LX(24,7) LX(25,7) LX(26,7) LX(27,8) LX(28,8)
LX(29,9) LX(30,9)
FR LX(31,10) LX(32,10) LX(33,10) LX(34,11) LX(35,11) LX(36,11)
LX(37,12) LX(38,12) LX(39,12)
FR LX(41,14) LX(42,14) LX(43,14) LX(44,14) LX(45,15) LX(46,15)
LX(47,15) LX(48,15)
FR LX(49,16) LX(50,16) LX(51,17) LX(52,17) LX(53,17)
FI LX(40,13) LX(54,18) TD(40,40) TD(54,54)
VA 1 LX(40,13) LX(54,18)
VA 0 TD(40,40) TD(54,54)
PD
OU
```

Appendix 4: LISREL Program for Structural Equations Modeling (SEM)

```
TI SEM7
DA NI=50 NO=456 MA=KM
RA FI='...'
SE
38 39 40 41 42 43 44 45 46 47 48 49 50 1 2 3 4 5 6 7 8 9 10 11 12 13 14
15
16 17 19 20 21 22 18 23 24 25 26 27 28 29 30 31 32 33 34 35 36 37
MO NY=13 NE=5 NX=37 NK=13 TD=DI,FR TE=DI,FR BE=FU,FI
GA=FU,FI
LE
JSC JFC JA JL TOVL
LK
OSC SR JC JP BCI BFT BLH JE OJ JI PC EM CR
FR LY(1,1) LY(2,1) LY(3,1) LY(4,1) LY(5,2) LY(6,2) LY(7,2) LY(8,3)
LY(9,3) LY(10,4) LY(11,4) LY(12,4)
FR LX(1,1) LX(2,1) LX(3,1) LX(4,1) LX(5,2) LX(6,2) LX(7,2) LX(8,3)
LX(9,3) LX(10,3)
FR LX(11,4) LX(12,4) LX(13,4) LX(14,4) LX(15,5) LX(16,5) LX(17,5)
LX(18,6) LX(19,6) LX(20,6) LX(21,6)
FR LX(22,7) LX(23,7) LX(24,7) LX(25,7) LX(28,10) LX(29,10)
LX(30,10)
FR LX(31,11) LX(32,11) LX(33,11) LX(34,12) LX(35,12) LX(36,12)
FI LY(13,5) LX(26,8) LX(27,9) LX(37,13) TE(13,13) TD(26,26)
TD(27,27) TD(37,37)
VA 1 LY(13,5) LX(26,8) LX(27,9) LX(37,13)
VA 0 TE(13,13) TD(26,26) TD(27,27) TD(37,37)
FR GA(1,1) GA(1,2) GA(1,3) GA(1,4) GA(1,5) GA(1,6) GA(1,7)
GA(1,8) GA(1,10)
```

FR GA(2,1) GA(2,2) GA(2,3) GA(2,4) GA(2,5) GA(2,6) GA(2,7) GA(2,8) GA(2,10)
FR GA(3,1) GA(3,2) GA(3,3) GA(3,4) GA(3,5) GA(3,6) GA(3,7) GA(3,8) GA(3,10)
FR GA(4,1) GA(4,5) GA(4,6) GA(4,8) GA(4,11) GA(4,13)
FR GA(5,4) GA(5,9) GA(5,11) GA(5,12)
FR BE(2,1) BE(3,1) BE(4,1) BE(3,2) BE(5,4) BE(5,3)
PD
OU AD=OFF EF

Appendix 5: LISREL Standardized Estimation Coefficients of Model M2

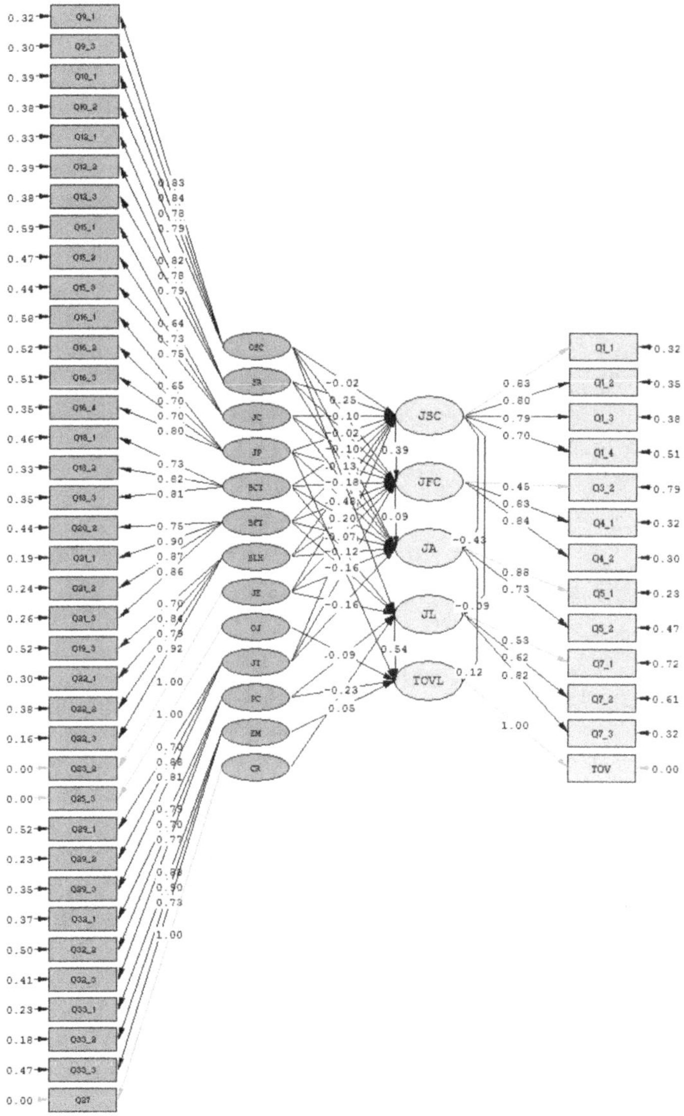

Chi-Square=2471.02, df=1058, P-value=0.00000, RMSEA=0.054

Bibliography

Abelson, M. A. and Baysinger, B. D. (1984). Optimal and dysfunctional turnover: Toward an organizational level model. Academy of Management Review, 9(2): 331-341.

Ajzen, I and Fishbein, M. (1977). Attitude-behavior relations: a theoretical analysis and review of empirical research. Psychological Bulletin, 84(5): 888-918.

Ajzen, I. (2002). Perceived behavioral control, self-efficacy, locus of control, and the theory of planned behavior. Journal of Applied Social Psychology, 32(4): 1-20.

Akerlof, G. (1970). The market for lemons: quality uncertainty and the market mechanism. Quarterly Journal of Economics, 84(3): 488-500.

Alcover, C. M., Rico, R., Turnley, W. H. and Bolino, M. (2017). Understanding the changing nature of psychological contracts in 21st century organizations: a multiple-foci exchange relationships approach and proposed framework. Organizational Psychology Review, 7(1): 4-35.

Allen, C. and Bluedorn. (1978). A taxonomy of turnover. Academy of Management Review, 21: 647-651.

Allen, D. G. and Griffeth, R. W. (1999). Job performance and turnover: a review and integrative multi-route model. Human Resource Management Review, 9(4): 525-548.

Allen, D. G. and Griffeth, R. W. (2001). Test of a mediated performance-turnover relationship highlighting the moderating roles of visibility and reward contingency. Journal of Applied Psychology, 86(5): 1014-1021.

Allen, D. G., Weeks, K. P. and Moffitt, K. R. (2005). Turnover intentions and voluntary turnover: the moderating roles of self-monitoring, locus of control, proactive personality, and risk aversion. Journal of Applied Psychology, 90(5): 980-990.

Aquino, K., Griffeth, R. W., Allen, D. G. and Hom, P. W. (1997). Integrating justice constructs into the turnover process: A test of a referent cognitions model. Academy of Management Journal, 40(5): 1208-1227.

Aryee, S., Kim, T. Y., Chu, C. and Ryu, S. (2017). Family supportive work environment, perceptions of the employment relationship and employee work outcomes. Academy of Management, forthcoming.

Aryee, S., Walumbwa, F. O., Seidu, E. Y. M. and Otaye, L. E. (2016). Developing and leveraging human capital resource to promote service quality: Testing a theory of performance. Journal of Management, 42(2): 480-499.
Auriol, E., Friebel, G. and Bieberstein, F, V. (2016). The firm as the locus of social comparisons: Standard promotion practices versus up-or-out. Journal of Economic Behavior and Organization, 121(1): 41-59.
Balfour, D. L. and Neff, D. M. (1993). Predicting and managing turnover in human service agencies: a case study of an organization in crisis. Public Personnel Management, 22(3): 473-486.
Barnard, C. I. (1938). The function of the executive. Cambridge, MA: Harvard University Press.
Barrick, M. R. and Mount, M. K. (1996). Effects of impression management and self-deception on the predictive validity of personality constructs. Journal of Applied Psychology, 81(3): 261-272.
Batt, R. and Colvin, A. (2011). An employment systems approach to turnover: HR practices, quits, dismissals, and performance. Academy of Management Journal, 54(4): 695-717.
Batt, R. (2002). Managing customer services: Human resource practices, quit rates, and sales growth. Academy of Management Journal, 45(3): 587-597.
Bauer, T. N., Maertz, C. P., Dolen, M. R., and Campion, M. A. (1998). Longitudinal assessment of applicant reactions to employment testing and test outcome feedback. Journal of Applied Psychology, 83(6): 892-903.
Becker, G. S. (1964). Human Capital. New York: Columbia University Press.
Becton, J. B., Carr, J. C., Mossholder, K. W. and Walker, H. J. (2016). Differential effects of task performance, organizational citizenship behavior, and job complexity on voluntary turnover. Journal of Business and Psychology, (July): 1-14.
Bench, S. W., Schlegel, R. J., Davis, W. E. and Vess, M. (2015). Thinking about change in the self and others: the role of self-discovery metaphors and the true self. Social Cognition, 33(3): 1-15.
Benson, G. S., David, F., Susan, M. A. (2004). You paid for the skills, now keep them: tuition reimbursement and voluntary turnover. Academy of Management Journal, 47(3): 315-331.
Berdett, K. and Mortenson, D. T. (1980). Search, layoffs, and labor

market equilibrium. Journal of Political Economy, 88(4): 652-72.
Berkman, L. F., Liu, S. Y., Hammer, L., Moen, P., Klein, L. C. and Kelly, E. (2015). Work-family conflict, cardiometabolic risk, and sleep duration in nursing employees. Journal of Occupational Health Psychology, 20(4): 420-433
Berle, A. A. and Means, G. C. (1932). The modern corporation and private property, New York: The Macmillan Company.
Bettencourt, L. A., Gwinner, K. P. and Meuter, M. L. (2001). A comparison of attitude, personality, and knowledge predictions of service-oriented organizational citizenship behaviors. Journal of Applied Psychology, 86(1): 29-41.
Bhide, A. (1999). The origins and evolution of new businesses. Oxford University Press.
Bies, R. J. and Moag, J. F. (1986). Interactional justice: Communication criteria of fairness. In Lewicki R J, Sheppard B H and Bazerman M H (Eds.). Research on negotiations in organizations, Greenwich, CT: JAI Press, (1): 43-55.
Bijlsma, K. and Koopman, P. (2003). Introduction: Trust within organizations. Personnel Review, 32(5): 543-555.
Blau, P. (1964). Exchange and power in social life. New York: Wiley.
Bogg, J. and Cooper, C. (1995). Job satisfaction, mental health, and occupational stress among senior civil servants. Human Relations, 48(3): 327-341.
Bontempo, R. and Rivero, J. C. (1992). Cultural variation in cognition: the role of self-concept in the attitude behavior link. Paper presented at the meeting of the American Academy of Management, August, Las Vegas.
Bosma, N., Hessels, J., Schutjens, V., Praag, M. V. and Verheul, I. (2012). Entrepreneurship and role models. Journal of Economic Psychology, 33(2): 410-424.
Boswell, W. R., Gardner, R. G. and Wang, J. (2017). Is retention necessarily a win? Outcomes of searching and staying. Journal of Vocational Behavior, 98(2):163-172.
Bowling, N. A. (2010). A meta-analysis of the predictors and consequences of organization-based self-esteem. Journal of Occupational and Organizational Psychology, 83(3): 601-626.
Bozeman, D. P. and Perrewe, P. L. (2001). The effect of item content overlap on organizational commitment questionnaire-turnover cognitions relationships. Journal of Applied Psychology, 86(1): 161-173.
Brief, A. P. and Weiss, H. M. (2002). Organizational behavior: affect in the workplace. Annual Review of Psychology, 53(1): 279-307.

Brief, A. P. (1998). Attitudes in and around organizations. Thousand Oaks, CA: Sage.
Brockner, J. and Chen, Y. R. (1996). The moderating roles of self-esteem and self-construal in reaction to a threat to the self: Evidence from the People's Republic of China and the United States. Journal of Personality and Social Psychology, 71(3): 603-615.
Brown, A. D. (2015). Identities and identity work in organizations. International Journal of Management Reviews, 17(1): 20-40.
Burke, P. J. (1991). Identity processes and social stress. American Sociological Review, 56(6), 836-849.
Cai, Z., Guan, Y., Li, H., Shi, W., Guo, K. and Liu, Y. (2015). Self-esteem and proactive personality as predictors of future work self and career adaptability: an examination of mediating and moderating processes. Journal of Vocational Behavior, 86(2): 86-94.
Campion, M. A. (1991). Meaning and measurement in turnover: comparison of alternative measures and recommendations for research. Journal of Applied Psychology, 76(2): 199-212.
Cappelli, P. (2000). A market-driven approach to retaining talent. Harvard Business Review, 78(1): 103-111.
Cascio, W. F. (1976). Turnover, biographical data, and fair employment practice. Journal of Applied Psychology, 61(5): 576-580.
Cassar, V. and Buttigieg, S. C. (2015). Psychological contract breach, organizational justice and emotional well-being. Personnel Review, 44(2): 217 - 235
Castro-Casal, C., Neira-Fontela, E. and Álvarez-Pérez, M. D. (2013). Human resources retention and knowledge transfer in mergers and acquisitions. Journal of Management and Organization, 19(2): 188-209.
Cavanaugh, M. A., Boswell, W. R., Roehling, M. V. and Boudreau, J. W. (2000). An empirical examination of self-reported work stress among U.S. managers. Journal of Applied Psychology, 85(1): 65-74.
Chandler, A. D. (1978). The visible hand: the managerial revolution in American business. The Belknap Press of Harvard University Press.
Charles, A. O., Caldwell, D. F. and Barnett, W. P. (1989). Work group demography, social integration, and turnover. Administrative Science Quarterly, 34(1): 21-38.
Chatman, J. A. (1989). Improving interactional organizational research: a model of person-organization fit. Academy of Management

Review, 14(3): 333-349.
Chen, J. Q., Hou, Z. J., Li, X., Lovelace, K. J., Liu, Y. L. and Wang, Z. L. (2016). The role of career growth in Chinese new employee's turnover process. Journal of Career Development, 43(1): 11-25.
Chen, L. (1998). Information characteristics, transaction cost and clannish organization. Economic Research Journal, (7): 28-34.
Chen, X. P., Hui, C. and Sego, D. J. (1998). The role of organizational citizenship behavior in turnover: Conceptualization and preliminary tests of key hypotheses. Journal of Applied Psychology, 83(6): 922-931.
Chen, Z. X. and Aryee, S. (2007). Delegation and employee work outcomes: an examination of the cultural context of mediating processes in China. Academy of Management Journal, 50(1): 226-238.
Chen, Z. X. and Francesco, A. M. (2000). Employee demography, organizational commitment, and turnover intentions in China: Do cultural differences matter? Human Relations, 53(6): 869-887.
Chen, Z. X., Tsui, A. S., Farh, J. (2002). Loyalty to supervisor vs. organizational commitment: Relationships to employee performance in China. Journal of Occupational and Organizational Psychology, 75(2): 339-356.
Cheng, A. and Brown, A. (1998). HRM Strategies and labor turnover in the hotel industry: a comparative study of Australia and Singapore. The International Journal of Human Resource Management, 9(1): 136-155.
Chu, X. and Li, H. (2003). Trust and the growth of family business. Management World, (6): 98-104.
Chu, X. and Liu, Q. (2005). An explanation for professional managers' job embezzlement by psychological ownership theory. Management World, (7): 83-93.
Chu, X. (2002). Professional managers and the growth of family business. Management World, (4): 100-108.
Chu, X. (2000). The research on family business: a topic with modern significance. Social Sciences in China, (12): 51-58.
Churchill, N. C. and Hatten, K. J. (2010). Non-market-based transfers of wealth and power: a research framework for family businesses. Family Business Review, 10(1): 53-67.
Cohen, A. (1999). Turnover among professionals: a longitudinal study of American layers. Human Resource Management, 38(1): 61-75.
Colquitt, J. A., Long, D. M., Rodell, J. B. and Halvorsen-Ganepola, M. D. (2015). Adding the "in" to justice: a qualitative and quantitative investigation of the differential effects of justice rule adherence

and violation. Journal of Applied Psychology, 100(2): 278-297.
Colquitt, J. A., Scott, B. A., Rodell, J. B., Long, D. M., Zapata, C. P. and Conlon, D. E. (2013). Justice at the millennium, a decade later: a meta-analytic test of social exchange and affect-based perspectives. Journal of Applied Psychology, 98(2): 199-236.
Connie, W. R. and Kammeyer-mueller, J. D. (2000). Predictors and Outcomes of Proactivity in the Socialization Process. Journal of Applied Psychology, 85(3): 373-385.
Cotton, J. L. and Tuttle, J. M. (1986). Employee turnover: a meta-analysis and review with implications for research. Academy of Management Review, 11(1): 55-70.
Craig, E., Kimberly, J. and Bouchikhi, H. (2002). Can loyalty be leased? Harvard Business Review, 80(9): 24-31.
Cropanzano, R., Anthony, E. L., Daniels, S. R. and Hall, A. V. (2017). Social exchange theory: a critical review with theoretical remedies. Academy of Management Annals, 11(1): 1-38.
Cropanzano, R., Rupp, D. E. and Byrne, Z. S. (2003). The relationship of emotional exhaustion to work attitudes, job performance, and organizational citizenship behaviors. Journal of Applied Psychology, 88(1): 160-169.
Currivan, D. B. (1999). The causal order of job satisfaction and organizational commitment in models of employee turnover. Human Resource Management Review, 9(4): 495-524.
Dabos, G. E. and Rousseau, D. M. (2004). Mutuality and reciprocity in the psychological contracts of employees and employers. Journal of Applied Psychology, 89(1): 52-72.
Dai, Y. (2005). The miracle of Chinese economy: private economy rising. People's Publishing House.
Davis, P. (1983). Realizing the potential of the family business. Organizational Dynamics, 12(1): 47-56.
Davison, M. L., Kwak, N., Seo, Y. S. and Choi, J. (2015). Using hierarchical linear models to examine moderator effects: person-by-organization interactions. Organizational Research Methods, 5(3): 231-254.
DeJong, B. A., Dirks, K. T. and Gillespie, N. (2016). Trust and team performance: a meta-analysis of main effects, moderators, and covariates. Journal of Applied Psychology, 101(8):1134-1150.
Deconinck, J. B. and Stilwell, C. D. (2004). Incorporating organizational justice, role states, pay satisfaction and supervisor satisfaction in a model of turnover intentions. Journal of Business Research, 57(3): 225-231.
Delcampo, R. G. (2006). The influence of culture strength on

person-organization fit and turnover. International Journal of Management, 23(3): 465-477.
Delery, J. E. and Doty, D. H. (1996). Modes of theorizing in strategic human resource management: Tests of universalistic, contingency, and configurational performance predictions. Academy of Management Journal, 39(4): 802-835.
Deng, H. (2002). A game model of entrepreneur flow: economic implication and entrepreneurial capacity allocation. Economic Science, (3): 94-102.
Dess, G. G. and Beard, D. W. (1984). Dimensions of organizational task environments. Administrative Science Quarterly, 29(1): 52-73.
Dess, G. G. and Shaw, J. D. (2001). Voluntary turnover, social capital, and organizational performance. Academy of Management Review, 26(1): 446-456.
Dickter, D. N., Roznowski, M. and Harrison, D. A. (1996). Temporal tempering: An event history analysis of the process of voluntary turnover. Journal of Applied Psychology, 81(6): 705-716.
Dorfman, P. and Howell, J. (1988). Dimensions of national culture and effective leadership patterns: Hofstede revisited. JAI Press.
Du, J. J., Zhou, J., Liu, C. and Picken, D. (2006). Exploring turnover intention of construction managers in China. Journal of Construction Research, 7(1): 191-205.
Dulebohn, J. H., Wu, D. and Liao, C. (2016). Does liking explain variance above and beyond LMX? A meta-analysis. Human Resource Management Review, 27(1): 149-166.
Earley, P. C. (1989). Social loafing and collectivism: A comparison of the United States and the People's Republic of China. Administrative Science Quarterly, 34(4): 565-581.
Eisenberger, R. and Stinglhamber, F. (2011). Perceived organizational support. Journal of Applied Psychology, 71(3): 500-507.
Eisenberger, R., Armeli, S., Rexwinkel, B., Lynch, P. D. and Rhoades, L. (2001). Reciprocation of perceived organizational support. Journal of Applied Psychology, 86(1): 42-51.
Eisenberger, R., Stinglhamber, F., Vandenberghe, C., Sucharski, I. L. and Rhoades, L. (2002). Perceived supervisor support: contributions to perceived organizational support and employee retention. Journal of Applied Psychology, 87(3): 565-573.
Ekrot, B., Kock, A. and Gemünden, H. G. (2016). Retaining project management competence: Antecedents and consequences. International Journal of Project Management, 34(2): 145-157.
Erdogan, B., Liden, R. C. and Kraimer, M. L. (2006). Justice and

leader-member exchange: the moderating role of organizational culture. Academy of Management Journal, 49(2): 395-406.

Ertürk, A. and Vurgun, L. (2015). Retention of IT professionals: Examining the influence of empowerment, social exchange, and trust. Journal of Business Research, 68(1): 34-46.

Fairbrother, K. and Warn, J. (2013). Workplace dimensions, stress and job satisfaction. Journal of Managerial Psychology, 18(1): 8-21.

Farh, J. and Cheng, B. S. (2000). A cultural analysis of paternalistic leadership in Chinese organizations. In Li, J. T., Tsui, A. S. and Weldon, E. (Eds.). Management and organizations in the Chinese context. London: MacMillan: 84-127.

Farh, J. and Zheng, B. (2000). Paternalistic leadership in Chinese organization: an analysis from cultural perspective. Local Psychology Research (Taiwan). Quoted in Li, X. and Zhang, S. (2005). Family enterprises: organization, behavior and Chinese economy, Shanghai: Shanghai Joint Publishing Press, Shanghai People's Publishing House: 379-430.

Farh, J., Earley, P. C. and Lin, S. (1997). Impetus for action: a cultural analysis of justice and organizational citizenship behavior in Chinese society. Administrative Science Quarterly, 42(3): 421-444.

Farh, J., Hackett, R. D. and Liang, J. (2007). Individual-level cultural values as moderators of perceived organizational support-employee outcome relationships in China: comparing the effects of power distance and traditionality. Academy of Management Journal, 50(3): 715-729.

Farh, J., Tsui, A., Xin, K. and Cheng, B. S. (1998). The influence of relational demography and Guanxi: the Chinese case. Organization Science, 9(4): 471-488.

Farmer, S. M. and Aguinis, H. (2005). Accounting for subordinate perceptions of supervisor power: an identity-dependence model. Journal of Applied Psychology, 90(6): 1069-1083.

Farrell, D. and Rusbult, C. E. (1981). Exchange variables as predictors of job satisfaction, job commitment, and turnover: The impact of rewards, costs, alternatives, and investments. Organizational Behavior and Human Performance, 28(1): 78-95.

Fei, X. (2005). Rural China and fertility system. Beijing: Peking University Press.

Ferreira, L. C. D. M. and Almeida, C. B. D. A. (2015). Employee turnover and organizational performance: a study of the Brazilian retail sector. Brazilian Business Review, 12(4): 27-56.

Fitz-Enz, J. (1997). It's costly to lose good employees. Workforce, 50.

Fleishman, E. A. (2010). Some new frontiers in personnel selection research. Personnel Psychology, 41(4): 679-701.

Forrier, A., Verbruggen, M. and Cuyper, N. D. (2015). Integrating different notions of employability in a dynamic chain: The relationship between job transitions, movement capital and perceived employability. Journal of Vocational Behavior, 89(8): 56-64.

Frazier, M. L., Johnson, P. D., Gavin, M., Gooty, J. and Snow, D. B. (2016). Organizational justice, trustworthiness, and trust: a multifoci examination. Group and Organization Management, 35(1): 39-76.

Fu, N., Flood, P. C., Bosak, J., Rousseau, D. M., Morris, T. and O'Regan, P. (2017). High performance work systems in professional service firms: examining the practices resources uses performance linkage. Human Resource Management, 56(2): 329-352.

Fukuyama. (1998). Trust: social morality and prosperity creation. Shanghai: Distance Press.

Gaertner, S. (1999). Structural determinants of job satisfaction and organizational commitment in turnover models. Human Resource Management Review, 9(4): 479-493.

Gardner, D. G., Van Dyne, L. and Pierce, J. L. (2004). The effects of pay level on organization-based self-esteem and performance: A field study. Journal of Occupational and Organizational Psychology, 77(3): 307-322.

George, C. (2015). Retaining professional workers: what makes them stay? Employee Relations, 37(1): 102-121.

George, J. M. and Brief, A. P. (1992). Feeling good-doing good: A conceptual analysis of the mood at work-organizational spontaneity relationship. Psychological Bulletin, 112(2): 310-329.

George, J. M. (2000). Emotions and leadership: the role of emotional intelligence. Humanity Relation, 53(8): 1027-1055

Gerhart, B. (1990). Voluntary turnover and alternative job opportunities. Journal of Applied Psychology, 73(5): 467-476.

Glebbeek, A. C. and Bax, E. H. (2004). Is high employee turnover really harmful? An empirical test using company records. Academy of Management Journal, 47(2): 277-286.

Gomez-Mejia, L. R. and Balkin, D. B. (1989). Effectiveness of individual and aggregate compensation strategies. Industrial Relations A Journal of Economy and Society, 28(3): 431-445.

Granovetter, M. (1985). Economic action and social structure: a theory of embeddedness. American Journal of Sociology, 91(3): 481-510.

Greenberg, J. (1990). Organizational justice: Yesterday, today, and tomorrow. Journal of Management, 16(2): 399-432.

Griffeth, R. W., Hom, P. W. and Gaertner, S. (2000). A meta-analysis of antecedents and correlates of employee turnover: update, moderator tests, and research implications for the next millennium. Journal of Management, 26(3): 463-488.

Griffeth, R. W., Steel, R. P., Allen, D. G. and Bryan, N. (2005). The development of a multidimensional measure of job market cognitions: the employment opportunity index (EOI). Journal of Applied Psychology, 90(2): 335-349.

Guest, D. (2005). Managing the career deal: the psychological contract as a framework for understanding career management, organizational commitment and work behavior. Journal of Organizational Behavior, 26(7): 821-838.

Gupta, V., Agarwal, U. A. and Khatri, N. (2016). The relationships between perceived organizational support, affective commitment, psychological contract breach, organizational citizenship behavior, and work engagement. Journal of Advanced Nursing, 72(11): 2806-2817.

Guthrie, J. P. (2001). High-involvement work practices, turnover, and productivity: evidence from New Zealand. Academy of Management Journal, 44(1): 180-190.

Hackman, J. R. and Oldham, G. R. (1975). The development of the job diagnostic survey. Journal of Applied Psychology, 60(2), 159-170.

Hancock, J. I., Allen, D. G., Bosco, F. A., Mcdaniel, K. R. and Pierce, C. A. (2013). Meta-analytic review of employee turnover as a predictor of firm performance. Journal of Management, 39(3): 573-603.

Harris, J. and Brannick, J. (1999). Finding and keeping great employees. New York: AMACOM.

Harris, M. and Weiss, Y. (1984). Job matching with finite horizon and risk aversion. Journal of Political economy, 92(4): 758-79.

Harrison, D. A., Daniel, N. A. and Philip, R. L. (2006). How important are job attitudes? Meta-analytic comparisons of integrative behavioral outcomes and time sequences. Academy of Management Journal, 49(2): 305-325.

Harrison, D. A., Virick, M. and William, S. (1996). Working without a net: Time, performance, and turnover under maximally contingent rewards. Journal of Applied Psychology, 81(4): 331-345.

Harter, J. K., Schmidt, F. L. and Hayes, T. L. (2002). Business-unit-level relationship between employee satisfaction, employee engagement, and business outcomes: a meta-analysis.

Journal of Applied Psychology, 87(2): 268-279.
Haslam, S. A. (2001). Psychology in organizations: the social identity approach. London: Sage Publications.
Hau, K. T., Wen, Z. and Cheng, Z. (2004). Structural equation model and its applications. Beijing: Educational Science Publishing House.
Herriot, G. and Pemberton, J. (1994). An empirical model of managerial careers in organization. British Journal of Management, 5(2): 113-121.
Hofstede, G. (1991). Culture and organizations: Software of the mind. London: McGraw-Hill.
Hogan, R., Raskin, R. and Fazzini, D. (1990). The dark side of charisma. In Clark K E and Clark M B (Eds.). Measures of leadership. West Orange, NJ: Leadership Library of America: 343-354.
Holt, D. T., Rehg, M. T., Lin, J. H. S. and Miller, J. (2007). An application of the unfolding model to explain turnover in a sample of military officers. Human Resource Management, 46(1): 35-49.
Holtom, B., Goldberg, C. B., Allen, D. G. and Clark, M. A. (2017). How today's shocks predict tomorrow's leaving. Journal of Business and Psychology, 32(1): 59-71.
Hom, P. W. and Griffeth, R. W. (1991). A structural equations modeling test of a turnover theory: cross-sectional and longitudinal analysis. Journal of Applied Psychology, 76(3): 350-366.
Hom, P. W. and Griffeth, R. W. (1995). Employee turnover. Cincinnati, OH: South-Western.
Hom, P. W. and Kinicki, A. J. (2001). Toward a greater understanding of how dissatisfaction drives employee turnover. Academy of Management Journal, 44(5): 975-987.
Hom, P. W. and Xiao, Z. (2006). Structural holes in Guanxi networks: do they increase employee turnover in the People's Republic of China? Academy of Management Best Conference Paper, (1): F1-F6.
Hom, P. W., Lee, T. W., Shaw, J. D. and Hausknecht, J. P. (2017). One hundred years of employee turnover theory and research. Journal of Applied Psychology, 102(3): 530-545.
Hoppock, R. (1935). Job Satisfaction. New York: Harper.
House, R. J. and Javidan, M. (2004). Overview of GLOBE. In House, R. J., Hanges, P. J., Javidan, M., Dorfman, P. W. and Gupta, V. (Eds.). Culture, leadership, and organizations: The GLOBE study of 62 societies. Thousand Oaks, CA: Sage: 9-28.
Huang, K. (2004). Face: power game of Chinese people. Beijing:

China Renmin University Press.
Huang, M. and Wang, Q. (2007). Annual report on non-state-owned economy in China (2006-2007). Beijing: Social Sciences Academic Press.
Huang, W. (2007). Organizational factors affecting professional manager's entry into private enterprises. PhD. Thesis, Sun Yat-Sen University.
Hulin, C. L., Roznowski, M. and Hachiya, D. (1985). Alternative opportunities and withdrawal decisions: empirical and theoretical discrepancies and an integration. Psychological Bulletin, 97(2): 233-250.
Hulin, C. L. (1991). Adaptation, persistence, and commitment in organizations. In Dunnette, M. D. and Hough, L. M. (Eds.). Handbook of industrial and organizational psychology (vol.2, 2nd ed.). Palo Alto, CA: Consulting Psychologists Press: 445-505.
Hunt, S. D., Wood, V. R. and Chonko, L. B. (1989). Corporate ethical values and organizational commitment in marketing. Journal of Marketing, 53(3): 79-90.
Iverson, R. D. and Roy, P. (1994). A causal model of behavioral commitment: evidence from a study of Australian blue collar employees. Journal of Management, 20 (1): 15 - 41.
Jackofsky, E. F. (1984). Turnover and job performance: an integrated process model. Academy of Management Journal, 9(1): 74-83.
Ji, Y. and Zhang, J. (2010). Determinants of the professional manager's low loyalty to family enterprise: an empirical test of personal, organizational and employer's characteristics. Economic Management, 32(3): 55-62.
Ji, Y. and Zhang, J. (2007). On the adverse selection problem during the process through which private enterprise hires professional managers. South China Journal of Economics, (9): 12-29.
Ji, Y. (2008). On the factors affecting the honesty level of private enterprisers: based on the perception of managers. Social Sciences in Yunnan, (2): 105-109.
Jiang, Z. (2016). The relationship between career adaptability and job content plateau: The mediating roles of fit perceptions. Journal of Vocational Behavior, 95-96:1-10.
Johnson, R. C. (2007). Wage and job dynamics after welfare reform: The importance of job skills. Research in Labor Economics, 26: 231-298.
Jones, D. A. and Skarlicki, D. P. (2003). The relationship between perceptions of fairness and voluntary turnover among retail employees. Journal of Applied Social Psychology, 33(6):

1226-1243.
Joseph, D. L., Jin, J., Newman, D. A. and O'Boyle, E. H. (2015). Why does self-reported emotional intelligence predict job performance? a meta-analytic investigation of mixed EI. Journal of Applied Psychology, 100(2): 298-342.
Jovanovic, B. (1979). Job matching and the theory of turnover. Journal of Political Economy, 87(5): 972-90.
Judge, T. A., Bono, J. E., Ilies, R. and Werner, M. W. (2002). Personality and leadership: A qualitative and quantitative review Journal of Applied Psychology, 87(4): 765-780.
Judge, T. A., Piccolo, R. F., Podsakoff, N. P., Shaw, J. C. and Rich, B. L. (2010). The relationship between pay and job satisfaction: A meta-analysis of the literature. Journal of Vocational Behavior, 77(2): 157-167.
Kahn, W. A. (1990). Psychological conditions of personal engagement and disengagement at work. Academy of Management Journal, 33(4): 692-724.
Kammeyer-mueller, J. D. and Wanberg, C. R. (2003). Unwrapping the organizational entry process: disentangling multiple antecedents and their pathways to adjustment. Journal of Applied Psychology, 88(5): 779-794.
Kammeyer-mueller, J. D., Wanberg, C. R., Glomb, T. M. and Ahlburg, D. (2005). The role of temporal shifts in turnover processes: it's about time. Journal of Applied Psychology, 90(4): 644-658.
Kao, C. S. (1990). The role of personal trust in large businesses in Taiwan. In Hamilton G G (Ed.). Business groups and economic development in East Asia. Hong Kong: Center of Asian Studies.
Kevin, M., Loan-clarkez, J. and Wilkinsonz, A. (2004). The role of shocks in employee turnover. British Journal of Management, 15(4): 335-349.
Khan, K., Abbas, M., Gul, A. and Raja, U. (2015). Organizational justice and job outcomes: moderating role of Islamic work ethic. Journal of Business Ethics, 126(2): 235-246.
Kinicki, A. J., McKee-Ryan, F. M., Schriesheim, C. A. and Carson, K. P. (2002). Assessing the construct validity of the Job Descriptive Index: A review and meta-analysis. Journal of Applied Psychology, 87(1): 14-32.
Kirchler, M. and Palan, S. (2017). Immaterial and monetary gifts in economic transactions: evidence from the field. Experimental Economics, (6): 1-26.
Kirkman, B. L. and Shapiro, D. L. (1997). The impact of cultural values on employee resistance to teams: Toward a model of

globalized self-managing work team effectiveness. Academy of Management Review, 22(3): 730-757.

Kirschenbaum, A. and Mano-Negrin, R. (1999). Underlying labor market dimensions of "opportunities": the case of employee turnover. Human Relations, 52(10): 1233-1255.

Kollock, P. (1994). The emergence of exchange structures: an experimental study of uncertainty, commitment, and trust. American Journal of Sociology, 100(2): 313-345.

Konovsky, M. A. and Pugh, S. D. (1994). Citizenship behavior and social exchange. Academy of Management Journal, 37(3): 656-669.

Konovsky, M. A. (2015). Understanding procedural justice and its impact on business organizations. Journal of Management, 26(3): 489-511.

Korff, J., Biemann, T. and Voelpel, S. C. (2017a). Differentiating HR systems' impact: moderating effects of age on the HR system-work outcome association. Journal of Organizational Behavior, 38(3): 415-438.

Korff, J., Biemann, T. and Voelpel, S. C. (2017b). Human resource management systems and work attitudes: The mediating role of future time perspective. Journal of Organizational Behavior, 38(1): 45-67.

Koys, D. J. (2001). The effects of employee satisfaction, organizational citizenship behavior, and turnover on organizational effectiveness: a unit-level, longitudinal study. Personnel Psychology, 54(1): 101-114.

Krau, E. (1981). Turnover analysis and prediction from a career developmental point of view. Personnel Psychology, 34(4): 771-790.

Krishnan, H. A., Park, D. and Kilboume, L. (2006). The development of a conceptual model to explain turnover among women in top management teams. International Journal of Management, 23(3): 470-477.

Kristof, A. L. (1996). Person-organization fit: an integrative review of its conceptualizations, measurement and implications. Personnel Psychology, 49(1): 1-49.

Lance, C. E. (1991). Evaluation of a structural model relating job satisfaction, organizational commitment, and precursors to voluntary turnover. Multivariate Behavioral Research, 26(1): 137-162.

Lance, C. E. (1988). Job performance as a moderator of the satisfaction-turnover intention relation: an empirical contrast of two perspectives. Journal of Organizational Behavior, 9(3): 271-280.

Lang, L. H. P. (2004). Corporate governance. Beijing: Social Sciences Academic Press.

Laroche, P. and Salesina, M. (2017). The effects of union and nonunion forms of employee representation on high - performance work systems: new evidence from French microdata. Human Resource Management, 56(1): 173-189.

Latham, V. M. and Leddy, P. M. (1987). Source of recruitment and employee attitudes: An analysis of job involvement, organizational commitment, and job satisfaction. Journal of Business and Psychology, 1(3): 230-235.

Lazear, E. (1998). Personnel economics for managers. New York: Wiley Allen.

Lee, K., Carswell, J. J. and Allen, N. J. (2000). A meta-analytic review of occupational commitment: relations with person- and work-related variables. Journal of Applied Psychology, 85(5): 799-811.

Lee, T. W. and Mitchell, T. R. (1994). An alternative approach: the unfolding model of voluntary employee turnover. Academy of Management Review, 19(1): 51-89.

Lee, T. W. and Mowday, R. T. (1987). Voluntary leaving an organization: an empirical investigation of steers and Mowday's model of turnover. Academy of Management Journal, 30(4): 721-743.

Lee, T. W., Mitchell, T. R., Wise, L. and Fireman, S. (1996). An unfolding model of voluntary employee turnover. Academy of Management Journal, 39(1): 5-36.

Lee, T. W., Terence, M. R., Chris, S. J., James, B. P. and Brooks, H. C. (2004). The effects of job embeddedness on organizational citizenship, job performance, volitional absences, and voluntary turnover. Academy of Management Journal, 47(5): 711-722.

Leong, C. S., Fumham, A. and Cooper, C. L. (1996). The moderating effect of organizational commitment on the occupational stress outcome relationship. Human Relations, 49(10): 1345-1363.

Li, N., Zheng, X., Harris, T. B., Liu, X. and Kirkman, B. L. (2016). Recognizing "me" benefits "we": investigating the positive spillover effects of formal individual recognition in teams. Journal of Applied Psychology, 101(7): 925-939.

Li, X. (2003). The dysfunction of markets of managing agents, and the control of clannish enterprises. Management World, (4): 87-95.

Li, X. (2002). Trust, loyalty and the predicament that clannishness is in.

Management World, (6): 87-93.
Liang, M. (2003). Analysis on the personnel system characteristics of Chinese family enterprises on managing level. Shanghai Economic Review, (3): 75-79.
Liang, S. (2005). Highlights of Chinese culture. Shanghai: Shanghai Century Publishing Group, Shanghai People's Publishing House.
Liang, X., Liao, J. and Zeng, Q. (2005). Extending and tests of core employees organizational performance-voluntary turnover models based on job embeddedness. Management World, (7): 106-115.
Lim, B. T. H., Loosemore, M. (2017). The effect of inter-organizational justice perceptions on organizational citizenship behaviors in construction projects. International Journal of Project Management, 35(2): 95-106.
Liu, Y., Wang, M., Chang, C. H., Shi, J., Zhou, L. and Shao, R. (2015). Work-family conflict, emotional exhaustion, and displaced aggression toward others: the moderating roles of workplace interpersonal conflict and perceived managerial family support. Journal of Applied Psychology, 100(3): 793-808.
Ljungqvist, L. and Sargent, T. J. (2000). Recursive macroeconomic theory. Cambridge, Massachusetts: The MIT Press.
Locke, E. A. (1976). The nature and causes of job satisfaction. In Dunnette M D (Ed.). Handbook of industrial and organizational psychology. Palo Alto, CA: Consulting Psychologists Press: 1297-1349.
Loewenstein, M. and Speltzer, J. (1997). Delayed formal on-the-job training. Industrial and Labor Relations Review, 51(1): 82-99.
Lyness, K. and Judiesch, M. (2001). Are female managers quitters? The relationships of gender, promotions, and family leaves of absence to voluntary turnover. Journal of Applied Psychology, 86(6): 1167-1178.
Ma, S., Silva, M. G., Callan, V. J. and Trigo, V. (2016). Control and commitment hr practices, job satisfaction and turnover intentions: a comparison between local and multinational firms in china. International Journal of Human Resource Management, 27(9): 974-990.
Maertz, C. P. and Campion. M. A. (2004). Profiles in quitting: integrating process and content turnover theory. Academy of Management Journal, 47(4): 566-582.
Maertz, C. P. and Griffeth, R. W. (2004). Eight motivational forces and voluntary turnover: a theoretical synthesis with implications for research. Journal of Management, 30(5): 667-683.
Mai, K. M., Ellis, A. P., Christian, J. S. and Porter, C. O. (2016).

Examining the effects of turnover intentions on organizational citizenship behaviors and deviance behaviors: a psychological contract approach. Journal of Applied Psychology, 101(8): 1067-1081.

March, J. G. and Simon, H. A. (1958). Organizations. New York: Wiley.

Mark, S. A. and Canger, J. M. (2004). Effects of supervisor 'big five' personality on subordinate attitudes. Journal of Business and Psychology, 18(4): 465-481.

Markus, H. and Kitayama, S. (1991). Culture and self: Implications for cognition, emotion, and motivation. Psychological Review, 98(2): 224-253.

Maslach, C. A. (1982). Burnout: The cost of caring. Englewood Cliffs. NJ: Prentice Hall.

Masterson, S. S., Lewis, K., Goldman, B. M. and Taylor, M. S. (2000). Integrating justice and social exchange: The differing effects of fair procedures and treatment on work relationships. Academy of Management Journal, 43(4): 738-749.

Mathieu, C., Fabi, B., Lacoursière, R. and Raymond, L. (2016). The role of supervisory behavior, job satisfaction and organizational commitment on employee turnover. Journal of Management and Organization, 22(1): 113-129.

Mcelroy, J. C., Morrow, P. C. and Rude, S. N. (2001). Turnover and organizational performance: a comparative analysis of the effects of voluntary, involuntary, and reduction-in-force turnover. Journal of Applied Psychology, 86(6): 1294-1299.

Melenie, L. J. and Scandura, T. A. (2002). An investigation of personal learning in mentoring relationships: content, antecedents, and consequences. Academy of Management Journal, 45(4): 779-790.

Mercurio, Z. A. (2015). Affective commitment as a core essence of organizational commitment: an integrative literature review. Human Resource Development Review, 14(4): 389-414.

Meyer, J. P. and Allen, N. J. (1991). A three-component conceptualization of organizational commitment. Human Research Management Review, 1(1): 61-89.

Milgrom, P. and Oster, S. (1987). Job discrimination, market forces, and the invisibility hypothesis. Quarterly Journal of Economics, 102(3): 453-476.

Mirvis, P. H. and Lawler, E. E. (1977). Measuring the financial impact of employee attitudes. Journal of Applied Psychology, 62(1): 1-8.

Mitchel, J. O. (1981). The effect of intentions, tenure, personal, and organizational variables on managerial turnover. Academy of

Management Journal, 24(4): 742-751.
Mitchell, T. R., Holtom, B. C. and Lee, T. W. (2001). How to keep your best employees: Developing an effective retention policy. Academy of Management Executive, 15(4): 96-108.
Mitchell, T. R., Holtom, B. C., Lee, T. W., Sablynski, C. J. and Erez, M. (2001). Why people stay: using job embeddedness to predict voluntary turnover. Academy of Management Journal, 44(6): 1102-1121.
Mo, S. and Shi, J. (2017). Linking ethical leadership to employees' organizational citizenship behavior: testing the multilevel mediation role of organizational concern. Journal of Business Ethics, 141(1): 151-162.
Mobley, W. H., Griffeth, R., Hand, H. and Meglino, B. (1979). A review and conceptual analysis of the employee turnover process. Psychological Bulletin, 86(3): 493-522.
Mobley, W. H. (1982). Employee turnover: causes, consequences, and control. Menlo Park, CA: Addison-Wesley.
Mobley, W. H. (1977). Intermediate linkages in the relationship between job satisfaction and employee turnover. Journal of Applied Psychology, 62(2): 237-240.
Mohamad, H. A. and Nasurdin, A. M. (2006). Predicting turnover intentions of hotel employees: The influence of employee development human resource management practices and trust in organization. Gadjah Mada International Journal of Business, 8(1): 21-42.
Momani, H. M. A. (2017). The mediating effect of organizational commitment on the relationship between work-life balance and intention to leave: evidence from working women in Jordan. International Business Research, 10(6): 164-177.
Morrell, K., Loan-clarke, J. and Wilkinson, A. (2001). Unweaving leaving: the use of models in the management of employee turnover. International Journal of Management Reviews, 3(3): 219-244.
Morrow, P. C. (2011). Managing organizational commitment: Insights from longitudinal research. Journal of Vocational Behavior, 79(1): 18-35.
Morrow, P. C. (1993). The theory and measurement of work commitment. Greenwich, CT: JAI Press.
Mossholder, K. W., Setton, R. P. and Henagan, S. C. (2005). A relational perspective on turnover: examining structural, attitudinal, and behavioral predictors. Academy of Management Journal, 48(4): 607-618.

Motowidlo, S. J. (1996). Orientation toward the job and organization. In Murphy, K. R. (Ed.). Individual differences and behavior in organizations. San Francisco: Jossey-Bass: 175-208.

Murray, B. R. and Zimmerman, R. D. (2005). Reducing Voluntary, Avoidable Turnover Through Selection. Journal of Applied Psychology, 90(1): 159-166.

Nelson, B. (2001). Please don't just do what I tell you, do what needs to be done: Every employee's guide to making work more rewarding. New York: Hyperion.

Ng, K. Y. and Dyne, L. V. (2015). Antecedents and performance consequences of helping behavior in work groups: a multilevel analysis. Group and Organization Management, 30(30): 514-540.

O'Keefe, J. D. and Delia, G. J. (2016). Construct differentiation and the relationship of attitudes and behavioral intentions. Communication Monographs, 48(2): 146-157.

O'Reilly, C. A., Chatman, J. A. and Caldwell, D. E. (1991). People and organizational culture: A profile comparison approach to assessing person-organization fit. Academy of Management Journal, 34(3): 487-516.

Organ, D. W. and Near, J. P. (1985). Cognitive vs. affect measures of job satisfaction. International Journal Psychology, 20(2): 241-54.

Ostroff, C. (1993). The effects of climate and personal influences on individual behavior and attitudes in organizations. Organizational Behavior and Human Decision Processes, 56(1): 56-90.

Park, J. H., Newman, A., Zhang, L., Wu, C. and Hooke, A. (2016). Mentoring functions and turnover intention: the mediating role of perceived organizational support. International Journal of Human Resource Management, 27(11): 1173-1191.

Park, T. Y. and Shaw, J. D. (2013). Turnover rates and organizational performance: a meta-analysis. The Journal of Applied Psychology, 98(2): 268-309.

Parker, P., Wasserman, I., Kram, K. E. and Hall, D. T. (2015). A relational communication approach to peer coaching. Journal of Applied Behavioral Science, 51(2): 231-252.

Payne, S. C. and Huffman, A. H. (2005). A longitudinal examination of the influence of mentoring on organizational commitment and turnover. Academy of Management Journal, 48(1): 158-168.

Penrose, E. T. (1995). The theory of growth of the firm. Oxford University Press.

Pfeffer, J. (1998). The human equation: Building profits by putting people first. Boston: Harvard Business School Press.

Pi, J. (2013). A dynamic game analysis about family enterprises absorbing professional manager during the period of transformation. Jinan Journal (Philosophy and Social Science), (3): 53-58.

Pindek, S., Kessler, S. R. and Spector, P. E. (2017). A quantitative and qualitative review of what meta-analyses have contributed to our understanding of human resource management. Human Resource Management Review, 27(1): 26-38.

Pittino, D., Visintin, F., Lenger, T. and Sternad, D. (2016). Are high performance work practices really necessary in family SMEs? An analysis of the impact on employee retention. Journal of Family Business Strategy, 7(2): 75-89.

Porter, C. M. and Sang, E. W. (2015). Untangling the networking phenomenon: A dynamic psychological perspective on how and why people network. Journal of Management, 41(5): 1-24.

Posthuma, R. A., Maertz, C. P. and Dworkin, J. B. (2007). Procedural justice's relationship with turnover: Explaining past inconsistent findings. Journal of Organizational Behavior, 28(4): 381-398.

Prabhu, V. P. (2016). Proactive personality and organizational change: factors affecting retention. Journal of Organizational Psychology, 16(1): 11-23.

Price, J. and Mueller, G. (1986). Absenteeism and turnover of hospital employees, Greenwich, CT: JAI Press.

Price, J. L. (1999). Introduction to the special issue on employee turnover. Human Resource Management Review, 9(4): 387-395.

Price, J. L. (2001). Reflections on the determinants of voluntary turnover. International Journal of Manpower, 22(7): 600-624.

Price, J. L. (1977). The study of turnover. Ames: Iowa State University Press.

Prooijen, J. W. V. (2015). Beyond social exchange: Collectivism's moderating role in the relationship between perceived organizational support and organizational citizenship behaviour. European Journal of Work and Organizational Psychology, 24(1): 152-160.

Ramlall, S. (2003). Managing employee retention as a strategy for increasing organizational competitiveness. Applied HRM Research, 8(2): 63-72.

Randall, C. S. and Muller, C. W. (1995). Extensions of justice theory: Justice evaluations and employees' reactions in a natural setting. Social Psychology Quarterly, 58(3): 178-194.

Ravichandan, K. (2015). Application of multiple regressions in development of an employee turnover model. International Journal of Economics and Management Sciences, 4: 266,

doi:10.4172/21626359.1000266.
Raymond, S. T. (2006). Do leaders 'influence tactics relate to members' helping behavior? It depends on the quality of the relationship. Academy of Management Journal, 49(6): 1194-1208.
Redding, S. G. (1990). The spirit of Chinese capitalism. Berlin: Walter de Gruyter.
Rhoades, L., Eisenberger, R. and Armeli, S. (2001). Affective commitment to the organization: the contribution of perceived organizational support. Journal of Applied Psychology, 86(5): 825-836.
Robinson, S. L. (1996). Trust and breach of the psychological contract. Administrative Science Quarterly, 41(4): 574-599.
Roof, R. A. (2015). The association of individual spirituality on employee engagement: the spirit at work. Journal of Business Ethics, 130(3): 585-599.
Rousseau, M. D. (1990). New hire perceptions of their own and their employer's obligations: a study of psychological contracts. Journal of Organizational Behavior, 11(5): 389-400.
Rubel, M. R. B. and Kee, D. M. H. (2015). Perceived fairness of performance appraisal, promotion opportunity and nurses turnover intention: the role of organizational commitment. Asian Social Science, 11(9): 183-197.
Rudy, K. (2010). Calculating the cost of turnover. Employment Relations Today, 34(1): 33-36.
Rusbult, C. E. and Farrell, D. (1983). A longitudinal test of the investment model: the impact on job satisfaction, job commitment and turnover of variations in rewards, costs, alternatives and investments. Journal of Applied Psychology, 68(3): 429-438.
Russ, F. A. and Mcneilly, K. M. (1995). Links among satisfaction, commitment, and turnover intentions: the moderating effect of experience, gender, and performance. Journal of Business Research, 34(1): 57-65.
Salamin, A. and Hom, P. W. (2005). In search of the elusive u-shaped performance-turnover relationship: are high performing swiss bankers more liable to quit? Journal of Applied Psychology, 90(6): 1204-1216.
Schaubroeck, J., Lam, S. S. K. and Xie, J. L. (2000). Collective efficacy versus self-efficacy in coping responses to stressors and control: a cross-cultural study. Journal of Applied Psychology, 85(4): 512-525.
Schnake, M. and Dumler, M. P. (2000). Predictors of propensity to turnover in the construction industry. Psychological Reports, 86(3):

1000-1002.
Schriesheim, C. A., Neider, L. L. and Scandura, T. A. (1998). Delegation and leader-member exchange: main effects, moderators, and measurement issues. Academy of Management Journal, 41(3): 298-318.
Schwartz, S. J. (1992). Universals in the content and structure of values: Theory and empirical tests in 20 countries. In Zanna M (Ed.). Advances in experimental social psychology. New York: Academic Press, 25: 1-65.
Schwepker, C. H. (2001). Ethical climate's relationship to job satisfaction, organizational commitment, and turnover intention in the salesforce. Journal of Business Research, 54(1): 39-52.
Selmer, J. (2001). Psychological barriers to adjustment and how they affect coping strategies: western business expatriates in China. International Journal of Human Resource Management, 12(2): 152-65.
Shaw, J. D. and Shi, S. (2017). The neglected state of organizational-level turnover studies in the Chinese context: a call for research. Frontiers of Business Research in China, 11: 6, DOI 10.1186/s11782-017-0001-y.
Shaw, J. D., Delery, J. E., Jenkins, G. D. and Gupta, N. (1998). An organizational-level analysis of voluntary and involuntary turnover. Academy of Management Journal, 41(5): 511-525.
Shaw, J. D., Duffy, M. K., Johnson, J. L. and Lockhart, D. E. (2005). Turnover, social capital losses, and performance. Academy of Management Journal, 48(4): 594-606.
Shaw, J. D., Gupta, N. and Delery, J. E. (2005). Alternative conceptualizations of the relationship between voluntary turnover and organizational performance. Academy of management Journal, 48(1): 50-68.
Sheridan, J. E. and Abelson, M. A. (1983). Cusp catastrophe model of employee turnover. Academy of Management Journal, 26(3): 418-436.
Simon, H. (1945). Administrative behavior. New York: The Free Press.
Simons, T. and Roberson, Q. (2003). Why managers should care about fairness: the effects of aggregate justice perceptions on organizational outcomes. Journal of Applied Psychology, 88(3): 432-443.
Simpson, B. and Willer, R. (2015). Beyond altruism: sociological foundations of cooperation and prosocial behavior. Annual Review of Sociology, 41(1): 43-63.
Smith, C. A., Organ, D. W. and Near, J. P. (1983). Organizational

citizenship behavior: Its nature and antecedents. Journal of Applied Psychology, 68(4): 653-663.
Snape, E. and Redman, T. (2003). An evaluation of a three-component model of occupational commitment: dimensionality and consequences among United Kingdom human resource management specialists. Journal of Applied Psychology, 88(1): 152-159.
Somers, M. J. (1995). Organizational commitment, turnover and absenteeism: an examination of direct and interaction effects. Journal of Organizational Behavior, 16(1): 49-58.
Spector, P. E. and Michaels, C. E. (1986). Personality and employee withdrawal: Effects of locus of control on turnover. Psychological Reports, 59(1): 63-66.
Spence, M. (1973). Job market signaling. Quarterly Journal of Economics, 87(3): 355-374.
Spreitzer, G. M. and Mishra, A. K. (2002). To stay or go: Voluntary survivor turnover following an organizational downsizing. Journal of Organizational Behavior, 23(6): 707-730.
Steel, R. P. and Ovalle, N. K. (1984). A review and meta-analysis of research on the relationship between behavioral intentions and employee turnover. Journal of Applied Psychology, 69(4): 673-686.
Steel, R. P. (2002). Turnover theory at the empirical interface: problems of fit and function. Academy of Management Review, 27(3): 346-360.
Steers, R. M. and Mowday, R. T. (1981). Employee turnover and post-decision justification. In Cummings, L. L. and Staw, B. M. (Ed.). Research in organizational behavior. Greenwich, CT: JAI Press, 3: 235-282.
Sturman, M. C. and Trevor, C. O. (2001). The implications of linking the dynamic performance and turnover literatures. Journal of Applied Psychology, 86(4): 684-696.
Sun, J. Y. and Wang, G. G. (2011). Integrating disparate literatures on voluntary career transition and voluntary turnover: Implications for research in the Chinese context. Journal of Chinese Human Resource Management, 2(1): 23-42.
Sun, L., Aryee, S. and law, K. S. (2007). High-performance human resource practices, citizenship behavior, and organizational performance: a relational perspective. Academy of Management Journal, 50(3): 558-577.
Susanna, L. and Aryee, S. (2003). Psychological contract breach in a Chinese. Journal of Management Studies, 40(4): 1005-1020.

Suzanne, P. J. and Luthans, F. (2006). The impact of financial and nonfinancial incentives on business-unit outcomes over time. Journal of Applied Psychology, 91(1): 156-165.

Swider, B. W., Zimmerman, R. D. and Barrick, M. R. (2015). Searching for the right fit: development of applicant person-organization fit perceptions during the recruitment process. Journal of Applied Psychology, 100(3): 880-893.

Takeuchi, R., Bolino, M. C. and Lin, C. C. (2015). Too many motives? The interactive effects of multiple motives on organizational citizenship behavior. Journal of Applied Psychology, 100(4):1239-1248.

Tang, R. (2003). On the elemental qualities of professional managers and loyalty development. Forum on Jiangsu Commerce, (8): 66-68.

Tett, R. P. and Meyer, J. P. (1993). Job satisfaction, organizational commitment, turnover intention, and turnover: Path analyses based on meta-analytic findings. Personnel Psychology, 46(2): 259- 293.

Tews, M. J., Michel, J. W. and Ellingson, J. E. (2013). The impact of coworker support on employee turnover in the hospitality industry. Group and Organization Management, 38(5): 630-653.

Thibaut, J. and Walker, L. (1975). Procedural justice: A psychological analysis. Hillsdale. NJ: Erlbaum.

Thomas, D. C., Ravlin, E. C., Liao, Y., Morrell, D. L. and Au, K. (2016). Collectivist values, exchange ideology and psychological contract preference. Management International Review, 56(2): 255-281.

Tillson, C. M., Sluiter, J. K., Blonk, R. W. B., Broersen, J. P. J. and Frings-Dresenm, M. H. W. (2004). Stressful Work, psychological job strain, and turnover: a 2-year prospective cohort study of truck drivers. Journal of Applied Psychology, 89(3): 442-454.

Tillson, T. (1997). Is your career killing you? Canadian Business, 70: 78-84.

Tong, C. K. (1990). Centripetal authority, differentiated networks: The social organization of Chinese firms in Singapore. In Hamilton, G. G. (Ed.). Business groups and economic development in East Asia. Hong Kong: Center of Asian Studies.

Trevor, C. O., Gerhart, B. and Boudreau, J. W. (1997). Voluntary turnover and job performance: Curvilinearity and the moderating influences of salary growth and promotions. Journal of Applied Psychology, 82(1): 44-61.

Trevor, C. O. (2001). Interactions among actual ease-of-movement determinants and job satisfaction in the prediction of voluntary turnover. Academy of Management Journal, 44(4): 621-638.

Tsang, W. and Eric, K. (1998). Can guanxi be a source of sustained competitive advantage for doing business in China? Academy of Management Executive, 12(2): 64-73.

Turan, A. (2015). Satisfaction with organization and intention to retain: the mediating role of organizational identity complexity/congruence of outsourcing labors. Anthropologist, 21(1-2): 300-310.

Turnley, W. H. and Feldman, D. G. (2000). Re-examining the effects of psychological contract violations: unmet expectations and job dissatisfaction as mediators. Journal of Organizational Behavior, 21(1): 25-42.

van Dick, R., Christw, O., Stellmacherw, J., Wagnerw, U., Ahlswedew, O., Grubbaw, C., Hauptmeierw, M., Hfeldw, C. H., Moltzenw, K. and Tissington, P. A. (2004). Should I stay or should I go? explaining turnover intentions with organizational identification and job satisfaction. British Journal of Management, 15(4): 351-360.

Vandenberg, R. J. and Lance, C. E. (1992). Examining the causal order of job satisfaction and organizational commitment. Journal of Management, 18(1): 153-167.

Vandenberghe, C. (1999). Organizational culture, person-culture fit, and turnover: A replication in the health care industry. Journal of Organizational Behavior, 20(2): 175-184.

Victor, B. and Cullen, J. B. (1988). The organizational bases of ethical work climates. Administrative Science Quarterly, 33(1): 101-125.

Vogel, R. M., Mitchell, M. S., Tepper, B. J., Restubog, S. L. D., Hu, C., Hua, W. and Huang, J. C. (2015). A cross - cultural examination of subordinates' perceptions of and reactions to abusive supervision. Journal of Organizational Behavior, 36(5): 720-745.

Wagner, J. A. (1995). Studies of individualism-collectivism: effects on cooperation in groups. Academy of Management Journal, 38(1): 152-172.

Waldman, D. A., Min, Z. C. and Hom, P. W. (2015). A multilevel investigation of leadership and turnover behavior. Journal of Management Official Journal of the Southern Management Association, 41(6): 1724-1744.

Wallace, J. E. (1995). Organizational and professional commitment in professional and nonprofessional organizations. Administrative Science Quarterly, 40(2): 228-255.

Wang, C., Yuan, Q. and Chen, L. (2016). The personnel earthquake

continuum: consequences of collective turnover—a case study of Qidian founders' collective turnover. Frontiers of Business Research in China, 10(1): 115-148.
Wang, D., Tsui, A. S., Zhang, Y. and Ma, L. (2003). Employment relationships and firm performance: Evidence from an emerging economy. Journal of Organizational Behavior, 24(5): 511-535.
Wang, L., Hinrichs, K. T., Prieto, L. and Howell, J. P. (2013). Five dimensions of organizational citizenship behavior: comparing antecedents and levels of engagement in china and the us. Asia Pacific Journal of Management, 30(1): 115-147.
Wang, Q. (2017). Annual report on non-state-owned economy in China (2015-2016). Beijing: Chinese Industry and Commerce Joint Press.
Wang, Z. and Jiang, H. (2004). An empirical study of the effects of Chinese employee's personal characteristics on satisfaction for company. Nankai Business Review, 7(1): 101-106.
Wasti, S. A. (2003). Organizational commitment, turnover intentions and the influence of cultural values. Journal of Occupational and Organizational Psychology, 76(3): 303-21.
Weiss, H. M., Suckow, K. and Cropanzano, R. (1999). Effects of justice conditions on discrete emotions. Journal of Applied Psychology, 84(5): 786-794.
Weiss, H. M. (2002). Deconstructing job satisfaction: Separating evaluations, beliefs and affective experiences. Human Resource Management Review, 12(2): 173-194.
Wen, R., Huang, G. and Feng, C. (2005). Coordinate: inquiry of Chinese professional managers. The Eastern Publishing Co., Ltd.
Wendy, B. R., Boudreau, J. W. and Tichy, J. (2005). The relationship between employee job change and job satisfaction: the honeymoon-hangover effect. Journal of Applied Psychology, 90(5): 882-892.
Weng, Q. and Mcelroy, J. C. (2012). Organizational career growth, affective occupational commitment and turnover intentions. Journal of Vocational Behavior, 80(2): 256-265.
Wiener, Y. (1982). Commitment in organizations: a normative view. Academy of Management Review, 7(3): 418-428.
Williams, C. R. and Livingstone, L. P. (1994). Another look at the relationship between performance and voluntary turnover. Academy of Management Journal, 37(2): 269-298.
Wong, C. S. and Kung, H. L. (1999). An exploratory investigation on commitment to specific constituencies in Taiwan. Chinese Journal of Psychology, 40(1): 1-13.

Wong, Y. and Wong, Y. (2013). Workplace guanxi and employee commitment to supervisor in Chinese international joint ventures. Journal of Chinese Human Resource Management, 4(1): 39-57.

Wong, Y., Wong, C. and Ngo, H. (2002). Loyalty to supervisor and trust in supervisor of workers in Chinese joint ventures: a test of two competing models. The International Journal of Human Resource Management, 13(6): 883-900.

Xiao, J. (2015). The effects of acquisition on the growth of new technology-based firms: Do different types of acquirers matter? Small Business Economics, 45(3): 487-504.

Xie, Y., Cao, J. and Zeng, Z. (2005). An early alarm system of knowledge employees' turnover based on staff loyalty. The Theory and Practice of Finance and Economics, 27(2): 69-72.

Xin, K. R. and Pearce, J. L. (1996). Guanxi: connections as substitutes for formal institutional support. Academy of Management Journal, 39(6): 1641-1658.

Xu, E., Huang, X. and Robinson, S. L. (2015). When self-view is at stake: responses to ostracism through the lens of self-verification theory. Journal of Management, 20(10): 1-22.

Yang, C., Lu, Y. and Yang, Y. (2014). Organizational justice and voluntary turnover: the roles of job embeddedness and equity sensitivity. Journal of Industrial Engineering and Engineering Management, 28(1): 16-25.

Yang, H. and Zhou, P. (2017). Risk predication in professional management in family business using support vector machine. Reform of Economic System, (5): 122-128.

Yao, X. and Wang, L. (2006). The predictability of normative organizational commitment for turnover in Chinese companies: a cultural perspective. The International Journal of Human Resource Management, 17(6): 1058-1075.

Yi, M. (2004). Assets complementarity, talents specificity and managers' loyalty. Social Science Research, (3): 42-44.

Yu, A., Matta, F. K. and Cornfield, B. (2017). Is LMX differentiation beneficial or detrimental for group effectiveness? a meta-analytic investigation and theoretical integration. Academy of Management Journal, Published online before print August 14, doi: 10.5465/amj.2016.1212.

Zagenczyk, T. J., Purvis, R. L., Shoss, M. K., Scott, K. L. and Cruz, K. S. (2015). Social influence and leader perceptions: multiplex social network ties and similarity in leader-member exchange. Journal of Business and Psychology, 30(1): 105-117.

Zhang, J. and Huang, W. (2003). The institutional factors about the private-owned enterprise's organizational-entry for professional executives in China: an empirical research. Economic Research Journal, (10): 25-31.

Zhang, J. and Huang, W. (2007). The study on the influential factors on managers career development in private enterprises. Journal of Sun Yat-Sen University (Social Science Edition), 47(3): 91-96.

Zhang, J. and Wang, F. (2003). An empirical study about the determinants of professional manager's turnover in private enterprises. Management World, (9): 129-135.

Zhang, J. and Zhao, W. (2007). The relationship between learning approach and entrepreneurial capacity: evidence from private enterprises in Guangdong province. Economic Theory and Business Management, (10): 65-69.

Zhang, J., Ji, Y. and Wang, T. (2007). An empirical study about organizational career management and attraction of private enterprise. Working Paper, Sun Yat-Sen University.

Zhang, J. (2002). Mechanism of manager's betrayal and employer's strategies. Management World, (5): 104-108.

Zhang, J. (2001). Nature of human capital and residual distribution of firm. China Industrial Economy, (5): 70-74.

Zhang, M. and Li, S. (2001). An empirical study on the determinants of employee's job satisfaction. Statistical Research, (8): 33-37.

Zhang, M. and Zhang, D. (2003). New developments of employee voluntary turnover models. Foreign Economies and Management, 25(9): 24-28.

Zhang, M. (2006). Research and application of employee turnover intention model. Beijing: Tsinghua University Press.

Zhang, W. (1996). An entrepreneurial-contractual theory of the firm. Shanghai: Shanghai Joint Publishing Press, Shanghai People's Publishing House.

Zhang, W. (2003). Enterprisers and professional handlers: how to establish trust. Journal of Peking University (Humanities and Social Sciences), 40(5): 29-39.

Zhang, W. (2001). Growth of family enterprises and professional managers. China Industry and Commerce, (10):136-139.

Zhang, X. A., Li, N. and Harris, T. B. (2015). Putting non-work ties to work: The case of guanxi in supervisor-subordinate relationships. Leadership Quarterly, 26(1): 37-54.

Zhao, X., Liang, Q. and Liu, D. (2005). The game analysis of the demission of employees in state-owned enterprise. Soft Science, 27(2): 69-72.

Zheng, B. (1995). Differential pattern and Chinese organization behaviors. Local Psychology Research (Taiwan). Quoted in Li, X. and Zhang, S. (2005). Family enterprises: organization, behavior and Chinese economy, Shanghai: Shanghai Joint Publishing Press, Shanghai People's Publishing House: 297-378.

Zhou, H. (2014). Research on the relation of the supply-demand of entrepreneurial capacity and growth of family enterprise. Science and Technology Progress and Policy, 31(19): 92-96.

Zhou, Q. (1996). Firm in market: a specific contract between human capital and non-human capital. Economic Research Journal, (6): 71-80.

Zhu, Y. and Warner, M. (2011). An emerging model of employment relations in China: a divergent path from the Japanese? International Business Review, 9(3): 345-361.

Zhuo, Y. and Zhang, M. (2004). Trust, agent costs and the choice of family business. Journal of Finance and Economics, 30(2): 50-57.

Zimmerman, R. D., Swider, B. W., Woo, S. E. and Allen, D. G. (2016). Who withdraws? psychological individual differences and employee withdrawal behaviors. Journal of Applied Psychology, 101(4): 498-519.

Zinta, B. S. (2005). Fairness reduces the negative effects of organizational politics on turnover intentions, citizenship behavior and job performance. Journal of Business and Psychology, 20(2): 175-200.

Index

E

F

G

H

M

N

O

P

Q

R

S

T

Made in United States
Orlando, FL
04 November 2026

90206776R00213